HEROES AND HEROIC DEEDS
of
THE PACIFIC NORTHWEST

VOLUME I.

Elementary Grades

Sacajawea

Heroes and Heroic Deeds of the Pacific Northwest

VOLUME I: THE PIONEERS

Henry L. Talkington, A.M. LL.D.

HERITAGE BOOKS
2023

HERITAGE BOOKS

AN IMPRINT OF HERITAGE BOOKS, INC.

Books, CDs, and more—Worldwide

For our listing of thousands of titles see our website
at
www.HeritageBooks.com

A Facsimile Reprint
Published 2023 by
HERITAGE BOOKS, INC.
Publishing Division
5810 Ruatan Street
Berwyn Heights, MD 20740

International Standard Book Number
Paperbound: 978-0-7884-4388-6

The West

Men look to the East for the dawning things,
For the light of a rising sun;
But they look to the West, to the crimson West,
For the things that are done, are done!
The eastward sun is a new-made hope from the
Dark of the night distilled;
But the westward sun is a sunset sun,
Is the sun of a hope fulfilled!

So out of the East they have always come,
The cradle that saw the birth
Of all of the heart-warm hopes of man
And of all of the hopes of earth.
For out of the East a Christ arose,
And out of the East there gleamed,
The dearest dream and the clearest dream,
That ever a prophet dreamed.

Yea, into the waiting West they go
With the dream-child of the East,
And find the hopes that they hoped of old
Are a hundred fold increased.
For there in the East we dream our dreams
Of the things we hope to do,
And here in the West, the crimson West,
The dreams of the East come true!

—*Douglas Malloch.*

PREFACE

IT IS given to few people to be so close to history as are the people of the Northwest. Here, within the brief space of a hundred years are found the primitive man, the discoverer, the fur-trader, the explorer, the missionary, the immigrant, the pioneer, and the miner. Many of the facts may be obtained from the lips of living witnesses, who speak from personal knowledge, or from knowledge gained from a preceding generation.

Sacajawea, the noted Indian guide of the Lewis and Clark expedition, according to good authority, has been dead only a few years, and the Indian we have ever had with us. McLoughlin, the great fur-trading governor, Meek, Craig, and Newell, the mountain men, were well known by some who are still living. The children of the first missionaries are yet with us. The last survivor of the convention which organized the first government in the Northwest died but recently. Men and women who came in the early immigrant trains continue to tell of their experiences.

Pioneer life is so near us as to excite little wonder or attention. Men who mined in the early sixties, men who served as members of miners' courts or were members of vigilante committees may be met with frequently; so may early packers, freighters, and stage drivers. A few of the old fiddlers who played for the "hurdy-gurdy" girls are here to entertain us with their experiences; pioneer railroad builders and steamboat men give us vivid pictures of early travel, and the pioneer farmers and stock raisers depict some of their difficulties. The "whipsaw" may yet be seen and some of the old "grist mills" stand as souvenirs of a former generation.

The "Indian War Dances," occasionally seen at fairs, are reminders of grim realities to some present. The old post trader cites many incidents of the Indian's honesty in the payment of bills. Banks with a million dollars on deposit, exhibit, as a curiosity, the old scales used in early days for weighing "gold dust." The old Wells Fargo stamped envelopes, costing seventy-five cents and used in the early delivery of mail, still may occasionally be found; the old account book and hotel register tell their stories of the high cost of living, and the old ferry sign, the high cost of transportation. The old school register and reports of school officials throw much light on educational conditions, while the files of early newspapers are mirrors of every phase of the life of preceding generations.

It has been the author's good fortune during his many years' residence in the Northwest either to come in personal contact with every phase of life here depicted or to know intimately those who had. The period or periods of history here mentioned are of great interest, fascination, and value because they show so well "history in the making" and afford splendid opportunities for dealing with "source materials." But this material has not been compiled with the view of writing a "narrative history," for such histories, when compressed within the compass of one volume, are little more than topical indexes, dry abstract statements, bald conclusions without sufficient facts to develop the topic, justify the statement, or establish the conclusions. Then, too, there are oftentimes vain repetitions.

In this work we have sought to tell the larger story by a series of smaller "type" stories, each complete in itself yet an integral part of the whole. This is not done by making statements or deducing conclusions, but by giving facts sufficient to enable the reader to form his own conclusions; not repeating something, simply because it occurred at another time or place yet was not essentially different from what had been given.

The question, too, of adaptation has been kept steadfastly in mind. Children, at different periods of their lives, are interested in and prepared for different kinds of material, and should be given that for which they are best suited. Fortunately the many periods represented in Northwestern history, in so short a time, make adaptation comparatively easy.

It is important to keep in mind that "History is not mere past politics"; and "politics is not mere present history." It is far more. "History is the science of the evolution of man in his activities as a social being" and embraces his industrial, social, educational, and religious life as well as his political life, and these phases of life are more interesting and better adapted to child life in the elementary grades than is the political phase.

A large use has also been made of what may be termed "empirical" material, that is, material that will appeal to the child through his previous experiences; for the same reasons a large number of illustrations have been used. Last, but not least, the attempt has been made to make history real by allowing real persons to tell their own story, or if not to tell it, to supply the facts.

HENRY L. TALKINGTON.

Lewiston, Idaho, June 1, 1929.

CONTENTS

CHAPTER X.

MINING.

LIST OF ILLUSTRATIONS

Page

CHAPTER I.

The Primitive Indian.

The Story of Sacajawea.—In 1804 and 1805 there were few white people between the Mississippi River and the Pacific Ocean. Indians, Indians, Indians, everywhere! These Indians were not friends, but enemies, of each other. Like naughty children they were always quarreling and fighting, but they called their fights wars. In these wars the men who were captured were killed, but the women and children were made slaves by the conquerors.

The Nez Perce, the Flathead and Shoshone Indians used to go across the Rocky Mountains into Montana to hunt for buffalo and many were the fierce fights they had with the Indians of the plains. In one of these fights Sacajawea, a little Shoshone girl, was captured and carried away to Dakota, having been made a prisoner by the Blackfeet. Her girlhood friend who was captured at the same time, however, escaped.

When Sacajawea was thirteen or fourteen years old she became the wife of a half-breed Frenchman named Charbonneau. He was many years older than she and lived among the Crow Indians, near the present city of Bismarck, North Dakota.

Lewis and Clark came by there in the winter of 1805. They were compelled to stop because of the deep snows and because they were in need of a guide, as none of their party knew the country west of the Rocky Mountains. Fortunately they found Sacajawea who knew this country well. She was engaged as their guide and her husband as the cook. In the spring, when the snows and the ice in the rivers had melted, the party started up the river, Sacajawea directing. She knew the plains and the mountains as well as the canyons and river bottoms and kept the party from getting lost. When food was scarce she knew how to find that stored away by the wild animals. She knew well the Indians and their ways; she could speak two or three dialects, and her husband two or three more; by this means it was possible for Lewis and Clark to converse with most of the Indians whom they met. She knew also how to prepare meat so as to preserve it; how to cook; how to dress skins and make clothes; was an expert in handling a canoe, was a fine swimmer, and rendered Lewis and Clark assistance in a thousand ways.

Sacajawea had a little baby boy who was a great care but also a great comfort, not only to her but to the whole party. His name was Baptiste and his mother carried him on her back all the way. He sometimes got very cold and hungry, because they not only had to travel through the cold but also had to sleep out at night as well. At one time the canoe in which little Baptiste and his mother were riding was tipped over by his father and the little papoose and his mother were thrown out into the cold river. However, Sacajawea could swim well and soon righted the canoe and had all safely back in it.

Near the present town of Three Forks, Montana, Sacajawea first caught sight of some of her own people. When she saw them she began to dance excitedly, and to suck her fingers which was her method of showing great joy. It also showed Lewis and Clark that the Indians were friends and not enemies. When they came up to the party she recognized the Chief, Cameahwait, as her brother, and threw her blanket over him, laying her head on his shoulder and weeping as only an overjoyed woman can. She also discovered her girlhood chum who had been captured but had escaped. They flew into each other's arms and laughed and cried just as all women do at such times. There was some sorrow as well as joy in the meeting, for Sacajawea learned that all of her family except the chief and one other brother, together with the son of her sister, had died. She adopted her nephew whose name was Basil.

Lewis and Clark found that they must now abandon their boats and secure horses, as their route lay across the mountains. The horses were bargained for from Sacajawea's people, but she soon discovered a plot, in which her own brother was engaged, to drive away the horses and leave the party stranded in the late summer. She did not hesitate a minute, but revealed the plot to Lewis and Clark. The trial was rather tedious, however, as there were so many languages spoken by all present. One of Lewis and Clark's men took the wording in English and translated it into French to Sacajawea's husband, who translated it into Hidatsa for Sacajawea. She, in turn, translated the message into Shoshone to the prisoner, who in his turn, adapted the Shoshone to Chopunnish for the contesting Indian chiefs.

The matter was finally settled; the party secured the horses, and resumed their journey westward toward the Rocky Mountains. There the route lay north and along the foot of the Rocky and Bitter Root mountains until the party came to Lolo Pass, where it crosses over to the headwaters of the Clearwater, which runs into the Snake, and thence on to the Columbia River.

The winter was spent near the mouth of this river and the next spring and summer Sacajawea, leaving with the Lewis and Clark party, returned to her Dakota home.

Although she had successfully piloted "the most hazardous and significant journey ever made on the western continent" she received nothing for her services except the satisfaction that comes from work well done.

We can imagine that little Baptiste was very tired after riding three or four thousand miles on his mother's back and would want a long rest, but he had a little playmate now in his cousin Basil. They both grew up to be useful men; Baptiste was educated in a Catholic school at St. Louis, Mr. Clark, whose expedition his mother had guided, paying the expenses of his education. He and his foster brother, Basil, could speak three languages, Shoshone, French, and English. They became noted guides in the Rocky Mountain section, directing Captain Bonneville, Fremont, and others. Finally, they, together with their mother, settled in

The Bull Boat.

The Primitive Home.

The Tepee.

Wyoming on the reservation now known as Wind River, where the noted guide, Sacajawea, according to some authorities, died in the late eighties.

She had seen many Indians during her lifetime and knew much of their manners and customs, their dress, their methods of securing food, their warfare, etc. She did not write anything, but if she had spoken of the Indians we can imagine that she would have told us the following:

The Indian's Food.—What the Indians ate depended upon where they lived. If they lived on the coast or the Columbia River, fish was their chief article of food, and there are many stories told of the abundance of fish in the early days of Oregon. One man said that they were so numerous that it was possible to walk across the Columbia River on their backs. Another told of stages being overturned by them in a little river

The Travois—An early mode of travel.

in southern Oregon, and still another, that the farmers in his locality fed them to their hogs. But these are all "fish stories" and indicate an abundance rather than exact facts.

The Indians in the Inland Empire lived on wild game, elk, deer, moose, and fowls being abundant. They also had great fields of kamas and kouse, while on the plains east of the Rocky Mountains, buffalo meat furnished the chief article of diet.

Practically everywhere, at certain seasons of the year, extensive use of berries was made. In the Puget Sound country especially, berries were very plentiful, it being claimed that there were eighteen different varieties to be found there, lasting from the early summer until the late fall. During these seasons the Indians lived in the berry patches and gorged themselves with luscious fruit, doing little but eating and sleeping, it being a veritable lazy man's country. Farther back in the interior, toward the east and in the mountainous districts, there was an abundance of huckleberries and service berries, which were gathered in large quantities during their season. While much of the fruit was eaten direct from the bush or vine, some of it was also dried and stored away in baskets, and used to season the meat diet which was prepared for the winter's consumption.

Fish were caught in various ways. The Indians contrived to make nets by weaving together strips of hemp or reed, and since the fish, at certain seasons, crowd up the small streams to spawn, great quantities were caught by this method. Spearing, too, was a very common method of catching the fish. The Indian prepared a long pole, sharpened at one end, on which was fastened the tip of a deer's horn, ground down to a very sharp point, a hole being bored through this and a thong or leather string attached to it and to the pole. The Indian would stand where the fish had to pass through shallow water, or he would find them in small streams and throw the spear through them; as he pulled his pole back the tip of the deer's horn would slip off and he could thereby hold his fish securely. The Indians were experts at spearing fish and still catch them in this way.

Fish were caught in the summer season when they were very plentiful. The Indians removed the intestines and placed the fish on stones or strung them on strips of leather; or they made a frame by setting up four sticks with a fork at the top and then passing sticks from one to the other, thereby forming a square across which other sticks could be laid, and the fish put upon these. A small fire placed under this would smoke or dry the fish. They were then stored in baskets and kept for winter use.

Another large source of food supply for the winter was what was termed jerked meat, that is, meat cut into thin strips, dried in the same manner as the fish, and preserved for winter use in the same way. Sometimes the dried meat, together with the tallow or fat of the animal, and a quantity of dried berries was put into a mortar and ground to a powder with a pestle. This was called pemmican and could be stored in baskets and kept for months. Another source of food supply was the wild potato—which the Indians called wapato—and the kamas and kouse. All of these belonged to the potato family and grew in large quantities in many places. These the Indians pulled or dug up, dried, and stored away in baskets. Later they could be taken out, put into the mortar and with a pestle ground into meal, which was used to make a kind of bread, or to season the soup which was prepared much as a housewife prepares soup today.

The Mortar and Pestle.

Cooking Utensils.—The Indians used a water proof basket woven from reeds. Into this, which was partially filled with water, the food to be cooked was placed, and then red hot stones were dropped into it; or, they dug a hole in the ground, lined it with clean grass and into this put the food to be cooked. The food was covered over with grass and dirt, then a fire was built over all of it. By making a proper selection of the twigs to be used, the food might be flavored to suit the individual taste. In the course of time, the Indians also came to use certain kinds of crude pottery. Many stories are told of how they learned to make it. One is to the effect that an Indian woman stepped into the mud and, on returning after the mud had dried saw the hole she had made with her foot. She cut out the piece of hard mud inclosing the opening and thereby forming a sort of vessel in which she could store things. Later, having set this by the fire, she saw that it hardened and thus learned how to construct and fire certain kinds of cooking utensils. The mortar and pestle were made as follows: They secured a rock, eight to twelve inches in diameter and perhaps six to eight inches deep; they gradually hollowed out a depression in the center in which they could place kamas, kouse or pieces of meat which they desired to pulverize. The pestle is a piece of long, round stone eight to ten inches in length and two to three inches in diameter. The Indians, by using the mortar and pestle, could pulverize any article of food in the same way in which the druggist pulverizes a drug.

Clothing.—The Indians' clothing consisted either of leather or of cloth woven from the bark of a tree. They tanned the skins of the deer or the elk in such a way

The Primitive Indian Loom.

that the hide was soft and pliable. They had certain crude instruments which enabled them to cut this leather into any required shape, and with a bone for a needle and sinews taken from the animal they could sew the garments and moccasins. The cloth made from reeds or the soft inner bark of trees is a form of weaving practiced today in practically all the schools where manual training and domestic science are taught. It is nothing more than a form of platting, on the same principle as the weaving of a chair bottom with rawhide or cane, where strips are first run across one way and then the other, by weaving them over and under until the opposite side is reached.

House.—The Indian's house consisted of two general styles: first, the tepee made of hides, mats of woven grass or reeds, and after the white man came, of cloth.

It is conical shaped, stretched tightly over a certain number of tepee poles which come together at a point twelve or fifteen feet above the ground. The size of the tepee varies, but as a rule is fifteen or twenty feet in diameter. There is a loose "flap" at the center of the top which may be opened or closed at will, allowing smoke to escape through the opening. There is another loose "flap" at the side which serves as a door.

The Indian's bed in the early days was simply the hides of animals, spread over grass, moss, or leaves.

Another kind of house was a sort of community building where several families lived together, one tepee being placed right beside the other and built of bark or twigs. This was in some respects like the lean-to which the miner built against the hill or overhanging cliff. These houses were designated by the number of fires that were kindled in them, as ten, twenty, or thirty fires might be burning at the same time. Here the various families lived, cooked, ate, and slept, if not in perfect harmony, at least with a great deal less discord than one would expect under such conditions. Lewis and Clark, on their return home, were entertained in one of these large houses by the Nez Perce Indians near Kamiah.

**The Peace Pipe.*—When one tribe wished to make a treaty of peace with another, a number of warriors or perhaps the whole band would move to a selected spot and send the peace pipe to those with whom they wished to enter into a treaty. This was a sort of flag of truce and was so regarded. When the Indians wished to treat with the white man they sent not only the peace pipe but a white flag as well. If the pipe were accepted then it was known that the other tribe was willing to

*See page 276.

treat, and the chiefs and the principal men met in council. Sometimes this meeting was in a wigwam and sometimes out in the open where a platform was built. Such was the arrangement when Governor Stevens held his great council at Walla Walla in 1855 with all of the Indian tribes in the Inland Empire.

When all were assembled, the Indians seated themselves on the ground in a circle. If there were any presents they sometimes were distributed in the beginning. In the case of the white man's treating with the Indians there were practically always presents, but they were not often distributed until something had been accomplished. After the preliminaries had been gone through with, the peace pipe was lighted. This was done by some one appointed especially for the purpose. He lit the pipe and handed it to the chief, who pointed the stem to the east, to the west, to the north, and to the south, toward heaven and then toward earth; then he took a few puffs—three or four—and passed the pipe to the next, who in turn took the required number of puffs, and so on until the pipe had passed around the entire circle. Each of the smokers inhaled the smoke and expelled it through his nose toward the sky. This was regarded as a very solemn ceremony, in which the will of the gods was invoked, and it was conducted in a very dignified manner. Any one who disturbed it or did not properly observe it was severely punished.

After the smoke, the big talk or the real work of the council began, when the questions under consideration were discussed. Each one spoke, much as the Quaker—as the spirit moved him.

When war was declared it began and closed with a council of the chiefs and leading men. The pipe was brought into use in the declaring of war just as in the council of peace, though used in a little different way. The council for war was opened by a big smoke from the pipe by all present. This was supposed to soothe and quiet each one so that questions could be properly and deliberately considered. If the council was of a warlike character, as the smoke was inhaled each Indian went through the pretense of catching the smoke and rubbing it upon his body; this was supposed to make him immune from the darts of his enemies. In brief, the pipe of the Indian had, in many respects, the same significance as the flag of civilized man.

Children.—The baby Indian soon after his birth is carried in a tecat, which consists of a board about thirty inches long, about ten inches wide at one end and six at the other, much in the shape of a small ironing board.

The Tecat.

Indian Basketry.

This is covered with a piece of skin under which is placed moss or grass, making a soft bed. On the front of the board is fastened a shoe-shaped basket made of soft skin, open at the top and down the front, being held together by a lace much like a shoe lace. The child is placed in this and laced up; it may then be carried on its mother's back wherever she goes, or it may be hung to the horn of her saddle or suspended from the limb of a tree, so that "when the wind blows the cradle will rock." But the mother is very careful to not hang this precious package to a limb that will break and allow the baby, cradle and all, to come down.

Indian children soon learn to take care of themselves; they engage in games just as do other children; are taught what constitute "good manners," and when naughty are "spanked" just as are other children.

Bathtub or Sweat House.—As we view the Indian's tepee, his food and clothing, as well as his general manner of living, hygiene seems an unknown science to him. Yet this is not altogether true.

He has his "bathroom," which is a hole dug into the ground, near the bank of the river, into which the water rises. This is covered with brush or grass. When the Indian is ready for his bath he drops red hot stones into his tub and when the water is sufficiently warm he jumps into it, and he may get a Turkish bath as well as a hot one. From this he sometimes jumps into the river for his "shower bath."

Dress.—The Indians are frequently very fastidious about their dress, especially the men. They will spend hours patiently painting or "coaxing" a silk handkerchief or scarf into a proper shape for their hats, or necks, and they make extensive use of beads, belts, tassels, feathers, and trinkets of various kinds in the adornment of their persons.

The Potlatch.—The Indians have many queer customs, but none more interesting than the Potlatch. This is a sort of a feast to which some Indian invites all of his friends, and at which he gives away all of his earthly possessions—knives, blankets, tepees, scarfs, handkerchiefs, and war implements, in short, everything that he possesses. This open-hearted generosity is not all prompted by the spirit of self-sacrifice, for it entitles him not only to the gratitude of all his friends, but it gives him the right ever afterwards to live with any one of them at their expense. In short, it is a form of insurance.

The Totem Pole.—"The totem pole is made to illustrate the 'blue blood' of the tribe and there is no race of people so proud of its genealogy as the Indian. An Indian crest is the symbol of his origin and it is the mark of subdivisions of the tribe into social clans that are closer and more rigid than even tribal union. Indians

The Totem Pole.

of the same crest never intermarry, and when a squaw marries into a distant tribe her children go back to her own people. It is not unusual to find an Indian's crest on everything that belongs to him, from his canoe to his household kettle, and it is the foundation and the cap sheaf of the totem poles of all the Alaskan Indians.

"The most grotesque totem poles seen on the trip were in Wrangle, some as high as fifty feet. These poles represented the history of the family and the ancestry as far back as it could be traced. If they are of the wolf tribe, a huge wolf would be carved at the top of the pole, and then on down with various signs to the base of the pole are recorded the great events of the family and the intermarriages, not forgetting to give place to the good and bad gods who assisted them. The genealogy of a tribe is always traced back through the mother's side. The totem poles are sometimes very large, perhaps four feet at the base, and have been known to cost $2,000. When the carving is completed they are planted firmly in front of the family hut, there to stay until they decay and fall away. At the base, some four feet from the ground, there is often an opening into the already hollowed pole, and in this are put the bones or ashes of the burned bodies of the family. It is only the wealthier families who support a totem pole, and any amount of money could not induce an Indian to part with his family tree."—*Fifteen Thousand Miles by Stage, by Carrie A. Strahorn*

Indian Mythology.—"In Indian mythology all created beings descend from the bird, fish, toad, bear, or wolf, and each has its influence upon the descendant. To the wolf ancestors are attributed all the features of cunning and the sly characteristics of their warriors in battle or in outwitting their fellows in time of peace. The bear indicates power and strength of muscle. The eagle is a leader, one who migrates and travels far. The frog descendants are savants and philosophers. Those who are from the raven are crafty, wise, and full of intrigue. The whale denotes a clan of plenty of food, who live well and peaceably. The salmon indicates ambition and desire to achieve. The seal gives grace and willowy motion and endows its descendants with charms and occult powers, and the duck gives a phlegmatic, even temperament, a command of seas, and a charmed life in waters."—*Fifteen Thousand Miles by Stage, by Carrie A. Strahorn.*

The Indian's Religion.—"The religion of these Indians is much the same as that of the other tribes of America. They believe in one superior presiding influence, which they call the Great High Chief. They believe also in an Evil Spirit and in numerous inferior spirits, both good and evil, which inhabit the earth and air, and are invisible or assume the form of smoke or vapor; the evil spirits afflict mankind with misfortune, disease and death. They also believe in the spiritualization of beasts, birds and fish, and even of their clothes, ornaments, canoes, tools, implements of war, etc., of fruits, flowers, and numerous other inanimate things; and we are inclined to the belief that they extend this spiritualization to all organized bodies. It is on account of this opinion that they bury their dead in their canoes, with many of the articles which belonged to them, while living—such as arms, clothing, ornaments, etc.—and furnish them with a supply of food, which they suppose sufficient to last them to the Spirit

Land. For the same reason a horse or a dog is frequently butchered beside the grave of a hunter. The spirits of all of which things, according to their opinion, will be required for their comfort and subsistence when they themselves have come to be disembodied spirits.

They are in many respects very superstitious; one instance of which is shown in the removal of a large stone, which lay in the way of some men who were taking saw-logs into the river, a mile below Oregon City. The workmen were about to remove it, when they were forbidden by some of the Indians, and told that it was once a man, and if they removed it, the river would rise up to it. They, however, removed it, and it happened that soon after the river rose higher than it had ever been known, which accidental circumstance was attributed by them to the removal of the stone, and of course strengthened their superstition."—*Oregon Historical Society. Vol. 7, page 180.*

CHAPTER II.

THE FUR TRADE.

Origin.—Fur trading is almost as old as the human race. The skins of animals were among the first articles of clothing and their flesh furnished the first kinds of food.

The Russians obtained furs from Siberia. England, from the beginning, obtained them from the Russians. When America was discovered, a new source for supplying furs was found. France, for a time, profited most largely of all the European nations in her trade with the American Indians. The French fur-trader and the missionary went hand in hand in their work with the Indian. Neither wanted his land. Both to a certain extent, adopted his way of living, and in the case of the former, intermarried. The fur-trader furnished the Indian with blankets, guns, powder, shot, and other things necessary to kill and capture the wild animals and took furs in exchange for them.

France lost her fur-trading business on the St. Lawrence and the Great Lakes, by the French and Indian War. England enlarged and extended the business both to the North and the West and the French retired to the west of the Mississippi and continued their trapping and trading in furs.

By the Revolutionary War the United States gained all of the territory south of the Great Lakes, and by the Louisiana Purchase all of the Mississippi Valley west of the river to the Rocky Mountains, thereby coming into a large share of the fur-trading business of North America.

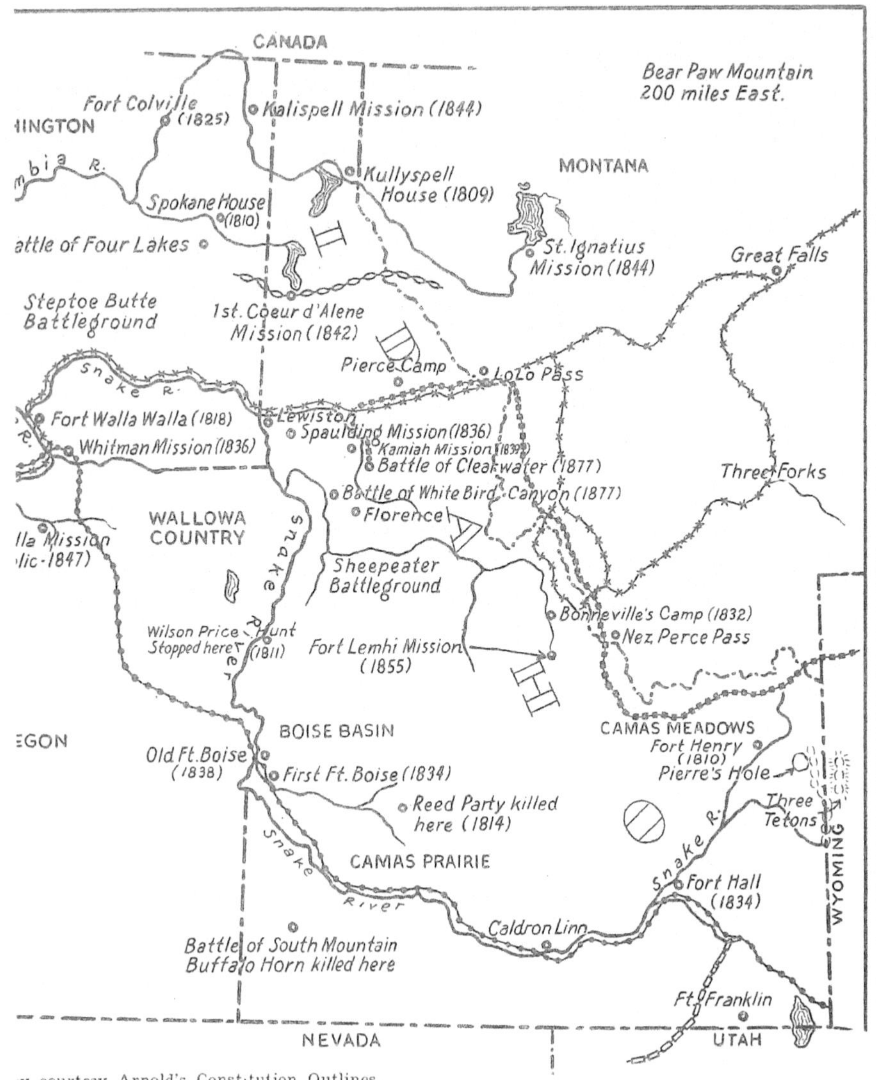

By courtesy Arnold's Constitution Outlines.

-x-x-x-x-x- LEWIS AND CLARK TRAIL—Began at St. Louis and ended at mouth of Columbia River.

OREGON TRAIL—Began at Independence, Missouri and ended at Oregon City, Oregon.

CALIFORNIA TRAIL—Left Oregon Trail at Bear River Bend near Fort Hall.

MULLAN ROAD—From Fort Benton, Montana, through Idaho mining district, to Ft. Walla Walla.

JOSEPH'S RETREAT—Began at Clearwater Battleground and ended at Bear Paw Mountain, Mont., where Chief Joseph's Band surrendered to General Miles, October 4, 1877.

FREMONT'S TRAIL—Fremont passed through Idaho and mapped route for the Oregon Trail.
CAMAS MEADOWS—Here Joseph's warriors stampeded Howard's mule herd.
CAMAS PRAIRIE (South Idaho)—Destroying of camas here caused the Bannock War.
SOUTH MOUNTAIN—Battle of Bannock War —Indians retreated into Oregon.
SOUTH PASS OF ROCKIES—(Discovered by Coulter) is just over Idaho line in Wyoming —the Oregon Trail follows it through the Rockies.
WHITMAN MISSION (or Waiilatpu) near Walla Walla—noted Indian Mission of Washington.
FORT FRANKLIN (1860)—First permanent settlement in Idaho—founded by Mormons.
FORT HALL (1834)—Built by Captain Wyeth. Most noted settlement.
FORT BOISE (temporary)—Was noted trading post.
LAPWAI—Founded by Spaulding. Noted Indian Mission.
"OLD MISSION" at Coeur d'Alene (Catholic) most noted mission in Idaho.
LEWISTON—Was Idaho's first capital.
PIERCE CITY—Was Idaho's first great mining camp. (1860).
FLORENCE (1861)—Richest of mining camps.
BOISE BASIN—Was one of nation's richest placer camps.

THE GREAT FUR-TRADING COMPANIES.

The Missouri Fur Company.—This company was organized by Manuel Lisa, a man of Spanish descent, with his headquarters at St. Louis. The expedition of Lewis and Clark had revealed that the habitat of the fur-bearing animals lay along the Missouri and its tributaries and the Columbia and its tributaries. In the spring of 1807 Lisa went up the Missouri and built a fort at the mouth of the Big Horn River, and called it Manuel in honor of himself. From this point he sent out trappers in every direction to gather furs and to invite the Indians to trade with him. Three years later another party was sent out by the same company under the command of Andrew Henry, who estabished another fort at Three Forks; still later another post was

A Fur-Trading Post, Old Fort George at Astoria, Oregon.

established on the headwaters of the north fork of the Snake River.

There were many powerful Indian tribes in the field selected by this company and it was not long until game became scarce and a conflict arose between the trappers and the Indians. Then came the War of 1812. This deprived the trappers of military protection; so after a few years, this company gave up its work.

The Pacific Fur Company.—John Jacob Astor was one of New York City's most successful merchants during the last quarter of the eighteenth century. His ships were seen on all seas and in almost every commercial center of the world. One of the most profitable lines of commerce in which he engaged was furs. At the beginning, his greatest source of supply was Montreal, the headquarters of the Northwest Company. Astor was a very able man and soon mastered the details of the fur trade and trapping.

When Lewis and Clark returned Astor saw an opportunity for conducting a fur-trading business on an extensive scale. He organized the Pacific Fur Company and furnished the capital and executive ability by employing the stock holders and trappers of the old Northwest Company, as they understood perfectly the trapping of animals and the preparation of their hides for the market. Astor's plan was to establish a line of forts from the mouth of the Missouri to the mouth of the Columbia. The furs collected east of the mountains would be brought back to St. Louis, while those collected west of the mountains could be taken down to the mouth of the Columbia where he established a post named Astoria. To this post he intended to send each year all the goods needed by the trappers in their trade with the Indians. After unloading this cargo he would take on board all of the furs collected at that point and take them to China, where he found a ready market at an immense profit. The ship would then be loaded with tea, silks, and other things which he would need for his store in New York City.

The War of 1812 came, and the Northwest Company was a very stiff competitor, so Astor's plan failed. He sold out his post at Astoria, and abandoned the field to the Hudson's Bay Company.

The Rocky Mountain Fur Company.—This company was organized in 1821, by Ashley, Jedediah Smith, Sublette, and others.

Their base of supplies was St. Louis, and their chief field was the Missouri River and its tributaries, but they soon discovered a new and unoccupied field along the Platte River and around Salt Lake. For a decade they had absolute control over the territory mentioned, extending their operations down to and even into the Mexican possessions which now constitute our southwestern states.

The Hudson's Bay Company.—By far the most successful of the fur-trading companies, was the Hudson's Bay Company, chartered in 1670 with exclusive rights on the Hudson Bay and all the rivers flowing into it. Later this company transferred its operations to the Pacific Coast with headquarters at Vancouver, absorbed its great rival, the Northwest Company, and as previously stated forced Astor out of the field. The Hudson's Bay Company had forts reaching from the Spanish possessions on the south to the Russian possessions on the north, covering all the territory east to the Rocky Mountains, and was absolute master in what was known as the Oregon Country. Toward the south it had posts on the Umpqua, toward the east was Wallula, Boise, and Fort Hall, to the north was Colville in the Okanagan Country and Nisqually on Puget Sound. McLoughlin was the general manager of the Company in the Northwest and was very successful in holding Indian tribes in subjection, and when the white settlers came to the country he aided them in many ways. He forced the Indians to respect them and he supplied them with live stock and seed grain and various other things needed by the early pioneers. This Company continued to hold full sway until Oregon was acquired by the United States and it is still a strong organization engaged in the fur trade and trapping in all the British possessions in the North.

St. Louis, the Great Fur-Trading Center of the Mississippi Valley—In 1762 the French director general

Old Fort Hall, near Pocatello, Idaho.

of Louisiana Territory granted to Pierre Laclede, the head of a company of merchants, the exclusive right to trade with the Indians on the Missouri River. Two years later the city of St. Louis was founded by his company. It is located at the mouth of the Missouri, which drains practically all of the northwest part of the Mississippi Valley, and is near the point where the rivers draining the northeastern part of the valley empty into the Mississippi. Later the trails leading from the southwest terminated at St. Louis, also.

LaSalle, Marquette, and other French explorers, who traversed the Mississippi Valley as well as many of its rivers, used the present site of St. Louis as a central point, and at the close of the French and Indian War, when the French surrendered all of their territory east of the Mississippi, the inhabitants of the town moved west across the river. The French were great fur-traders and had conducted their operations for many years around the Great Lakes. Later, when they immigrated westward, they continued in the same business. They were good friends of the Indians and were able to control all of the trade in furs conducted by them.

In 1803, when the United States purchased the Louisiana Territory, they also inherited the fur-trading privileges heretofore enjoyed by the French. Four great companies were organized to continue this business, all with headquarters at St. Louis. The Missouri Fur Trading Company, with a capital stock of $40,000, was organized in 1808-9, and operated on the upper Missouri; the American Fur Company, organized by Astor in 1810, had St. Louis as one of its stations; the Rocky Mountain Fur Trading Company, organized in 1832, had the same city as its headquarters.

These companies had hundreds of trappers in the field and there were many men besides called free trappers who engaged in trapping independent of the companies. The Indians also collected many furs and all of this trade found its way toward St. Louis. In short, the fur-trading business west of the Mississippi, up to 1810 or later, was controlled by companies operating in and out of St. Louis. Here all parties were organized, here all outfits were made up and through this place all furs passed to their market.

In 1821, the year of the Missouri Compromise, $600,000 worth of furs were handled in St. Louis. By this time steamboats had been placed on the Missouri and the trade on the Santa Fe Trail had assumed large proportions. This was the golden age of the fur-trader. The Missouri Fur Company, in October, 1822, brought out the first cargoes, the first being valued at $14,000, the second at $10,000. It was estimated that the beaver packs alone of this company amounted to $250,000 during the next few years; from 80 to 180 trappers were employed by them, and they worked the whole country west of the mountains, from the mouth of the Columbia down to California.

Some idea of the extent of the fur-trading business may be gained from the description given of one of the wholesale houses located in St. Louis at that time. It consisted of two large fireproof buildings, with spacious vaults, and basements constructed of stone. Upon the first floor, ranging level with the street, were the directors' rooms and the offices of the clerks, together with an immense iron compartment, with vents in the wall to allow the heat to escape, all setting upon a solid foundation of stone. Above this was a large room running the entire length of the building, where large bales of blankets, boxes of hardware and other necessaries of the trade were stored. The floors above were divided into wholesale and retail departments, some being used exclusively for the traders, others for the Indians.

About 1834 the fur-trading business began to decline. Formerly fine hats were made from the fur of the beaver, but at the time mentioned silk was substituted. The extensive scale on which the fur trade was conducted gradually almost exterminated the fur-bearing animals. The land, too, was being settled up by farmers. This drove the wild animals away. The Indians were being placed on reservations and cared for by the government, so that they did not hunt so much, and the Franco-Prussian War, a few years later, deprived the fur-trader of one of his best customers.

However, the fur-trading industry has been revived, and today St. Louis enjoys the largest trade in its history. This is due to two factors: (1) the South entering into the market, supplying raccoon, mink, fox, opossum, house and wild cat skins, and wolf and deer skins, and (2) the organization of great fur-trading houses which deal directly with the trapper.

Thousands of men all the way from the northern part of British America to Mexico, are engaged in trapping, some on a large scale, but most of them on a small scale. The average catch is estimated at less than $50 annually. Many of the animals trapped thrive in thickly settled communities. Parcel post allows the trapper to send his pelts directly to the great fur-trading houses of St. Louis.

The extent and value of this industry is illustrated by an account of a sale which took place there in the spring of 1916: "Six thousand skins were sold for a total of about $300,000 here today at the second session of the fur auction at which approximately 800,000 pelts, including every known variety and coming from every part of the globe, are to be disposed of. Yesterday about 250,000 smaller and inferior skins brought approximately $250,000.

"Today's sales were at varying advances over last year's prices with the single exception of silver fox furs, which sold at a decline of from 10 to 25 per cent over the record prices of last October. One pair of silver fox skins today brought $2,450, while the highest price for these skins in October was $2,600 a pair.

"In all, 350 silver fox pelts were sold, some as low as $75 a pair. Three hundred Russian sables brought $25 to $60 each, 3,500 white foxes, $8 to $20 each, 566 blue foxes, $25 to $190, 725 cross foxes, $10 to $100, and 287 chinchillas, $5 to $60."

One of the leading fur-trading companies of St. Louis, Missouri, under date of April 29, 1929, writes the author as follows:

"In 1920 we discontinued holding large public auction fur sales of furs which we received from all parts of the world. However, since 1920 we have been conducting only two raw fur sales each year and at these sales we sell only United States Government seal skins, blue foxes, etc., and we are not accepting any shipments from private concerns. However, we hold two private sales each week during the active fur season and these sales are attended by a large number of fur buyers and brokers who represent manufacturers in the United States and other parts of the world. At these sales we sell from $50,000.00 to $100,000.00 worth of furs twice each week and there are a number of other fur houses here in the big St. Louis market who conduct private sales in the same manner.

"The reason we discontinued the large public auction fur sales was due to the fact that this encouraged speculation in furs and they were not being turned into the manufactured garments as fast as they should have been. However, public auction fur sales are being held now in New York, Montreal, Seattle, and one or two other places in this country and Canada, but the sales are not as large in size and the volume of furs offered is much smaller than the offerings at our large public auction fur sales conducted between the years 1914 and 1920."

The Beaver.—When the white man came to America beavers were very numerous. They live largely in or near the water, so that other animals can only with difficulty, catch or kill them. The Indians did not care

The Beaver—His Dam and Lodges.

for the flesh for food nor for the skin for clothing, so they were found in large numbers in all the streams in what is now the United States and Canada.

The Beaver is as large as a small shepherd dog weighing 30 or 40 pounds. His legs are short; the front ones are small, while the hind ones are large and very powerful. His paws are well supplied with long claws and he is very handy with his front paws; he can carry an object much as a little girl carries a bag or a bucket. His hind feet are webbed and aid him greatly in swimming. He has a large flat tail which he is said to use in plastering his dam or to splash in the water as a signal of danger, and, in some instances, so spank the little beavers when they do not do as he wishes. The beaver has four large front teeth which he uses to gnaw down a tree and cut it into suitable lengths for his dam, or to gnaw his food. His coat is a beautiful chestnut brown of rich, thick fur about an inch long.

The beaver builds his house in or beside a stream of water. If the stream is swift he builds his house in the bank, the entrance being beneath the water, but if the stream is not swift he builds a dam across it of sticks and mud and grass and rocks. Thus a pond or lake is formed. In this lake he builds his house which is dome-shaped and is made of sticks and mud, the dome being about four or five feet above the water level. The interior is about six feet wide, 16 inches high and 16 feet long. The sides are four to five feet thick while the top is three feet thick, built rather loosely to admit the air. The floor is just above the water line and is kept perfectly clean; it usually is covered with soft grass.

For food the beaver cuts down the cottonwood and other trees whose bark he likes, cuts off the limbs which he divides into suitable lengths and then pushes them into the water and steers them up to the side of his house where they are sunk until desired as food. He makes a tunnel from his house down into the bed of the stream and through this he goes and gets his stick of wood when he desires food, and through it also, he pushes the stick back again when he has used all of the bark from it.

A beaver family consists of the father and mother and all the little beavers not over two years old, but no family will allow a bachelor beaver to live with it. He is always driven away after he becomes two years old.

The little beavers are taught how to build dams and houses, how to cut down trees and select their winter supply of food, and how to guard against their enemies; and if they are very careful what they eat and where they go they sometimes live to the ripe old age of fifteen years.*

The Tail of a Beaver.—The beaver's tail is not the useless object that some people think. *The Youth's*

**Breaking of the Wilderness,* p. 13.

Companion tells about a beaver named Diver. "Diver," says this authority, "would sometimes thrust his tail under him and use it for a seat. Sometimes, when standing up he used his tail for a rear brace to prop himself on his hind legs. In swimming he occasionally turned it on edge and used it for an oar; besides, it served in the water as a rudder whenever a rudder was needed. But out of the water when he was walking about, it appeared to drag behind him as if it were not a part of him. When he was stationed he usually tipped his tail on edge, doubled it round and rested it against his side. On one occasion, he thrust it between his legs, scooped up a mess of mud and carried it up on a small fallen tree near by and then dumped it. One time he carried two small sticks by clasping them between his tail and his stomach."

Trapping Animals.—The fur-bearing animals are the beaver, fox, lynx, mink, muskrat, marten, bear, coon, ermine, rabbit, coyote and sable. Furs are best where cold is most intense, so trappers usually go to the mountains. The beaver was the standard of value for American trappers; by the price of beaver, the price of all other furs and merchandise was measured. So many beavers for so many otter, fox, etc., or so many beavers for the price of a gun, blanket, or trinkets desired by the Indians.

Fall, winter, and spring are the hunting seasons; then trappers, in groups of two or three, accompanied by their squaws and children, could be found from Mexico to Canada, and from the Mississippi to the Pacific.

The trapper's dress consisted of a buckskin shirt and trousers, a coonskin cap, capote or flexible hat, and moccasins. He carried a gun, powder horn, and a shot pouch, containing bullets, bullet molds, and patching; also a large knife, whetstone, and tobacco. On his pack horse he had an axe, steel traps, and all sorts of trinkets to trade with the Indians.

He, like the prospector, went up and down stream looking for signs—dams, lodges, fallen trees, etc.—and when the beaver was located he would set his trap. If near a pond in which there were lodges, the traps would be fastened to a block of wood and the chain to a stake driven into the bottom of the pond in such a way that the trap would be held just under the water through which the beaver would have to swim to get to his lodge. The trap would be baited with some "medicine." This medicine was an oil taken from the groin of a beaver, the odor of which attracted the beaver; and very soon he would be caught. Then he would struggle until he drowned, or he would get to land and gnaw his foot off and free himself.

The trapper stopped but a short time in one place; sometimes if he discovered a colony of beavers he would break their dam, expose their lodges and then with his dog, capture the inmates. If the beaver made his home in the bank, sticks would be driven down through the passageway leading to the water and by this means escape was cut off and he would be captured.

As soon as he was caught the hide was removed, as only the tail and the liver were good for food. The flesh and fat were taken from the hide and it was stretched on a frame until it became dry; after drying the skins were put up in bales of 100 each, taken to the nearest post or rendezvous, and marketed.

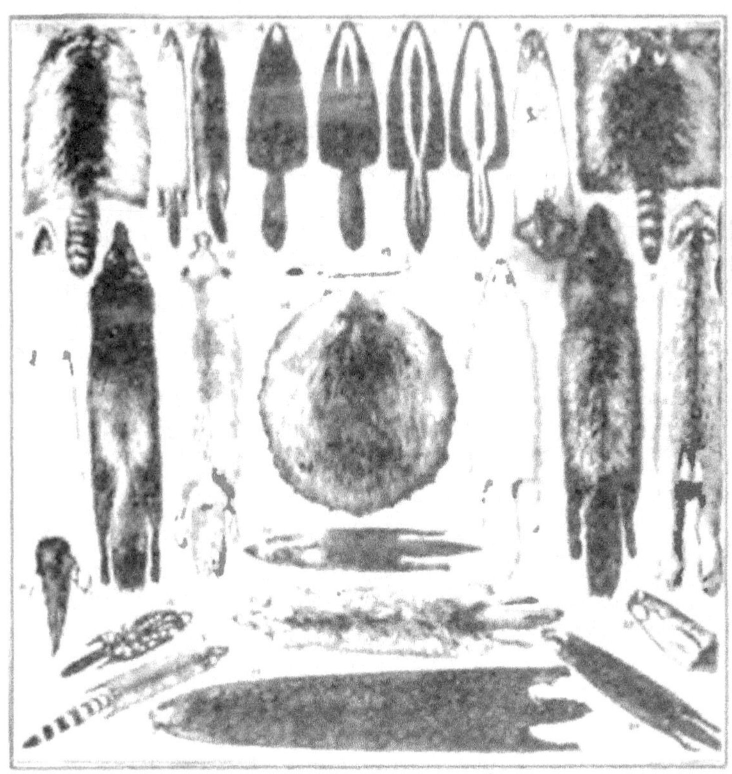

Pelts of Fur-Bearing Animals.

HOW TO REMOVE THE SKINS FROM ANIMALS.

Funston Brothers of St. Louis, Missouri, maintain that the following kinds of furs should be taken off cased, that is, not cut open down the belly: mink, marten, skunk, opossum, land otter, all kinds of foxes, ermine (or white weasel), lynx, civet, ring tail cat, fisher, sea otter, muskrat and house cat.

Wolf may be either cased or open. The fine skins from mountain or northern sections sell better cased, while the wolf and coyote skins from western and southern prairie sections sell better open.

To remove skins that are taken off cased, a cut should be made crosswise just under the tail, and lengthwise down the back of the hind legs, so as to get the skins free from fat or meat by scraping if necessary, but the skin should not be cut or damaged. Skins should be stretched with Funsten Invincible Fur Stretchers if available; if not, a thin board cut to the natural shape of the skin, but a trifle larger may be used. Skins should not be stretched too much with the hope of getting a large skin out of a small one; too much stretching spreads the fur over a larger surface and makes it appear thin and lacking in richness of color.

NOTE—Tails of opossum and muskrat *only* should be cut off. All other tails should be left on, removing the bone by splitting the tail part of the way down if necessary. It is best to remove the tail bone, especially on fine or high priced skins, to prevent the tail from becoming tainted. All legs should be left on lynx.

The following kinds of skins should be taken off *open:* raccoon, bear, badger, beaver, wolverine and wild cat (mountain lion or lynx cat may be taken off either open or cased). In taking off skins open, they should be cut down the center of the belly from chin to tail. No fat or meat should be left on the skin. Skins should be stretched to shapes shown in the picture and dried carefully.

No. 1. Raccoon. Should be taken off open, as picture shows. This style of handling is popular with the northern trappers.

No. 2 and No. 3. Mink. Should be cased pelt side out, but the fine dark skins from the extreme north should be cased fur side out.

No. 4. Black Skunk.

No. 5. Short Stripe Skunk.

No. 6. Narrow Stripe Skunk.

No. 7. Broad Stripe Skunk.

All skunks should be cased pelt side out. The fur side is shown in the picture only to point out the difference between black, short, narrow, and broad stripe skunk.

No. 8. Opossum. Should be cased pelt side out.

No. 9. Square Handled Coon. This is one of the best shapes for coons, especially for central and southern sections. It is very popular with all manufacturers.

No. 10. Land Otter. Should be cased pelt side out, but fine dark skins should be cased fur side out.

No. 11. Silver Fox. Should always be cased fur side out. This picture is taken from a very valuable skin.

No. 12. Red Fox. Should be cased fur side out.

No. 13. Ermine (or White Weasel). Should be cased fur side out.

No. 14. Beaver. Should be open and stretched as nearly round as possible.

No. 15. White Fox. Should be cased fur side out.

No. 16. Cross Fox. Should be cased fur side out.

No. 17. Lynx. Should be cased fur side out. All legs should be left on.

No. 18. Civet. Should be cased pelt side out.

No. 19. Ring Tail Cat. Should be cased pelt side out. Picture shows civet and ring tail cat fur side out to show nature and color of the fur.

No. 20. Fisher. Should be cased fur side out.

No. 21. Wolf. Should be cased fur side out from mountain and northern sections, but should be taken off open from western and southwestern sections.

No. 22. Sea Otter. Should always be cased fur side out.

No. 23. Muskrat. Should be cased pelt side out.

No. 24. Marten. Should be cased fur side out.

Some trappers deviate slightly from above suggestions in details of handling.

The Rendezvous.—Professional men have their associations where they meet and discuss questions of common interest. Farmers have their fairs and live stock shows, in order that they may exchange ideas on the subject of stock raising. Various labor organizations meet and plan for their common good. Representatives of the churches of the same denominations hold their annual conventions and conferences and reports are received and future work planned. In brief, kindred spirits in every walk of life seek the associations of their fellow laborers.

The trapper and the fur-trader were no exception to this rule. They had their rendezvous where there might be an exchange of furs for traps, firearms, ammunition, blankets, trinkets, and so on. East and west of the Rocky Mountains, everywhere, thousands of men scattered over hundreds of miles in every direction, engaged in the trapping and trading business, working either alone or in parties of two or three or more. They led a hard life. Almost half of their number met death from famine, cold, or accident, or from wild beasts or savage Indians. So they looked forward to their annual rendezvous, when they might again see and mingle with their fellowmen.

The place selected would be one that would accommodate the largest number, and furnish the best in the way of climate, water, and wood for the men and pasture for the pack horses. Such a location was found near South Pass in Wyoming. This was a midway ground between the traders on the eastern and the western slopes of the mountains, and both could meet the representatives of the great fur-trading companies, who brought them their necessary supplies.

The gathering was made up from many classes; the Indian, representing every grade from the naked savage to the proud Nez Perce, dressed in all the gaudy trappings of which he was so fond; the white trader with his Indian wife and half-breed children; the fur trapper, as well as those in the employ of the great companies; the Mexican from the south, and the Frenchman from the north, all met at the appointed time and place.

Their sports were such as gave expression to the wild nature of the men and women who roamed through the forests the greater part of the year. The days were spent in trading, horse racing, gambling, etc., and the nights in feasting, drinking, and carousing. Fights were of frequent occurrence, and murders not uncommon. There was whiskey in abundance; everybody carried firearms and dangerous knives; and clashes between the representatives of the different companies, between whites and Indians or Mexicans were a common occurrence. The free trappers, and those engaged by the companies, all represented a life so strenuous that such a meeting could not last long; the trapper soon squandered his year's earnings and was eager to get back to his work; the gamblers soon won everything to be had in a company of that kind, and the trader disposed of his goods and started on his return to market with the furs which he had received for them. Thus the wild carousal ended, and the men again returned to their lonely life in the forests.

A Cache.—Trappers, explorers and travelers through the country frequently found it necessary temporarily to abandon some of their equipment and supplies. Since there were no buildings where such materials could be stored, other means had to be provided. The hiding place or cache had to be so constructed that its location would escape the sharp eye of the Indian or unscrupulous traveler, and in some cases the keen scent of the wild animal.

The usual method was to dig a hole in the ground. A well-drained location was selected, and an opening a little larger than a man's body was started; as it increased in depth, it was enlarged, sometimes being fashioned in the shape of a jug. The size of this would depend upon the amount of material to be stored. The dirt removed was carefully carried away and thrown into a stream of water or otherwise disposed of so as not to excite the curiosity of passers-by. When the hole was of sufficient size it was lined with dry grass or leaves or sometimes the hides of animals; then the materials to be stored were placed; these might be provisions, bales of furs, the instruments of explorers, clothing, etc. On top of this was piled grass or hides, and the opening into the cache was carefully filled and tamped with dirt. Last of all, the sod which had been taken off at the beginning was carefully replaced, and as far as possible, all trace of the existence of such a storehouse would be blotted out.

The place was then carefully noted in the mind or in an account book, so that it could be recognized readily by the natural surroundings, when the one who had made the cache should return to it.

Joe Meek, Mountain Man.—The mountain men were those engaged in trapping, and spent their lives on the plains and in the hills. Usually they wore moccasins of buckskin, corduroy trousers, buckskin coats or capote and fur caps; they went heavily armed; had one horse to ride and one to pack provisions. They experienced all kinds of danger and endured all manner of hardships; frequently they met with accident and sometimes death.

They, like all children of the forest, delighted in recounting their exploits by means of stories which were strange mixtures of fact and fiction. While these stories are not to be taken too seriously as history, yet they present a vivid picture of the lives of men who kept no diaries, wrote no letters and made no reports; who lived much alone in the wilds of nature.

About 1828, a young Virginian, 18 years of age, arrived at St. Louis. His name was Joe Meek. He was looking for a job, having run away from home because of his stepmother. As he walked along the street he saw a sign "Trappers Wanted." He went in and met the great trapper, Sublette, to whom he offered his services. The trapper laughed; he was looking for old, experienced men; not gawky, green boys. He said to

Meek, "Young man, you would be killed before you were half way up." Meek replied, "Wal, I reckon that I'd be dead." This pleased Sublette, so he said, "Well, we'll take you if you keep your wits about you." "All right," said Meek, "there is no other place for 'em."

So, about March 1st, a company consisting of sixty horsemen and forty-three pack horses, started west from St. Louis, Missouri, which then was very sparsely settled, and at Independence left the last vestige of settlement. Another young man by the name of Newell, who afterwards became famous in Idaho and Oregon, was also in the party. He and Meek became fast friends. Just before leaving Independence they were out walking and passed a farmer's wife carrying some milk in a gourd. They made some humorous remark about the milk pail. She turned and said, "You are running away from home, who'll mend your clothes in the wilderness?" This did remind Meek that he was getting into a wild country and leaving friends behind, but he could not turn back now.

The route was along the old Oregon Trail, and in July Meek had his first experience with wild Indians. Suddenly one day a band of warriors came at terrible speed towards the party. They were brandishing their tomahawks, swinging war clubs, and in every way indicating that they were a war party. Sublette, who was in charge, understood what to do. He knew one should never show fear, so he told his men to lay down their arms, yet be ready to fight. When the Indians were about fifty yards from the trappers, they threw down their guns right in front of Sublette and dismounted, which was a signal for a powwow. Sublette soon arranged for the Indians to pass on, otherwise the trappers would have been completely annihilated, and we should never have known of Joe Meek and Newell.

Later in the summer, the party moved on up to the head of Big Horn River, where a rendezvous was held. Here, those who had been trapping through the winter and spring met the new party bringing supplies. The traders took possession of all the pelts collected, paid the men their wages, and entered into contracts for the next year.

A trading company is in charge of a leader, termed a "bushway." He subdivides the party into groups of a few men, who go out in every direction in such a way as not to interfere with each other's ground.

Meek came to the head waters of the Snake River in the vicinity of Pierre's Hole, just opposite the Hudson's Bay Company Post in the Blackfoot Country. At first he was delegated to do guard duty, but he was young and got very tired and sleepy. The first night he went to sleep. This was a very serious offense and was visited with severe punishment. But Meek's fellow-guard saved him. It was the custom of the captain to go out at any hour of the night and shout to see if any guard was asleep. When this guard heard the shout and knew that Meek was asleep and ought to answer, he ran up to the captain and cautioned him to be still, that the Indians were near. He then slipped back and woke Meek. Since all trappers wore moccasins, Meek made tracks to make the captain believe that the Indians had approached.

In the fall of 1829 when the party started back east, it was attacked on the Yellowstone River. Two men were killed, and Meek was separated from the party. He had only his gun, his mule, and blankets. He wandered through the mountains for three or four days, floundering in the snow, not daring to kindle a fire to cook food or for warmth. Finally, he had to abandon his mule. On the third day he killed a mountain sheep, kindled a fire, ate a hearty supper, then slept soundly all night. Soon after he resumed his journey he came upon some boiling springs, and, while admiring them he was startled by a war whoop and the report of a gun. His fright, however, was only momentary, for some one said, "It is only old Joe"; then he knew he had overtaken his party.

At one time Meek and his two companions were attacked by a bear. They threw down their guns and made for a tree. All succeeded in getting up the tree, but the tree climbed by one of the men, had another very near it. The bear climbed up the tree where this man was, by bracing his back against one tree and holding to the other. As he neared the man, the tree bent and Mr. Bear fell to the ground. He repeated this many times, Meek and his friend, in the meantime, making all sorts of fun of their companion.

The party broke camp and started for the rendezvous, but Meek was compelled to remain behind, for Sublette had been stabbed and Meek had to remain with him for forty days. As they traveled through the mountains they came upon a band of Snake Indians who also saw them. It was two men against thousands, so they did not attempt to get away, but mounted their horses and made a dash for the lodge of the Medicine Man, which was located in the center of the village. They charged right through the village to the tent door. Once within the tepee they knew they would not be disturbed until they departed. The lodge was full of Indians, and a discussion arose as to what to do with the white men. Meek and Sublette understood the Indian language and at the close of the day learned that the decision was to kill them. But neither of them dared show signs of fear. The Indians departed to carry out the decision of the court as soon as darkness fell. As they passed out of the tepee, one old chief remained for a moment. As he he went out he pointed up and down, a sign that possibly the white men might be saved but that probably they would be killed.

Soon there was a great commotion among the horses. Every one ran to see what the trouble was. At the same time the old chief came into the tent and motioned for the men to follow quickly, which they did. Running down to a thicket of bushes, they found a beautiful Indian girl holding two horses. The chief told the men to mount and ride for their lives. By riding all that night and the next day they outdistanced the Indians.

The mountain men at times were driven to great need, depending as they did upon the killing of game for meat. If game in the locality was scarce, they sometimes ate ants, grasshoppers, and mice, or they killed their horses, or even toasted their moccasins or buckskin coats. Again, if game was plentiful, they had an abundance.

There are three grades of trappers. (1) The skin trapper, (2) the hired trapper, and (3) the free trapper, who furnished supplies and sold to whom he pleased. Meek passed through all stages, the last in 1835. About that time, Sublette had to go east for medical attention. This annulled the marriage between him and his Indian wife, and Meek immediately married her. It was she who had furnished the horses for the escape of himself and Sublette. She was called the Mountain Lamb, and was described by her husband as follows: "She had a bodice and leggings of scarlet cloth. Her hair was braided and fell down on her shoulders; a scarlet silk handkerchief was tied around her head. She wore the finest embroidered moccasins. She, like all Indian women, rode astride, carrying on one side of her saddle a tomahawk for war, on the other the 'Pipe of Peace.' Her horse was a fine dappled gray, costing $300.00, the saddle, $150.00, the bridle $50.00, the musk-a-moots $50.00. All were ornamented with cut glass beads and hawks bells that tinkled at every step. She was a bright and very self-controlled woman." At one time she was captured by a band of Indians but was rescued by Meek; again she escaped by swimming a river; and at still another time, she made a big Irishman apologize because he threatened to whip her. She was finally killed by Blackfoot Indians.

When the Whitmans and Spauldings came west, a party of which Meek was a member met them at the South Pass of the Rocky Mountains. Meek was very favorably impressed with Mrs. Whitman, who was a beautiful woman and the first white woman he had seen for many years. He loitered around her tent that he might talk with her. Mrs. Whitman was also interested in him because, with him as an interpreter, she could talk with the Indians. A few years later Meek placed his little daughter in the Whitman school. His second wife had left him and he had kept the daughter, who was named Helen Mar, from a hero in "Scottish Chiefs."

In 1840, after Meek had been in the trapper's business for twelve years, and had traveled from Canada to Mexico, and from the Mississippi to the Pacific; over deserts and mountains, he decided to settle down to farming in the Willamette Valley. "We are done with mountain life, done with wading beaver dams, done with Indian fighting and fur trading, done with the Rocky Mountains," said he. So, he, Newell, and a friend named Craig, who was at Fort Hall, obtained three wagons and left for the Willamette Valley. Meek put his family in one wagon, Newell and his family occupied another, and Craig accompanied the third. They followed the Oregon Trail, and stopped at Fort Boise and Payette, the Hudson's Bay leader being then in charge. He received Newell into the Fort, but, being an aristocrat, would not allow the rest of the party in. He sent them a piece of meat but they refused it. The party moved westward and stopped at Whitman station where other men joined them. The total number was now six. Meek's party went on to the Willamette Valley, settling not far from the present city of Salem. Each family took up land and began farming. The Methodists had already established missions, and had considerable live stock and fruit. So, also, had a number of retired Hudson's Bay trappers. Vancouver was about 100 miles to the north. These people, too, had made a good beginning in agriculture. However, the mountain men were not practical farmers and their Indian wives and children could do nothing. The settlers had driven the game away, so for the first few years "squaw men" lived a life of intense deprivation.

About 1843 there was a heavy immigration to the Oregon Country. Within a few years the American settlers formed a sort of government for their mutual protection. This provided for three departments. Meek was appointed sheriff. It was his duty to make all arrests, investigate all cases of unlawful character, and act as tax collector. After a time he resigned and was elected a member of the legislature. The legislature was in session when the Whitman massacre occurred, and the Territorial government attempted to raise a company of soldiers for protection from the Indians. They elected a messenger to go to Washington for aid. Meek was chosen for that journey of 3,000 miles. He was given a draft for $500.00 on the Methodist Missionary Society in New York, but this was of no value until he reached that city.

He immediately started on his journey with a party of seven. They adopted Hudson's Bay Company dress as that would insure protection from the Indians who feared the company. At Whitman Station they buried the dead including Mr. and Mrs. Whitman and Meek's daughter Helen Mar. From here they followed the Oregon Trail, two of them remaining at Fort Boise. At Fort Hall they stopped for a day or two, then pushed eastward. As it was winter they had to give up the horses and go afoot. Later Meek met old mountain friends, Smith and Bridger, who supplied them with horses, food and firearms. In March, two months after starting, they came to Independence, Missouri. It had been twenty years since Meek had passed through there. Now he felt his old social shortcomings. He had only a coon-skin cap and buckskin clothes. He was without money or friends. But he decided to be himself. "Joe Meek, you always have been, and Joe Meek you will always be. Go ahead Joe," he said to himself.

Here he met a sister whom he had not seen for twenty years.

He contrived to go down the river to St. Louis where the city papers published the account of the massacre and Meek's journey. This brought fame but no money. Penniless, he made his way to the wharf and went on board one of the best boats bound for Pittsburg. As prospective passengers came he stood on deck, dressed in western garb, shouting, "Ladies and gentlemen, board this ship which is going to carry Joe Meek. Hear all about the Indian wars, trappers, Whitman's massacre, etc." He finally arrived at Wheeling, Virginia, and moved toward Washington. He had no money and was beating his way. His strange dress made him the center of attraction, and his good nature won him friends. When he took the train for Washington he was without ticket or money. He was dressed like an Indian and looked like one, and when the conductor asked for his ticket, he replied, "Ha-ko any me-ca hunch?" The conductor, taking him for an Indian, passed on, but he soon came back and demanded the ticket. "Ka hrom hunch?" said Meek. There was uproarious laughter at the conductor's expense so he did not pass that way again.

Meek arrived in Washington, D. C., dressed as a western trapper. He signalled a cab and drove to the most fashionable hotel. He entered the dining room, and when presented with a bill of fare he refused it, saying, "I can't read," and asked the waiter to read it for him. Among other things listed on the menu was small game. Meek asked for antelope and the waiter replied, "Boss, I neber heard of dat." "Deer?" Same reply. Meek exclaimed, "That's small game in the

West. Big game is buffalo and grizzlies." He then asked for steak and got it at last. Gulping it down in four bites he said, "That'll do, bring me four pounds." That attracted the attention of all diners. At the close of the meal a number came forward to meet him. Some one asked him who he was. He replied, "I am 'envoy extraordinary' and minister plenipotentiary from the Republic of Oregon."

Without changing clothes he went to the White House. Upon his arrival he met the doorkeeper, a negro, who was reared on Meek's old plantation home. Polk's private secretary was a relative of Meek's. Although there were many who had appointments with the president, all had to step aside for the Oregon representative, and he was ushered into the presence of the president who also was a relative. After they had a short conference the President insisted on sending for his wife and other ladies. Meek said the rustle of silk frightened him more than the growl of a grizzley. The president put Meek in the hands of a barber and tailor, gave him money, and entertained him. Meek proceeded to see the sights, meet people, and enjoy himself. He met Benton, Fremont, Houston, Kit Carson, and others. His friends all supplied him liberally with cash which he freely spent in entertainment.

The president prepared a message for Congress, describing the conditions in the Oregon Country and recommending the organization of a Territorial government. This was done and Meek was appointed first United States Marshal for the territory. He filled this office creditably for a few years, but after acting as hangman of the Whitman murderers, he retired to private life and lived to a ripe old age, honored by all who knew him.*

What the West Owes to the Fur-Trader.—The people of the West owe the fur-traders a very great debt. They were our nation's first great explorers. There is not a creek or a branch which they did not ascend or descend repeatedly. There is not a range, a hog-back, or a hill which they did not go over. There is not a pass which they did not find, a wilderness which they did not penetrate, nor a desert which they did not cross.

The fur-trader with his Indian wife and half-breed children did much to prepare the Indian for the coming of the white man, as he understood both, and was, to a certain extent, understood by both.

The fur-trader mapped out regular routes which later became the roads traveled by the white man. At regular intervals, posts were located. They consisted of a store and a block house, which were surrounded by palisades. These were about one hundred yards square, and were made of logs sunk in the ground eighteen inches or two feet and rising some fifteen or twenty feet above it. (In treeless sections the walls and buildings were made of sod or adobe.) Watchtowers were erected at opposite corners. In these forts were mounted from two to six guns—four to six pounders. Every one, before entering the gates, was examined by the keeper, and only one at a time was admitted. Here was kept the merchandise needed by the trader in his work, as well as in his trade with the Indians. Here, also were stored the bales of furs until they were ready for shipment to some central point.

*Based on account given in *The River of the West.*

These posts later became the stations where the westward immigrant could get needed supplies and guides, and sometimes protection from the Indians. The most noted of these posts were: Forts Laramie, Bridger, Hall, Boise, Wallula, Colville, Umpqua, and Vancouver.

Trails to the Pacific.

This map on which the trails are traced was engraved and printed by the U. S. Geological Survey and is used by courtesy of this department.

CHAPTER III

Trails To The Pacific

When the United States purchased Louisiana Territory, there was not a single road, river, or trail used for travel; there was nothing but the unexplored plains, deserts, and mountains. Routes across this country had to be found, and the first were called trails. They were made at different times and for different purposes. Those like the Lewis and Clark were for the explorer and trader. The Oregon Trail was for the immigrant, and the Santa Fe Trail for the commerce of the Southwest, while the California Trail was for the gold seeker who went to California in 1849.

The Lewis and Clark Trail.—This trail might more properly be spoken of as a route, as it was as often on the water as on the land. The starting point was St. Louis, and the general course was up the Missouri River to its source in the Rocky Mountains, then crossing these mountains, to the headwaters of the Salmon River, which was named by Lewis and Clark, "The Lewis." The explorers were unable to push their way down this river, so they turned back and wandered through the mountains and down the Bitter Root River for some distance. They then turned southward across the mountains at Lolo Pass and came to a branch of the Clearwater River, which they followed to the Snake, thence down the Columbia to the Pacific Ocean.

The Oregon Trail.—From Westport, now Kansas City, this trail followed the Missouri River up to its junction with the Platte, or went diagonally across by land to the Platte. In either case the Platte River was followed up to the Rocky Mountains. Crossing at South Pass, the route was down the north tributaries of the Snake River to Fort Hall, descending the Snake to a point near where Huntington is now located; thence across by the present cities of Baker, La Grande, and Pendleton, reaching the Columbia at Fort Walla Walla, now Wallula, and on down the Columbia to the Willamette River. This was the route taken by most of the early immigrants to the Northwest, and the one best known in American history.

The Santa Fe Trail.—This trail, too, started from the same point as the Oregon, and extended in a southwesterly direction. It led up the Kansas River for several miles then crossed over to the Arkansas, which it followed up to the Rocky Mountains; or it crossed the Arkansas and went on to the Cimaron and followed this up to the Rocky Mountains; in either case, after reaching the mountains the route led along the foothills south to Santa Fe, the present capital of New Mexico.

The Gila Trail.—Santa Fe is located on the Rio Grande, and the trapper and explorer traveled largely along the river. By going down the Rio Grande a few miles, a point was reached only fifty miles from the Gila River, which furnished a route to Lower California.

The Utah or California Trail.—There were two of these. They both branched off from the Oregon Trail. One, a short distance east of Fort Hall and the other west of the same place. Both ran through northern Utah, and both followed the Humboldt River until it disappeared into the ground, then up the Truckee River to its source, through the mountains at the Truckee Pass, thence down the Bear River to the Sacramento River.

The Old Spanish Trail.—This was laid out by a trapper in 1830. Starting at Santa Fe it ran in a northwesterly direction, across the Grand and Green rivers, then up the Seiver River, later intersecting the Mormon Trail which ran southwesterly to San Diego, California.

The Bozeman Trail.—The discovery of gold in Montana made necessary a road across the mountains from the east to these mines. A trail had been made by John Bozeman who went to Montana in the early sixties; later when it was made a military highway it took his name. The starting point was Fort Kearney in southern Nebraska; it passed by Red Buttes in northeastern Colorado on to Fort Laramie, thence northwesterly through Wyoming, passing east and north of Yellowstone Park and on to Virginia City in southern Montana.

The Cradle Home of the Pacific Northwest.

The Cradle Home of the Pacific Northwest.—"Louisville, Kentucky, February 17.—Just south of Louisville, between the Newberg road and the Bardstown pike, stands a log house more than a century old, which is one of the landmarks of American history, and which may be designated the cradle of the great Northwest, for it was from this house that Lewis and Clark started on their journey through the then unexplored wilderness to the Pacific Coast, in 1803.

"The house stands today almost as it did in the dawn of the last century when the intrepid young explorers set out on their journey which was to open an empire. It was then an outpost in the wilderness. Today the city has swept all around it and it is within a short distance of the center of population of the United States.

"The house was built by Gen. Jonathan Clark, the father of William Clark, of the Lewis and Clark expedition, and of George Rogers Clark, one of the mighty figures in the history of the Northwest Territory. It was erected about the year 1784.

"William Clark served as lieutenant under his brother, George Rogers Clark, from 1793 to 1796, and then went to St. Louis. When he was commissioned a member of the expedition to push through the Northwest to the Pacific he came to Louisville and met Meriwether Lewis. The leaders gathered the first members of their expedition here and starting from the Clark homestead, proceeded to St. Louis and thence on their historic journey.

"The homestead, which was known as Mulberry Hill, was occupied by the Clark family for many years, and is now in the possession of its descendants. Around the original log cabin other structures were erected and the slave quarters are as they were in the days before the war. The log cabin itself is unchanged except that the roof has undergone repairs made necessary by the wear of time. But the logs, culled from the primeval forest, are as sound as they were when the pioneers shaped their home from them."—*The Indianapolis News.*

Lewis and Clark Exploration.—No party for the exploration of the West was ever more carefully organized than that of Lewis and Clark, which consisted of the following:

"There were fourteen soldiers selected from a large number who had volunteered from the regular army. There were nine young frontiersmen from Kentucky, men who had used the rifle from boyhood in hunting and in Indian warfare. There were two French canoemen, or 'voyageurs,' one of whom could speak many Indian languages, while the other was a skilled hunter. These men were all enrolled as privates in the army, and with a negro servant of Captain Clark they made up the force. Three of the men were appointed sergeants. In addition, a corporal and six soldiers with nine boatmen were sent to accompany the expedition until they should reach the Mandan Indians, who dwelt near the the present site of Bismarck, North Dakota."

The Lewis and Clark party during the first summer pushed on up the Missouri River, using poles and sails when possible for propelling their boats. But this was a very slow method of travel, and winter overtook them at Fort Mandan, near the present site of Bismarck, North Dakota. Here they went into winter quarters. Some of the most powerful as well as hostile tribes of Indians resided in this vicinity. The British fur-traders to the north, too, were looking on with a jealous eye, none too friendly to the American invasion of what heretofore had been their trapping ground.

Lewis and Clark realized their precarious position, so they set their men to work and built a stockade, getting cottonwood logs from the river bottoms, splitting them in two, and making a triangular palisade, within which they erected houses for the men. This is a cold and bleak section of the country and it was rather a severe trial for the men, some of whom were from the south, where they had been accustomed to a milder climate. Lewis and Clark, however, spent most of the time gathering all the information they could in regard to the number and condition of the Indians in that immediate locality, as well as of those farther west. At the opening of the spring, however, they were ready and anxious to resume their journey, and they were most fortunate in securing for a guide an Indian woman, "Sacajawea," a member of the Shoshone tribe, who had been stolen in her childhood, and was now married to a half-breed Frenchman, who was engaged as cook for the party. Their journey was continued up the Missouri to Great Falls. Passing around these Falls, they then swung far toward the south arriving in due time at Three Forks located in what is now southern Montana. By this time the Indian woman was quite familiar with the country and she guided them up the middle fork of the Missouri, which the party named Jefferson, to its source. At this point Clark was worn out and ill, so Lewis took the party and pushed on to the south looking for the Shoshones.

At a point in Montana where the town of Armstead is now located, Sacajawea recognized the place of her capture, explaining to the party its details. Lewis marched on, and soon came in sight of some Indians, with whom he tarried until Clark and the rest of the party came up. Sacajawea was very much excited as she recognized the Indians of her tribe. Soon an Indian girl, leaning over and looking at Sacajawea, recognized her, and they flew into each other's arms.

"They had been children together, had been captured in the same little band, and shared the same captivity. The one had escaped to her own people while the other, Sacajawea, was sold as a slave and was now returning to them."

Lewis was impatient to push on as it was getting late in the summer, and he knew he had to cross the Rocky Mountains; so, selecting for his guide a Shoshone Indian whom he named Toby, he crossed over the mountains toward the south into what is now Idaho, and on to the headquarters of the Salmon River. He was warned by the old Indian that it was a river of "high rocks, and all a river of foam, no man or horse can cross, no man can walk along the shore, we never travel that way." However, Clark continued for seventy miles. Lewis at length turned his party back and crossed the Bitter Root Mountains. He followed down the river of that name to near the present site of Missoula, then turned west, crossed the Bitter Root Mountains at Lolo Pass, then down the Locksaw and the Clearwater rivers to the present town of Weippe. There he surprised three little Nez Perce boys while gathering kamas. The boys ran and hid as they had never before seen a white man. Coming on down the river to the present site of Orofino, they met other Indians, who gave them a fine salmon, while they, in turn, tore off a piece of red cloth—some say a piece of the flag—and bound it around the Indians' heads.

The party was anxious to continue their journey, so they chopped down trees for the purpose of making log canoes. It is said by some that the stumps* of some of these trees were removed by the builders of the Northern Pacific Railroad, when the road was built into Orofino. Lewis and Clark continued their journey down the Clearwater to its junction with the Snake, thence to the Columbia, and on down to the Pacific, arriving there in the late fall.

A fort, called Fort Klatsop, built of logs, was established near the mouth of the river. It was enclosed in the usual way with pickets and a gate, and had log buildings within the enclosure for housing the men. This was completed by Christmas Eve, and the party moved in. At daylight on the next morning, salutes were fired, presents were distributed, and other means of merry-making indulged in. The members of the party spent the winter in resting and hunting elk, killing over one hundred. The flesh was used for food, the skins for preparing clothes and the tallow for the manufacture of candles.

On Sunday, March 23, 1806, the party broke camp and started on their homeward journey. The trip up the Columbia was much like that made down the same river but a big reception had been prepared by the Nez Perces for the party on its return to the Nez Perce country. The place selected was in the Kamiah Valley. A house 150 feet long, made of sticks, straw, and dried

---

*One of these stumps, called in the Indian language *piouit* or white man's stump is still pointed out on Lot 3, Block 1, Gorman's Addition to Orofino, Idaho, and the old adz used in the making of these canoes is still in the possession of Charles Adams, a descendent of the family to whom it was given by Lewis and Clark. The adz is of the hoop-pole variety used in barrel making, is small, and can be easily stored.

grass was the place in which they were received. There were twenty-four fireplaces in a straight line through the middle of the house, and on these were placed kettles in which various kinds of food were prepared for the coming of the white men. Lewis and Clark's party were very tired and hungry when they arrived, and in a humor to do full justice to the meal. Here they remained for some days, as it was too early in the spring to start across the mountains. Then, too, horses for packing purposes had to be secured, and a guide to direct them across the mountains was also desired.

On the trip the party had many amusing experiences with the Indians, who had not seen white men before. When they arrived in the Shoshone country, east of the Bitter Root Mountains, the Indians thought the men were in a starved and frozen condition, so they built enormous fires, and threw blankets over the men. When the perspiration poured over their faces and they could no longer endure the intense heat the white men would throw off the blankets only to have them thrown on again, and the fires kindled anew, the Indians not understanding the reason for the pale faces of the white men. Poor York, a negro servant, had a different experience. The Nez Perce Indian women took him down to the river and tried to wash the black off his face, and he, being unable to explain the impossibility of such a thing, had to stand by and submit meekly to the unmerciful scrubbing given him.

But when the summer was sufficiently far advanced that the snow on the mountains would allow the crossing over, Lewis and Clark resumed their journey and in due time arrived at St. Louis.

All members of the party were well rewarded by Congress, which voted Lewis fifteen hundred acres of land and Clark a thousand. The officers were allowed double pay and each of the other members of the party received three hundred acres of land.

The results of this journey cannot be overestimated. They had traveled eight thousand miles and had brought back much information in regard to the entire section of country traversed by them; so that years afterward, when the Louisiana Territory was being settled, and the Oregon Country being contended for, suitable information was always at hand to show the value of both.

CHAPTER IV

Routes To The Pacific By Water.

The Cape Horn Route.—The Pacific Coast could be reached by water by four general routes. First, by Cape Horn. This was a long distance, yet it furnished a continuous route by water, and in the early days was used quite extensively.

The Panama Route.— The route by way of the Isthmus of Panama, greatly shortened the distance from the Atlantic to the Pacific, but was open to the objection of very poor accommodations across the Isthmus, as in early days there were no railroads, roads, or regular pack trains. Besides, it led through swamps and was very unhealthy and unsatisfactory.

The Nicaragua Route.—This took advantage of the lake and the river of this name on the east coast, while there was also a river on the west. It passed through high altitudes, was a healthier route, and had better transportation accommodations than had the Panama.

The Tehuantepec Route.—This route led through Mexico and furnished accommodations for continuous transportation, as a railroad had been constructed, connecting the river on the Atlantic with that on the Pacific Coast; but as it was not needed by the Americans until after the Mexican War, the feeling between the two nations at that time made it impracticable to make a large use of it.

A Journey by Water From the East to the Pacific Coast.—"When the report of the discovery of gold in California became quite generally known in the East, there was a great demand for some means of reaching the new mines. If the individual desired to escape the dreary journey across the plains and mountains, as well as the danger of being scalped by wild Indians, or held up by robbers, he must go by water. There were two general routes—one around by way of Cape Horn, the other by way of the Isthmus, but in either case the route was by water. The demand for accommodations on board the Pacific Coast bound ships became so great that all kinds of boats, manned by all kinds of men, and propelled in various ways were pressed into service. The typical boat would accommodate five or six hundred people, but frequently had a thousand or more on board. This meant that they were jammed into every bit of available space with little regard to age, class, or sex. The rooms were often poorly furnished, ventilated, and kept. The floors were unscrubbed, beds left unmade, the bed clothing being rarely changed.

"The officials and employes, knowing the great demand in which their boat was held, were frequently neglectful, arrogant, and extortionate. The fare demanded was from three to five hundred dollars, and in addition to this, the provisions were very high. Ice cost from twenty-five to fifty cents per pound. The food was poorly prepared and served in an unsatisfactory manner.

"Under such conditions, seasickness in its worst form was unavoidable. Women lay in their cabins too sick to move. Little children often crawled from place to place on deck uncared for. The odors from the engine room, as well as from the kitchen, mingled with the unkempt conditions on the boat generally, and the poorly ventilated conditions everywhere formed a combination of circumstances sufficient to stagger the bravest souls.

"To endure circumstances like these for a few days is possible, but when days become weeks and the weeks months, only the strong and the brave could hold up for such a journey.

"The boat was not only overcrowded with passengers, but the same was more true considering the standpoint of baggage. Trunks, boxes, bundles of clothing, picks and shovels, pumps and gold washing machines and sometimes household goods were piled and stored in scattered profusion everywhere. If the voyage was by way of the Isthmus, all of this baggage had to be unloaded and reloaded, with the same hurry, confusion, and lack of system incident to lack of organization, and brought about the same conditions previously mentioned.

"This description, however, applied largely to the boats on the Atlantic Coast. On the Pacific Coast the conditions were different. Here a well-organized company, the 'Pacific,' plied regular boats between San Francisco and the Isthmus. They had good boats, ably manned and well furnished. The service on these boats became more and more perfect until this Pacific Coast company had ships one-sixteenth of a mile long, and the service as a whole was equal to that of the best merchantmen of the world. It carried more passengers, had more reasonable rates, and went through a greater variety of climate than any other line of the time. But when the transcontinental railways were completed, and the rush to the Pacific Coast mines was through, this boat line was discontinued, to be resumed only when the Panama Canal was completed."—*Bancroft* Vol. 35: 125-135.

CHAPTER V.

Missionaries.

The Spanish Missions in California.—The soldier goes forth into new lands to acquire them for his nation. The business man to exploit their resources. But the missionary seeks new lands that he may heal the savage of his diseases, teach him better ways of living, and bring to him the message of the true God, the Savior of men, and the hope of eternal life. The priest ever went with the soldier in Mexico, Central, and South America, as well as along the Pacific Coast to the Northwest.

The Spanish king knew the power of the priest in civilizing the Indian, and making him obedient to the rule of the Spanish governor. He, therefore, encouraged the founding of missions.

Many missions were established in what is now California, first in lower California, but gradually extend-

Old Spanish Mission at San Luis Rey, California.

ing northward. The prefix "San," meaning "Saint," and "Santa," the feminine of this prefix, applied to the names of many towns and cities of the state of California, show how numerous were these missions. While they might differ in some respects, having the individuality of some strong man stamped upon them, yet in the main they were the same. A bell swung from a tree, a wooden cross erected, an altar built of brush, and a hut of some material, would answer all purposes until an adobe house could be built.

The mission represented a group of buildings arranged in the form of a rectangle, in some respects like a fur-trading post. There was a threefold purpose in the plan. It offered (1) Living quarters for the priest and other employes of the mission. (2) Work shops of various kinds, such as carpenter shop, blacksmith shop, shoe shop, etc. (3) Buildings to be used for schools and religious services, and it was arranged with a view of defense in case of attack.

Since the missions were built down in the valleys far away from the timber, and since the climate did not demand fuel except for cooking purposes, the material used in construction was adobe; that is, sun-dried brick.

The roof gave them the most trouble. First they tried brush or thatch made of straw or weeds, but these soon became dry and were always a great fire hazard. Finally, a priest developed a process by which tiles could be manufactured like those used in European countries, and the beautiful tiled roofs which are seen today in many parts of California are the result of his discovery.

The Indians were taught how to farm, raise gardens and fruit, care for live stock, tan hides, and make clothing; they also attended church services, many of them being baptized and received into the church. They gradually adopted the ways of the white man, and when gold was discovered in California they were prepared for the white man's coming. They were accustomed to his ways, having learned of them from the priests at the various missions. Vast fields of grain and herds of stock were there ready to feed the white man when he arrived following the discovery of gold.

The warm climate and the rich valleys made it possible, when the missionaries had learned how to irrigate the land, to raise almost any kind of fruit, vegetables, grains, or grasses. This was followed by the introduction of all kinds of live stock.

The American trader on his voyages to China by way of the Hawaiian Islands or the Oregon Country, learned to put into the ports of California, first to replenish his food and water supplies, but later to trade. Here he found hides, tallow, fruit, etc.

The Indians in the Northwest obtained their first horses from those raised by the Spanish missionaries, and when the first immigrants came to the Oregon Country they, too, went to California for horses, cattle, and sheep. The gold miners on the Pacific Coast were at first fed largely from the fields, the orchards, and the herds of stock found at the old Spanish missions. The debt which the Pacific Coast owes to these missions can be realized only when their work is understood.

A Trip of 4,000 Miles in Search of a Teacher and a Bible.—The red man had traditions of his own in regard to Creation and the explanation of the forces of nature which surrounded him, but these were all vague and uncertain. What he most wanted was the white man's

Hi-youts-to-Han (Rabbit-Skin Leggings).

Ta-Wis-Sis-Sim-Nim (No Horns on His Head.)

(From paintings by Catlin.)

Book which explained all these things, and a teacher who would read it to him and teach him how to read it for himself.

Lewis and Clark told the Indians something of the Great Spirit and the Bible. The Hudson's Bay Company hoisted their flag on Sundays and when the Indians inquired about the significance of this, the day of rest or Sunday was explained to them. Some Iroquois Indians, in the employ of the Company, had been east of the mountains and had seen the priests or "Black Robes," as they were termed. This they told to their brothers in the West. Other trappers, who came west from time to time, brought more news of the same kind.

The Indians were informed that their mode of worshipping the Supreme Being was radically wrong. They were also informed that the white people away toward the rising of the sun had been put in possession of the true mode of worshipping the Great Spirit. They had a Book containing directions how to conduct themselves in order to enjoy His favor and hold converse with Him; and with this guide, no one need go astray, but every one that would follow the directions there laid down could enjoy, in this life, the good will of the Great Spirit, and after death would be received into the country where He resided, and live forever with Him.

Of all the Indian tribes in the Northwest the Nez Perces were perhaps the most intelligent and progressive. Their physical constitution had not been undermined by the diseases which the white men had brought to the coast Indians, and as a tribe they had not been conquered or cowed by numerous wars. They owned horses and traveled readily from one part of the country to another.

Tradition relates how a council of Nez Perces was held in the spring of 1832 and a decision reached to send five men east to secure the Book. Three of the men chosen were old men, the other two were young. Their names were as follows:

1. Tip-ya-lah-no-jeh-nin (Black or Speaking Eagle).
2. Ka-ou-pa (Man of the Morning or Daylight).
3. Hi-youts-to-han (Rabbit-skin Leggings).
4. Ta-wis-sis-sim-nim (No Horns on his Head).
5. Name not given.

The distance was two thousand miles, the way unknown and the destination uncertain, but as the older men remembered Lewis and Clark, there is a probability that they meant to find the latter who was then Indian agent, stationed at St. Louis. By October, four of the party had arrived at St. Louis, the fifth had gone only one or two days' journey when he returned. Clark, who had been so kindly treated by the Nez Perces twenty-five years before, sent two of his officers to meet the Indians and bring them to the barracks where they would be entertained while in the city. They arrived, greeted General Clark with calm dignity, but said nothing of their mission. Clark understood Indians and awaited their pleasure.

Finally, they told him of the object of their journey. They wanted the white man's Book of Heaven. Would General Clark give it to them? They wanted to know of God as the white man knew him. Would he tell them? They wanted a teacher who would go with them to the Columbia and open to them the mysteries of life. Would he send one?

General Clark did not know just what to say. He told them a little about God—perhaps as much as he felt they could understand. He was a member of Christ Church (Episcopal), and he was eager to satisfy the seekers after God. But he had no Bible in any language that the seekers understood. Furthermore, he was not in command of missionaries, but of soldiers. So how could he satisfy the requests made by the children from the West?

The Indians were disappointed, but remained during the winter. The old men were taken sick and died. In the spring the two remaining Indians decided to return to their people. Before they started, General Clark gave them a banquet after which he asked Ta-wis-sis-sim-nim to speak to those present, and he replied as follows:

"I came to you over the trail of many moons, from the setting sun. You were the friends of my fathers, who have all gone the long way. I came with an eye partly open for my people who sit in darkness. I go back with both eyes closed. How can I go back blind to my blind people? I made my way to you with strong arms through many enemies and strange lands that I might carry back much to them. I go back with both arms broken and empty! Two fathers came with us; they were the braves of many snows and wars. We leave them asleep here by your great water and tepees. They were tired in many moons, and their moccasins were worn out.

"My people sent me to get the white man's Book of Heaven. You took me to where you allow your women to dance, as we do not ours; and the Book was not there! You took me to where they worship the Great Spirit with candles, and the Book was not there! You showed me images of the Great Spirit and pictures of the Good Land beyond, but the Book was not among them to tell me the way. I am going back the long trail to my people in the dark land. You make my feet heavy with gifts, and my moccasins will grow old in carrying them, and yet the Book is not among them! When I tell my poor people, after one more snow, in the big council, that I did not bring the Book, no word will be spoken by our old men or by our young braves. One by one they will rise up and go out in silence. My people will die in darkness, and they will go on a long path to other hunting-grounds. No white man will go with them, and no white man's Book to make the way plain. I have no more words."*

Only Hi-youts-to-han lived to tell the story of his trip to his people, a large band of whom came out many miles to meet him, but the only message that he brought was, "A man will be sent with the Book."

The Call For Missionaries For the Oregon Country.—The story of the visit of the Nez Perce Indians to St. Louis was published in the church papers of New York and created wide-spread attention. In the cities and villages of New York and Pennsylvania, and among the pioneers in Ohio, Indiana and Illinois, the people said the Nez Perces must have their missionaries.

Dr. Wilbur Fisk, President of Wesleyan University, wrote the following challenge which was printed in the church papers:

"HEAR! HEAR!

WHO WILL RESPOND TO THE CALL FROM BEYOND THE ROCKY MOUNTAINS?

"We are for having a mission established at once. Let two suitable men, unencumbered with families and possessing the spirit of martyrs, throw themselves into the nation, live with them, learn

*While this speech or lament, is undoubtedly the work of some of the missionaries of a later date, yet it is by one who thoroughly understood the Indian and the circumstance of their visit to St. Louis, and for this reason it has a certain value. Incidently it may be mentioned that the MacBeth sisters, who served for many years as missionaries among these Indians, were personally acquainted with many who knew of this Eastern Mission and today tradition relates how this one, that one, or the other, is a decendant of one of these four men sent east.—The Author.

their language, preach Christ to them, and, as the way opens, introduce schools, agriculture, and the arts of civilized life. The means for these improvements can be introduced through the fur-traders, and by the reenforcements with which from time to time we can strengthen the mission. Money shall be forthcoming. I will be bondsman for the Church. All we want is the men. Who will go? Who? I know of one young man who I think will go; and I know of no one like him for the enterprise. If he will go (and I have written him on the subject), we only want another, and the mission will be commenced the coming season. Were I young and healthy and unencumbered, how joyfully would I go! But this honor is reserved for another. Bright will be his crown; glorious his reward."

Methodist Mission Founded by the Lees.

The Marriage of Jason Lee and Miss Anna Marie Pitman, or the First Christian Marriage in the Oregon Country.—"It is not good for man to be alone." So thought Jason Lee, the noted missionary in the Oregon Country, who in 1837, was located on the Willamette River, 3,000 miles from home and friends. He wrote to the Board of the Methodist Chuch, setting forth his necessities. It is not recorded that he asked for a wife, but we all know that in his condition he was badly in need of one. The Board very likely took this view, too, and when, in the spring of 1837, reenforcements were sent to the mission, there were some marriageable young ladies among the number, Miss Anna Marie Pitman, of New York, being one of them.

She is said to have been "tall, dark, somewhat gifted with poetic genius, fervently pious, and full of enthusiasm for the missionary life." The party of which Miss Pitman was a member sailed from Boston in July, 1836, by way of Cape Horn, arriving at the Sandwich Islands in the winter, where they remained until the following spring. They then went aboard another ship

Jason Lee.

Anna Pitman.

(From *The Winning of the Oregon Country*, by courtesy of the publishers.)

which brought them to Vancouver. Lee heard of their arrival and hastened to meet them. In the meantime they were royally entertained by the great and good Dr. McLoughlin.

It was understood that Jason Lee and Miss Pitman were to become man and wife, if, after meeting, they were mutually satisfied with such an arrangement. Their introduction was therefore one of more than ordinary interest. With Lee, if not a case of "love at first sight," it was one in which he was very favorably impressed. With Miss Pitman the ordeal was more trying, as man is supposed to do most of the wooing. In this case the woman had come many thousand miles to meet the man. She acquitted herself most creditably, however. A light blush which rose to her cheek, and a slight trepidation, which added charm to her manner, were all the evidences, said an eye witness, that she was conscious of the peculiarity of her position.

Immediate arrangements were made for their departure by canoe for the mission which was located on the Willamette River about seventy-five miles above Fort Vancouver. Cupid rightly decreed that Miss Pitman and Mr. Lee were to ride in a boat manned entirely by Indians who knew not a word of English, but, as they were versed in the language of love they doubtless understood much, although they could not speak the language of the party whom they were taking to their new home. On the third day the party landed and completed the journey on horseback. Miss Pitman enjoyed the change from the cramped quarters of the canoe, and the flower-decked prairies, with singing birds and humming bees, were a welcome change from the lifeless monotony of the open seas.

The home-coming was anything but inviting. The house was a log structure, forty-eight by eighteen feet, with a sort of loft or attic for the second story. The furniture was home-made and scant. There were already thirty-eight children in the house, many of whom were sick. They were lying on mats or blankets in various places on the floor. The new comers of the mission party numbered sixteen, consisting of men, women, and children, representing the most cultured of the New England states. These were to mingle promiscuously in their domestic life with the children of the forest who knew nothing but primitive simplicity.

The Lee-Pitman couple did not constitute all the romance connected with this home-coming. One, Cyrus Shepard, had been left behind to look after the household duties while Lee went to Vancouver, and he, too, was expecting a bride in the person of Miss Susan Downing. Dressed in a style befitting an eastern bride of culture and refinement, she suddenly appeared upon the scene and caught Mr. Shepard unawares, engaged in his household work and attired in a suit of linen whose cut and condition did not set off his figure to advantage. It was now the man's turn to blush and be embarrassed. But he soon recovered and proceeded to prepare a meal for the hungry travelers.

The table was laid with a brown linen cloth and tin plates. This pre-nuptial supper consisted of venison, sausage, bread of unbolted flour, butter, cheese, and fried cakes with strawberries and cream.

How this mixed company of fifty-four people were disposed of at night in a house with few if any partitions or beds is a question not answered by the historian, though presumably the good sense and good will of all found a satisfactory solution. Reverend Lee was in good health and spirits and so was Miss Pitman. They rode and roamed about the country and soon grew to understand and appreciate each other. The "course of true love" did not run so smoothly with poor Shepard. He was prostrated with a fever, whether from trouble over household duties or other reasons is not known. But the tender ministrations of Miss Downing soon restored him to health and happiness.

One Sunday in June, in a grove near the mission, the missionary family and the Indians met for what they thought was their usual service. Reverend Lee delivered a discourse on the propriety and duties of Christian marriage and closed by saying, "What I urge upon you by precept I am prepared this day to enforce by example." He then led Miss Pitman to the front of the congregation and they were married by his nephew who read the marriage service of the Episcopal Church. Mr. Lee then led his wife back to her seat and performed the marriage ceremony of Mr. Shepard and Miss Downing. A wedding breakfast followed, and thus was established the institution of Christian marriage in the Northwest.—*Bancroft's History of Oregon, Volume* I:156.

The Story of the First Two White Children Born West of the Rocky Mountains.—In 1836 Dr. Whitman, with his wife and Rev. H. H. Spalding with his wife, came as missionaries to the Indians in the Oregon Country. The former established a mission four miles west of the present city of Walla Walla, while the latter established one twelve miles east of the present city of Lewiston.

Mission of Waiilatpu, founded by Whitman, 1836.

During the next year we find this entry in the diary of Mrs. Whitman. "On the evening of my birthday, March 14, we received the gift of a little daughter, a treasure invaluable. The little stranger is visited daily by the chiefs and principal men in camp, and the women throng around the house continually, waiting an opportunity to see her. Her whole appearance is so new to them. Her complexion, her size and dress, etc., all excite a great deal of wonder; for they never raise a child here except they are lashed tight to a board, and the girls' heads undergo the flattening process. I have not yet described my babe to you. I think her grandmother would willingly own her as one of her number of babies, like her aunts Jane and Harriet. She is plump and large, holds her head up finely, and looks about considerably. She weighs ten pounds. Fee-low-ki-ke, a kind, friendly Indian, called to see her the next day after she was born. Said she was a Cayuse to-mi

(Cayuse girl), because she was expected by all the people of the country—the Nez Perces, Cayuses and Walla Walla Indians, and, now she has arrived, it would soon be heard of by them all, and we must write to our land and tell our parents and friends of it. The whole tribe are highly pleased because we allow her to be called a Cayuse girl."

This little girl was named Alice Clarissa, these being the names of her grandmothers. Little Alice had no white friends nearer than the Spaldings one hundred and twenty miles away. So when she was about seven months old, her parents took her on a visit to them. The Whitmans left their home on November 8, traveling on horseback. It took them about three days to reach the home of the Spaldings. They camped out by night and traveled through the day, frequently through sleet and snow. On the evening of the third day, they crossed the Snake River at the present site of Lewiston, where they camped for the night. Mrs. Whitman, speaking of this experience, said:

"We rode all day in the wind and rain, and came to the Snake River about the middle of the afternoon and thought to stop, but it cleared away and after making a fire and warming a little, we started again and came to the crossing place, and when the sun went down it found me sitting by the root of a large tree, on stones, with my baby in my arms, watching by moonlight the movements in crossing our baggage and horses. This was the only piece of wood in sight, and with a few bunches of wild sage a fire was made against it to warm me while waiting to cross. Soon I was seated in a canoe with my babe and landed across safely. At a little distance from the shore we found lodges and were supplied by them with fire-wood and lodge poles."

Little Alice enjoyed the visit at the Spaldings very greatly, Mrs. Spalding being the only white woman she had ever seen besides her mother, and at times she appeared to realize no difference between them. She would play with Mrs. Spalding, and kiss her with the same ardor and affection as she would her mother. While the Whitmans were there, a little baby girl, who was afterwards named Eliza, came to the home of the Spaldings. As little Alice was the first white child born in the present state of Washington, so Eliza was the first white child born in the present state of Idaho. The Whitmans, after a visit of a few weeks, returned to their home. Mrs. Whitman and her baby were taken down in a canoe to Fort Walla Walla, where they were met by Dr. Whitman who took them on horseback to their home, located twenty-five miles away.

The open air, the wholesome food, and the careful attention which the little Whitman girl received from her parents made her a very healthy child, and it is needless to say that she was much beloved by her parents. Her mother, in speaking of her, said: "My little Clarissa is my own little companion from day to day. She has saved me many melancholy hours while living here alone so long, especially when her father is gone for many days together."

When little Alice was about two and one-half years old she fell into the river and was drowned. The following description of this sad event is thus described by her mother: "It was half past two when we gave directions for supper, thinking to have it some earlier than usual because husband had not eaten anything since breakfast, when I sent Margaret to look for her.

Mungo went out with her at the same time and went to the river, but came back immediately and said there were two cups in the river. This startled us at once and as I made the inquiry, 'How did they come there?' Husband said, 'Let them be and get them out to-morrow, because of the Sabbath.' I asked again how they came there and what cups they were. He said 'I suppose Alice put them there,' and immediately went out and took some poles to get them out. Why I was not alarmed in an instant is to me astonishing. It was doubtless owing partially to my confidence in the girl I sent for her, because she did not come and tell me she could not find her. I trusted she had and had taken her with her to get radishes, etc. I looked to see if she was with her, husband at the same time going to see about the cups. I went to the other side of the house and inquired for her, but no one had seen her. Then it was pretty plain in my mind where she was, and by the time I got to the river's brink, it flashed across my mind like a dream, that I had a glimpse of her, while sitting and reading, entering the house and on seeing the table set for supper, she exclaimed with her usual animation, 'Mamma, supper is almost ready; let Alice get some water.' She went up to the table and took two cups that set by her plate and Margaret's (for we drank water instead of tea) and disappeared. This was like a shadow that passed across my mind, passed away and made no impression. Strange as it seemed to myself, I did not recollect it until I reached the place where she had fallen in. And now where is she? We thought if we could find her immediately she would not be dead entirely, so that we could bring her to again. We ran down on the brink of the river near the place where she was, and, as if forbidden to approach the spot, although accessible, we passed her, crossed a bend in the river far below and then back again, and then in another direction, still farther below, while others got into the river and waded to find her, and what was remarkable, all entered the the river below where she was at last found."

As one reads this sad event, he is almost ready to exclaim as the prophets did of old, that the Lord was asleep or away, or did not even exist to allow such a sad thing to happen to these devoted missionaries, depriving them of the only link between them and those of their own race and nationality. But a few years later, as the mother lay on a couch, having been struck down by the tomahawk of a ruthless savage and saw her husband who had been butchered in the same manner, what a blessing she must have thought it that her little Alice had been so painlessly taken away years before, rather than to have been left and butchered by these wild Indians.

The other little girl, Eliza Spalding, lived a very happy life at her home at Lapwai. She soon learned to speak the Nez Perce language, and she had many Indian playmates of her own age, and she, as well as her parents, had many friends among the Indians who lived near them.

When she was about ten or twelve years of age her father sent her to the Whitman mission to enter the school at that place, and while there the Whitman massacre occurred, she being one of the survivors of that terrible event. About fifty women and children were spared by the Indians but were held prisoners. Little Eliza was the only one who could speak the

Indian language readily and she had to act as interpreter in all that was communicated between the captives and their captors. These duties, and the continual nervous strain she was under, exhausted the little girl, and when she acted as interpreter she had to be held up in bed while she conversed with the one or the other. While here, she contrived to send word to her father who was down at Umatilla, and he escaped the fate that befell the others at Whitman station. She was greatly troubled, too, for fear her mother and other members of the family at home would be murdered by the Nez Perces, but one of the survivors of the Whitman massacre managed to escape and went to Lapwai and notified Mrs. Spalding of what had happened at Whitman station, and that her daughter Eliza, was yet safe.

Mrs. Spalding was taken to the home of Mr. Craig, located midway between the present site of Fort Lapwai and Culdesac, and she succeeded in getting two friendly Nez Perces, Timothy and Eagle, to go to Whitman station and try to get the release of her daughter. How happy little Eliza was when she saw these two old Indians, for she felt, of course, that she would be released, but the good old Indian, Timothy, told her it was impossible for him to get her away. "Then," she said, "for the first time, I cried." Old Timothy sympathized with her, and wiped her eyes with her apron, and said, "Eliza, don't cry. See mother soon. We'll fix it."

In the meantime, Peter Skene Ogden negotiated for the release of the captives. The price paid was sixty-two three-point blankets, sixty-three cotton sheets, twelve guns, six hundred loads of ammunition, thirty-seven pounds of tobacco and twelve flints. Seven oxen and sixteen bags of flour obtained from the Indians for the use of the captives were settled for. Later Mr. and Mrs. Spalding and other members of the family were brought down the Clearwater and Snake rivers to Fort Walla Walla where Eliza joined them. Their family as well as all of the whites, were taken down to the Willamette Valley.

Later, when the chief leaders in the Whitman massacre were brought to Oregon City to be tried for murder, little Eliza had to testify as a witness against these Indians, and in speaking of this she said: "I was almost as much frightened at the questions which the lawyers asked me and by the threatening looks of the Indians who were being tried, as I was in the days of captivity."

Mrs. Spalding died when her daughter was twelve or thirteen years of age, and Eliza then became the housekeeper for her father and brothers and sisters. When sixteen years of age, she was married to a Mr. Warren.

Sixty-two years after the massacre she revisited her old home at Lapwai, and how changed she found everything! She says: "I went out to the spot where the old house stood, and looked long and intently at the place where I had lived and played as a girl. The Indians had made many improvements in their methods of living, and were paying gratifying attention to better things. On the Sabbath I attended services in their little church, and talked to them through an interpreter, as I had forgotten their language during the years of absence from the tribe. Then they sang a song that father had taught them just before his death. After the meeting, we had a regular love feast and every one of them shook hands with me, and some of the older men remarked, 'This is Father Spalding's Eliza, I knew you when you were a little girl.'

"I am glad that father is buried right there among these Indians. As I looked at them, neatly dressed, quiet and civilized, I could not help comparing them with the Indians I knew when father first started his work. It had been worth the sacrifice and the lives and the heartaches of it all."

The Spalding Mission at Lapwai.—In 1830 the whole Oregon Country was inhabited by roving bands of Indians who were constantly at war with each other. The most powerful of these Indian tribes were the Nez Perces who lived in what is now northeastern Oregon and northern Idaho. Lewis and Clark had been entertained by them at their home on the Clearwater. By some means these Indians had heard of the white man's God and the white man's Bible, and were anxious to secure some one who could tell them of both.

About 1835 the American Board of Foreign Missions appointed Dr. Marcus Whitman and Samuel Parker to establish a mission among the Indians of the Northwest. They made the trip and investigated the field. Whitman returned, and in the following spring, he, accompanied by his bride, and Reverend H. H. Spalding and his bride, came to the Northwest for the purpose of establishing missions. The Whitmans settled among the Cayuses near the present city of Walla Walla, Washington, while Spalding came to the Nez Perces, settling at Lapwai. On January 27, 1837, we find the following entry in the diary of Mrs. Spalding: "By the blessing of God we are now in a comfortable dwelling." But one acquainted with pioneer conditions can easily picture to himself what that "comfortable dwelling" was like, a little one room log house with dirt or puncheon floor, stick and dirt chimney, one door, no windows, with household furniture and kitchen utensils much like that used by primitive man, and curious, child-like Indians "peeping" between the logs on every side.

"But the Mission after a few years consisted of a large and commodious dwelling with eleven fireplaces, an Indian reception room, weaving and spinning room, eating and sleeping rooms for the children, rooms for the family, and a school house, all under one roof. There were, besides, a church, saw mill, blacksmith shop, granary, store house, and all necessary farm buildings. The mission farm, besides supporting the family, as was at first anticipated, became a source of supply to travelers, natives, and other missions.

"Spalding had discovered as early at 1838 the fertility of the soil in the country east of the Cascades, and as early as 1845 that the plains were even more valuable for farming than the valleys. In a letter prepared by him in 1846 for the use and by the request of Joel Palmer, then on his way to the States, after giving the above opinion, he goes on to say: 'My place is one of the deepest valleys, and consequently the most exposed to reflection from the high bluffs around, which rise from 2,000 to 3,000 feet; but my farm, though prepared for irrigation, has remained without it for the last four years, I find the ground becomes more moist by cultivation. Three years ago I raised 600 bushels of shelled corn from 6 acres, and good crops of wheat on the same piece the two following years, without irrigation. Eight years ago I raised 1500 bushels of potatoes from one acre and a half, measuring some of the bags in which they were brought to the cellars, and so judging the whole amount. I gave every eleventh bag for digging and fetching, and kept a strict account of what every person brought, so that I was able to make a pretty accurate estimate of the whole amount. My potatoes and corn are always planted in drills. Every kind of grain or vegetable which I have tried in this country grows well.' "*

Mr Spalding was a very practical man as the above would indicate. He taught the Indian men how to plough, sow, reap, and thresh grain as well as how to grind it. They were also shown how to build houses and fence farms; how to raise and care for live stock.

His wife was equally practical; being the daughter of a farmer she had been taught how to card, spin, and weave cloth, how to cut, fit and make clothes, how to cook and do all other kinds of house work. These she taught to the Indian women.

Reverend and Mrs. Spalding were devout Christians and labored unceasingly for the conversion of the Indians, training them in ways of Christian living. The Whitman massacre which occurred about twelve years after the founding of their mission, also put an end to the Spaldings' work. Today there is very little evidence of the Spaldings ever having been at the site of their mission. The large stones showing the location of the chimneys to the main building may be seen on the right at the south end of the bridge as one going

*Bancroft's History of Oregon, Vol. I: 337.

south crosses the Clearwater River. Piles of stones show the location of the fence inclosing his corral. There may also be traced another fence-like enclosure where all the Indians are said to have sat while Spalding addressed them from the center.

The old mill race is plainly visible, as is the old mill site; while still buried in the sand, the Indians say, is one of the burrs used in the grist mill. But there is not a fruit tree standing in the orchard, nor has one of the stumps been preserved. There is a fine truck garden where Spalding raised the first vegetables in Idaho; and a garage, a filling station, and a grocery store are located on the site of what was very likely the front yard of the home. These things are all material and, as such, decay or give way to progress, but the real work of the missionary is shown in the advancement made in the civilization of the Indian.

The Last Remnant of the Spalding Mission.

The tepee has given way to the modern house and the blanket to modern dress. The reaper has taken the place of the kamas hook, and the Indian now transacts his political business by means of the Australian ballot, rather than the powwow. The medicine man has given way to the preacher; heathen paganism to Christian faith.

The citizens of Idaho are interested in this Mission for the further reason that here was organized the first church, established the first school, planted the first garden, sowed the first grain, set out the first orchards, built the first mill, brought the first poultry and live stock and founded the first Christian home within the boundaries of the present state of Idaho.

This, then, is a fitting site for the erection of a monument to commemorate these accomplishments, and this has been done by the synod (Presbyterian churches) of Washington. Another has also been erected by the local chapter of the D. A. R.

*Cyrus H. Walker, the First White Boy Born West of the Rocky Mountains and His Home.**—A year after the Whitmans and Spaldings had come west, two other couples took a wedding journey, Mr. and Mrs. Cyrus Hamlin Walker and Mr. and Mrs. Myron Eells. The site of their work was near the present city of Spokane, at a place called Tshimakain. But since there was no house they spent the winter with the Spaldings. During their sojourn here the missionaries made a study of the Spokane language, under the famous Nez Perce

*Mr. Walker in a letter addressed Albany, Oregon, Nov. 27, 1917, to Hon. Henry F. Ashlund, chairman of Senate Committee on Indian Affairs, says, "I was born at Whitman Mission, Dec. 7, 1838."

chief, Lawyer, who well understood that language. On the 5th of March, 1839, the wedding anniversary of both couples, they started for their new home. Upon their arrival a few days later their tents were pitched, but, upon the urgent invitation of Mr. Archibald McDonald, the Hudson's Bay trader at Fort Colville, the ladies and the baby boy became his guests until their husbands got the cabin homes ready for occupancy. On the last of April they went to their homes and began housekeeping.

"At first the houses had only earthen floors, and pine boughs served for roofs. As the spring rains quickly penetrated this rough shelter, earth was put upon the boughs; but still the roofs leaked, so bearskins were spread upon the beds to keep dry 'our first families' near Spokane.

"The luxury of a cookstove was unknown throughout the nine years' life of the mission at Tshimakain. In lieu of window glass, cotton cloth, and later, oiled deerskin, were used. A few years later there was much rejoicing over the receipt of a few panes of glass, sent in a sailing vessel around the Horn by Massachusetts friends, and transported with infinite care to the distant interior.

"For nine years the mission could boast of only a single chair. Three boards, three feet long, were packed 150 miles and by driving four stakes into the ground, a table was constructed. Timber, riven and hewn, was used for other furniture.

"In all the Oregon Country there were two flour mills, both owned by the Hudson's Bay Company, one at Colville, the other at Vancouver. Flour at the Whitman mission was worth $24 a barrel. With the harvesting of the first crop of wheat at Tshimakain, the grain was taken in buckskin bags to Colville for grinding. It was only seventy miles distant, and they could go and return in five days.

"The plough was homemade, with rawhide on the singletrees in place of iron, and for nine years the wheat crop was cut with sickles.

"The beef, according to Myron Eells, 'neither chewed the cud nor parted the hoof.' It was made out of the Indian pony. Cattle were very scarce. Neither love nor money could procure one from the Hudson's Bay Company. About half a dozen horses were killed for beef at Dr. Whitman's during the winter of 1838-39, and for several years Mr. Eells was accustomed to salt one down every winter. They were fattened on the rich bunch-grass, and with but few exceptions were eaten with relish, even by the fastidious.

"Mrs. Eells once wrote; 'I had the luxury of eating a a piece of the first cow that was driven into the country.'

"Fire was made with flint, steel, and punk. Mail from the East was brought out twice a year to Hawaii, and from there to Vancouver in the boat of the Hudson's Bay Company. That for the Mission was sent up the Columbia to old Fort Walla Walla, and when the missionaries learned of its arrival there, they would 'go to the postoffice,' 200 miles away, the round trip taking two weeks.

"In January, 1844, Mrs. Eells wrote to her sister in Massachusetts: 'Your letter dated September, 1841, I received July, 1843, a long time, sure enough, but, as the Indians say, 'I am thankful to get a letter of any date.' " To the same sister she wrote, in April, 1847: 'I have just been reading your sisterly letter of December, 1844, and although it was written more than two years ago, yet, since it is the last I have heard from you, it is like reviving conversation and talking of past events.' "—*Spokane and the Inland Empire,* by N. W. Durham, Vol. 1, Page 76.

Father DeSmet and Catholic Missions in the Oregon Country.—A large number of Hudson's Bay Company employes were French Canadians and members of the Catholic Church. From time to time they made requests of Dr. McLoughlin for a priest, and in 1839, during his absence, the request was made of the archbishop of Quebec, and he sent two priests, Fathers Blanchet and Demers. They came by land to Vancouver, the last few hundred miles being down the Columbia. Upon their arrival mass was celebrated. This rite had not been celebrated by the trappers for many years, and many of them, although rough backwoodsmen, were moved to tears. Missions were established on the Willamette River, near the Methodist Mission, and also on the Cowlitz River, north of Vancouver, good work being done at both places.

But perhaps the greatest Catholic missionary to the Northwest was Father DeSmet. The Indians, on their way to St. Louis to secure the Book and a teacher, passed by Council Bluffs, where they stopped for a few days. Here Father DeSmet was stationed. He met the Indians and became greatly interested in mission work among them. In March 1840, the way was opened up for him to go as a missionary to these people, and in the spring of that year he, with a party of the American Fur Company, left Westport, Missouri, for the Flathead country. An Indian by the name of

Ignace was his guide, and another went on ahead to announce his coming.

At Green River he and his party met a band of Indians, fur-traders, and trappers. Here, on the fifth of July, he celebrated mass. An altar was erected on a platform and decorated with the boughs of the cottonwood and the wild flowers of the plains.

From here Father DeSmet went to the Flathead country, where 16,000 Indians had assembled to meet him. Some of them had come 800 miles. The meeting was held at Pierre's Hole. The end of the first day was closed with a prayer and a chant, and the second day he transcribed for them the Ten Commandments and the Lord's Prayer. Within two weeks, 2,000 of them knew the Lord's Prayer and within six months, 600 were baptized. Such success stimulated DeSmet to extend his labors to the west. He visited the Coeur-d'Alene Indians and, as a result of his visit, there stands today "The Old Mission Church." He also visited Fort Colville, on the Columbia River, a little farther to the west, and then went down to Vancouver. The whole of the Oregon Country was organized into four dioceses with Oregon City, Fort Walla Walla, Fort Colville, and Fort Hall as centers.

Several times he crossed and re-crossed the continent, from the Atlantic to the Pacific; made a trip to Europe in the interest of his work; established missions wherever he went; baptized thousands of Indians, and with all exercised perhaps a greater influence than any other missionary of his time. He was, at different times, called upon by the national government to aid in quelling Indian disturbances and putting down Indian rebellions. The most noted mission which he founded is located on Coeur d'Alene River, Idaho, and is known as the Mission of the Sacred Heart. It was founded in 1846.

"It is vain to describe to an eye witness the beauty of the surrounding country. The property on which the church stands is situated at the head of navigation of the picturesque Coeur d'Alene River. What an intelligent man of the world would select as a site for a future town, the wise servants of God chose for the erection of a temple of divine worship. The church, standing on an elevation of some two hundred feet, commands the fertile valley which spreads out before it and presents a pastoral scene not easily to be forgotten. In the rear of the edifice rises gradually an amphitheatre of wild mountains and untraversed forests, contrasting strikingly with the evidences of civilization in the valley.

St. Mary's Mission on Coeur d'Alene River.

"This location was chosen for the headquarters of the new mission, that the Coeur d'Alene Indians, then under Chief Joseph Stellame, might be taught the elements of farming along with the knowledge of the true God. A large shanty made of bark served as a temporary place of worship and the work of building the cherished landmark was begun in the fall of 1848. Under the direction of Brother Magri, S. J. assisted by Brothers Huybrechts and McGinn and a large crew of Indians, Father Ravalli, S. J., later famous in the annals of Montana history, designed the church.

"But how was this church to be erected? In those pioneer days, they had no modern appliances and tools were very scarce. How could they build with but a few ordinary implements—no nails, no iron, no sawmill? Nevertheless, they did set to work and felled tall cedars of the neighboring forest. These they trimmed and shaped into timbers, sawing them in an improvised saw-pit, as the nearest mill was at Walla Walla, 210 miles distant. Thus were constructed enough uprights and rafters for the framework, the uprights being eighteen inches square and the rafters ten inches square. Boring holes in these logs, they inserted wooden pins in default of nails, and after such crude labor, the framework of the edifice was raised on high.

"The next problem was to cover this skeleton, as they had no shingles or clapboards or anything of that sort. The ingenuity of the missionaries who personally supervised the whole work did not even in this difficulty fail them. Willow saplings were cut and laced between the beams. These were interwoven with wild grass, making the wall about eight inches thick. The time now came for the plasterer to appear on the scene with his trowel and plaster. But no such luxury was theirs. They gathered large quantities of clay from the river's bank, and with their hands, smeared it on the grass, both inside and out. In fact, if you were to enter the sacristy of the church now, and ascend the ladder to the little garret above it, you would see the finger marks of the workmen and also the peculiar way in which the rafters and uprights were joined. The church was finished in a year and a half and was first used in the winter of 1849-50, the dedication being simple but solemn."*

Today, after three score and ten years, it stands in its rigid simplicity and the grandeur of its rugged surroundings, as a monument to man's faith in God and love for his fellow men.

The Old Mormon Fort in Lemhi Valley near Salmon, Idaho.

The remains of the mud wall at old Fort Lemhi, in Lemhi Valley, Idaho, which was erected in 1855, by the

*The Old Mission Church—Gonzaga University.

Mormons from Utah, is now part of a wheat field. This fort was made from a mortar composed of mud and rocks formed into a kind of natural cement. It was moulded in forms in place on the wall, a foot high at a round, by using two strips of timber thrown across the wall, about 12 feet apart. A hole was bored in each end of the strips about 2 feet apart. Upright pegs 12 inches high were placed in the bored holes, then a plank 12 inches high and about 15 feet long was placed against the pegs and the space between the planks on each side was filled with the mud. After the mud dried, the planks were removed, leaving the strips of timber in the wall. New strips were made and another form erected and so on, but the same plank was used several times or all the time. This mud wall was 16 rods square and about 9 feet high. It was used as a corral for stock and for the storing of crops and farm machinery; everything was put in here for safety.

The Mormon Mission at Lembi, Idaho, 1855.—History records many examples of people with sublime faith who made heroic sacrifice to attain the object of that faith. The children of Isreal, wandering through the deserts and the wilderness; the Pilgrims, landing on that bleak New England shore, on a cold December day; Roger Williams, in mid-winter going out into the wilderness, and many others might be cited. Such was the trek of one thousand miles across the trackless plains and snow-capped mountains of the eight hundred Mormons who came from western Missouri to Salt Lake, in the summer of 1847. They began their settlements in the midst of the Great American Desert, founding Salt Lake City.

From that day to this immigrant trains have treked out from this city to New and Old Mexico, Arizona, Nevada, Idaho, Oregon, Wyoming, and Montana to found Missions. One of the earliest of these missions was the Lemhi Mission and it is a good illustration of their methods and of the difficulties which all pioneers had to meet. It is thus described in the history of the Bannock Stake:

"It was at the annual conference of the Church, held in Salt Lake City, April 7, 1855, that a number of brethren were called to go and locate a settlement among the buffalo-hunting Bannock and Shoshone Indians in the far off north, in what was then Oregon Territory, and Elder Thos. S. Smith, of Farmington, Davis County, Utah, a man of considerable experience, was appointed to take charge of the colony. Most of the brethren who were called on this mission, made preparations at once to fill it, and on the 15th of May, 1855, President Smith, together with other brethren, left their home in Farmington forever, and arrived at their new home on June 14th, in the upper valley of the Salmon River, on the head-waters of the east branch of that river, now known as Lemhi River. Here President Smith called a halt. Selecting five brethren of the camp, he proceeded about thirty miles farther down the river to explore for a suitable place to locate a settlement. (Singularly this is the day on which the treaty between Great Britain and the United States, settling the Oregon question, was ratified and is designated 'Pioneer Day' in the States of the Northwest). On the 15th they selected a site for a fort and a tract for farming land, after which President Smith returned to the main camp, and on the 18th, moved upon the site chosen.

"With that energy and determination characteristic of Mormon pioneers the brethren immediately commenced to make improvements; they soon had a blacksmith shop in working order and also had coal burned, a plow made, and a corral built for their stock. By the 10th of August they had built a fort wall and gates, seven houses and the blacksmith shop, besides breaking and planting several acres of land, and doing a great deal of fencing. They called their location Fort Limhi, after Limhi, a Nephite king mentioned in the Book of Mormon.

"Fort Limhi (now spelled Lemhi) consisted of a neat stockade inclosing a space sixteen rods square, located on the bench land a short distance from the right bank of the east branch of Salmon River, now called Lemhi River, in what is now township 19 north of range 24 east of Boise Meridian. It is about twenty miles above the point where that stream unites with the main Salmon River.

"August 13th and 14th, 1855, twelve of the company were sent to Utah for supplies, in charge of Captain Durfee; and B. F. Cummings and John Galligher were dispatched to Salt Lake City with the mail, being ordered to return as soon as possible.

"On the 17th of November, Captain Durfee and company returned to the fort with twelve wagons laden with supplies of wheat, corn and other seeds and several hundred pounds of flour. Five families also accompanied the brethren.

"By the beginning of December, 1854, a large amount of hay had been cut, the field enlarged, much more ground broken, and about fifteen acres of land sown with wheat, besides which several more houses had been built in the fort. The weather had been pleasant during the fall, but there was now two or three inches of snow on the ground.

"On the 5th of December, Thos. Butterfield, G. W. Hill, and seven others left the fort with two ox-wagons to return to the settlements in Utah, where they expected to spend the winter.

"In March, 1856, President Smith, accompanied by others, traveled to Utah with pack animals, and on arriving in Salt Lake City, reported the condition of the Salmon River mission to President Brigham Young, who was much pleased with what the missionaries had done, and concluded to strengthen the settlement by calling more brethren to go and locate there. This was done.

"President Smith returned to Fort Limhi July 8th, 1856, and found the missionaries in good health and spirits, 'notwithstanding they had witnessed the almost entire destruction of their crops by grasshoppers, whose unrelenting ravages had blasted all anticipations of an abundant harvest, the prospect of which could not have been more flattering previous to the inroad of the devourers. The grasshoppers left without depositing their eggs.' The loss of crops put the brethren to serious inconvenience, as they thereby were compelled again (like the previous year) to haul their flour and seed grain from the settlements in Utah. A company of brethren started for supplies on the 28th of July and arrived in Salt Lake City about the middle of August. Most of them returned in due course of time with provisions, seed grain, and other articles of food and clothing needed by the settlers.

"Considerable winter wheat was sown in the fall of 1856, when another small company of settlers arrived to strengthen the colony, having been called on missions to do this like the other brethren who had gone before them. Peace and good health prevailed among the brethren at Fort Limhi during the winter of 1856-57.

A New Company Arrives. Fort Built.—"The new company of settlers reached Fort Limhi at six o'clock on the evening of Friday, May 8th. This fort is a neat stockade inclosing a space sixteen rods square, and has a large securely fenced yard for animals, and a small grist mill not yet finished, though sufficiently so to be used. . . . . There are two good-sized fields, mostly plowed and sown, in which the crops look promising, considering the coolness and consequent lateness of the season. The big, red-sided salmon are said to be very plentiful here in their season, for which we were about a month too soon; but a few red-sided salmon were purchased from the Indians. They are a fine-flavored fish, and average about two and a half feet in length. A few Bannock Indians had pitched their lodges adjacent to the fort, among whom Governor Young distributed many presents of blankets, etc., on the 11th of May, which were very gladly received."

Attacked and Driven Out by the Indians.—President Smith, in his private journal, gives the following account of this sad affair:

"Thursday, February 25th, 1858. As I was returning from the field to the fort I saw a large party of Indians riding at full speed toward the point where our herd was grazing. Quick as possible I unharnessed my horses, and, mounting one of them, proceeded, in company with Ezra Barnard, who was also mounted, toward the herd. After going about a mile we discovered that the Indians had got possession of all our stock, and that they were driving back the brethren who had gone in pursuit ahead of us. As soon as the Indians saw us, six of their warriors took after us, and we changed our course toward the other brethren, but seeing that we could not gain the point where they were, we turned toward the fort, and as we rode down the bench, the Indians, who pursued us, fired upon us, one of the bullets passing through my suspenders and lodging in my horse's right jaw, a little below the joint. The horse jumped, whereby my left stirrup broke, and I, losing my balance, was thrown off the horse. In the fall I lost my pistol. Fortunately Brother Barnard caught my horse, but before I could reach him, a ball passed through the rim of my hat near my right ear, and while I was in the act of mounting, another ball passed through the upper part of my right arm, a little above the elbow; the Indians continued shooting all the time. We reached the fort without further difficulty, but in running in I had to hold my hand over the wound of my animal to prevent him from bleeding to death.

"Soon after we got in, the brethren who had gone out on foot also returned with Brother Welch, whom the Indians had shot in the small of the back, the ball lodging against the back bone. He had also been struck twice on the head with a gun; and after taking his gun and ammunition and stripping him of his shirt the savages left him for dead.

"The Indians who had chased us to the fort now joined their companions who were driving off our herd, and I sent out ten men to hunt for the missing herdsmen. While they were gone, Brother O. Rose, one of the herders, came in unhurt. The ten men returned a little before sunset with the dead body of Geo. McBride, who had been shot from his horse and stripped of everything except his socks, pants and under garments. He was also scalped. The ball that killed him had entered his body under the left arm and came out under his right arm. The ten men also found Brother Andrew Quigley, who was shot in the shoulder, the ball lodging against the collar bone. He had been struck several blows on the head and left by the savages for dead, but after they had gone, he came to and subsequently recovered.

"On the 20th the mail and several brethren arrived from Salt Lake City, bringing the news that 150 men were coming to help the missionaries away. On the 22nd this company, in command of Colonel Andrew Cunningham, arrived, and on the 24th the Colonel and President Smith, with sixty other men, visited the camp of the Indians, who delivered to President Smith three cows and calves and six ponies in payment for cattle they had killed.

"On the 26th ten men started from the fort for Salt Lake City with the mail and messages for President Young, stating the conditions of the camp, as it was feared at the headquarters of the Church in Salt Lake City that all the brethren of the mission had been murdered by the Indians.

"On the 27th the ox teams, with some of the missionaries and such effects as they could take with them, started for Utah, and on the 28th Fort Limhi was entirely vacated by the departure of the remaining

Survivors of the Whitman Massacre and their descendants.

Daughter of survivor—Mrs. Christenson, daughter of Mrs. Church.
Survivor—Mrs. Elizabetb (Sager) Helm. 1844.

Survivor—Mrs. Nancy (Osborn) Jacobs 1845.
Survivor—Mrs. Helen M. (Saunders) Church, 1845.

Daughter of survivor—Mrs. M. N. Stratton, daughter of Mrs. Helm.
Survivor—Mrs. Gertrude (Hall) Denny (Mrs. O. N.) 1847.

brethren who left with horse teams, together with their friends who had come to help them away. President Smith gave the friendly Indians about six hundred bushels of wheat and left about a thousand bushels with them to trade for horses. The two companies arrived in Utah safe and well. But the ten men who had left with the mail on the 26th, in charge of Elder B. F. Cummings, were suddenly and furiously fired upon by a party of Indians in ambush, while traveling up Bannock Creek, on the 31st of March, 1858. On this occasion Bailey Lake, one of the party, was killed by the Indians, who also robbed the company of eleven horses. The rest of the brethren reached the settlements in Utah a few days later.

"Thus ended the famous Salmon River mission which proved to be one of the most dangerous missions ever performed among the Indians in the North."

The Whitman Massacre, November 29, 1847.—As Whitman's coming was the beginning of missions in the Inland Empire, so was his massacre the end of the first period of Protestant Missions. Not only his mission but those of Spalding at Lapwai and of Eells and Walker near Spokane were abandoned.

The events leading up to the massacre are thus described by President Penrose of Whitman College:

"Hitherto the Indians had regarded the Whitmans as their friends—as angels sent to them from heaven. They had called the doctor 'the good doctor,' and had gone to him in every time of trouble. But now suspicions were planted in their minds. It was whispered to them that Dr. Whitman had a secret motive for his work; that he was trying to rob them of their lands and of their horses. In the fall of 1847 measles broke out, and Whitman treated his white patients and his Indian patients alike, but, strange as it may seem, his white patients recovered, while his Indian patients died. They took the same medicines, but the Indians taking his medicine would go and steep themselves in a sweat-box, a low lodge or hut of branches constructed by the edge of the river, in which they had placed hot stones and poured water over them to make a steam bath. Reeking with sweat, they rushed out and jumped into the ice-cold stream. They died by hundreds. But they were told, 'Whitman has poisoned you,' and they knew no better than to believe it. On the 29th of November, 1847, the plot reached its head and broke. On the afternoon of that day Dr. Whitman was indoors giving medicine to a sick Indian boy. An Indian stole through the door in moccasined feet, bearing in his hand under his blanket a hatchet. Quickly raising his arm, he struck the good doctor one blow on the back of the head. He fell to the ground with a groan, 'My God!' and his blood gushed out upon the bare board floor. Then the war whoop rang out, and guns were fired. Mrs. Whitman fell, pierced through the breast by a rifle bullet. She and the doctor were killed and scalped, besides twelve others of the missionary party. The rest were carried away into a captivity which was worse than death. The Indians, in their savage lust for destruction, burned the buildings to the ground, and hacked to pieces the very orchard which Whitman had planted, leaving not a vestige of civilization to mark the spot where Whitman had lived and died."

The incidents of the massacre were fully described by a survivor on the fiftieth anniversary year. Mrs. Osborne-Jacobs, in an interview published in the Portland *Oregonian* of June 20, 1897, says:

"We crossed the plains in '45. It was my father's intention to go straight on to the Willamette Valley, but we were out of provisions and stopped at Dr. Whitman's mission. When Dr. Whitman heard that my father was a millwright he wanted to hire father to look after his work. Hence we were at the Whitman mission when the massacre occurred.

"It was about noon on the 29th of November, 1847, when we began to notice and remark on the unusual number of Indians that seemed to be around the mission. My father and mother and their three children: myself, Nancy Osborne, a child of eight, and two little boys aged five and two and a half years, respectively, occupied a room on one side of the house near the kitchen. My little brother, John, was ill with the measles, and my mother was also weak and miserable from an illness a few weeks previous. In the house there were a number of the mission children, ill with the measles. An Indian came and knocked at the door, and Mrs. Whitman said: 'Let him come in and see that our children are sick, too, and perhaps then they will not think the doctor is poisoning their children.' The Indian asked for some medicine and went away. Shortly afterwards we heard firing in the yard, and Mrs. Whitman, who was standing near the window, exclaimed: 'The Indians are shooting. They are going to murder us all!'

"A few minutes later, Dr. Whitman was shot and Mrs. Whitman came into the room. She clung to the wall as though for support, and repeated in a dazed sort of a way, 'I am a widow! I am a widow!'

"When Mrs. Whitman left the room I suddenly thought of the cellar and said, 'Father, let us go to the cellar. The Indians will not see us there.' My father unloosened a board in the floor—they were but lightly laid—and I slipped under and crawled as far forward as I could. My father and mother then came under with the two children. I lay with my face in my hands, noiselessly, all through those long hours of the afternoon. I have often been asked to tell how I felt during those hours, but looking back upon that time I cannot remember more than lying there in silent awe. I do remember noticing that the cracks in the floor were very wide, and wondering if the Indians could see us through them.

"The noise and shooting continued for some time in the room beyond. It was during this time that Mrs. Whitman was shot, and others with her. During the greater part of the afternoon we could hear the wounded moaning as we lay there. We could recognize the voice of a young man—who was living at the mission and who intended to be a minister—raised in prayer, between the moans of pain. Soon we heard him say in a weak voice, almost a whisper: 'Come, Lord Jesus, come quickly,' and then there was silence.

"When night came on—about ten o'clock I think it was—we crept out of the cellar and went into the other room and slipped quietly out of the house. As we went out, I remember that the dead body of the young missionary was lying near the door. I can still see his pale face, as it looked in the dim light that came through the windows. We walked what seemed to us a very long way, although in reality only about two miles from the mission, and at last stopped to rest and hide in a clump of bushes on the opposite side of the Walla Walla River. The river was low at this time.

My father carried across the two little boys, then came back and got me, and lastly, my mother. We remained at this place the two following days. We took from the mission as we fled such food as we could hastily find, which consisted of a few pieces of bread and a plate of cold porridge. At the end of the second day my mother was very ill from the suffering she had endured. The weather was damp and chilly and we had few wraps. She said to father, very faintly:

" 'I am going to die. But you must save these children. Take one of them with you. Go to Fort Walla Walla. Get assistance and return for us.'

"My father at first declared that he could not leave us alone—that he would remain and we should all die together. Fort Walla Walla was thirty miles distant. He had only once made the journey before; and now, at night, it would be by the merest chance if he could make his way there. But my mother insisted that it was death to stay, and in going there was a chance for life. Then the question was, which child should he take?

"Have you read that poem, 'Which Shall It Be?' " asked Mrs. Jacobs, tears filling her eyes at the painful recollections. "I always think of it when I remember that night when my little brother and I lay close to mother on the cold earth, and a choice was to be made of who should go. They decided at last that father would better take Johnny, who was not yet well from the measles, and needed shelter more than the baby or myself. My father was gone two days. On the evening of the second day my mother gave up all hope of rescue. She had given us children the last bit of food early in the day, and the baby was crying of hunger. We heard shots fired not far in the distance during the afternoon, and mother said, 'That was father coming for us, and the Indians have shot him, and we will lie here until we die of cold and starvation.' But I said to mother: 'No, father isn't dead. When I was sleeping a little while ago I dreamed that we were living in a large white house, and brother was sitting on father's knees, and I am sure he is coming back to get us.' Not long after this we heard a noise, and, looking up saw an Indian coming toward us, and behind him a short distance, father.

" 'Hias clatawau! —hurry and go!' said the Indian. The Indian was not a Cayuse, but one of the Walla Wallas. When my father reached the fort he was refused admittance; was told to go to Umatilla. A stranger, an eastern man whom he met at the fort, pitying him, gave father a few provisions that he had; and with these and the friendly Indian accompanying him, my father returned to look for us. They had each brought a pony with them, and we at once started for Umatilla. We stopped at French farm—about five miles from where we had been hidden. The lumberman at this farm gave us milk to drink, but said he had nothing cooked. He told father to go again to the fort and demand admittance as an American citizen; that if he went to Umatilla the Indians would certainly kill him on the way, or when he reached there. Father said he had already been refused admittance at the fort and there was no use returning there. At this point my mother slipped off the pony and said that she would not go to Umatilla and see him murdered before her eyes. This settled the question. The horses' heads were turned and we began the journey to Fort Walla Walla.

"We journeyed on for several hours and then turned into a little valley shut in by hills—for the country all around about is hilly and rolling—to rest ourselves and horses. We know now that the delay probably saved our lives, for the Indians had come in pursuit of us, and passed on ahead while we rested. When we went on our way later we passed not far from their camp fires, where they had camped for the night.

"We arrived in safety at Fort Walla Walla a little later, demanded admittance and were not refused. We remained at the fort two months, and were then brought safely down to the valley."

CHAPTER VI.

Immigration To The Oregon Country

Westward Immigration.—From the establishment of settlements at Jamestown and Plymouth to the present day, wave after wave of immigration has swept westward. First to the foothills of the Alleghenies, then over these mountains into the valleys of Tennessee and Kentucky; only in a short time to cross the Mississippi to Missouri and Arkansas, where the tide was stayed for a time to gather force which would enable it to make the great leap to the Pacific Northwest.

The riches of this country had gradually become known to the people of the East through the explorer, the fur-trader, and the missionary, as well as agents of the United States government. This knowledge, together with the commercial stagnation of the Mississippi Valley, caused the restless pioneer to turn his attention to this new land, where the possibilities of trade with

The Immigrant.

China seemed to offer much, hence the great immigrant trains to the West.

Westport in Immigration Days.—Two geographical names stand out prominently in immigration to the Oregon Country—Westport and Vancouver—Westport being the starting point, and Vancouver, the terminal of the Oregon Trail.

The grand old pioneer, Ezra Meeker, has firmly placed in history that historic highway, the Oregon Trail, which he marked with his prairie schooner and an ox-team, when celebrating the semi-centennial of his westward trip, having gone back over the trail eastward in the same manner that he had come west. Vancouver's place in history was fixed by another grand old man, Dr. McLoughlin. Moreover, its future commercial importance would not allow it to be forgotten. But not so with Westport. No great names in history are associated with it, and its name and identity are both lost by being made a part of Kansas City, whose commercial importance completely overshadows Westport's historical significance. But the old town should not be forgotten. It served its day and generation well.

St. Louis was the first gateway to the West, the Lewis and Clark Expedition starting from there. Later, St. Joe became the starting place, and still later, Independence. But all finally yielded the field to Westport, which served as outfitting point for both the Santa Fe and the Oregon Trail; the one leading to the Southwest, the other to the Northwest. The one meant commerce, the other homes.

Westport was the gateway to the great West; it was a frontier town where might be seen the traveler, the post trader, the Indians, and the soldiers who kept the Indian tribes in subjection. But all of these were overshadowed by the great immigrant trains which were formed and outfitted here.

It was a town of tents; of straggling houses, hastily put together, without paved streets or sidewalks, churches or schools; inhabited by a motley array of traders, travelers, and Indians—in short, all of those affected with the "wanderlust," and coming from all over the United States as well as from many other countries.

The stores contained chiefly those things needed for the Indian trade—paint, powder, firearms, highly-colored scarfs and handkerchiefs, blankets and beads, knives and hatchets, beaded moccasins and leggings; while for the immigrants there were all sorts of cutlery and tinware, dried fruits and vegetables, bacon and lard, flour and meal, clothing and camping outfits, materials to make and repair wagons, as well as the wagons themselves, harness and ox yokes. For when the immigrant left Westport there was no place where he could buy a pound of sugar or coffee, a sack of flour or salt, a hammer or a horseshoe nail, a postage stamp or a sheet of paper, a yard of cloth or a paper of pins or needles, until he reached Vancouver on the Columbia, two thousand miles distant. (Perhaps this is overstated as a few articles could be had at the fur-trading posts.)

A day spent at Westport would mean seeing men, women and children engaged in the purchase of such things as were deemed necessary for their long journey. The town would also be "full of Indians. Their little shaggy ponies were tied by dozens along the houses and fences. Sacs and Foxes with shaved heads and painted faces, Shawnees and Delawares, Wyandots dressed as white men, and a few wretched Kansas wrapped in old blankets were strolling about the streets or lounging in and out of the shops and houses." The gunsmith, the blacksmith and the saddler would be just as busy as the merchant in supplying the needs of their various customers.

Outside the town would be seen men engaged in "breaking" oxen and horses to be yoked or harnessed, hitched and driven to the wagons. Others would be repairing and putting in readiness the wagons, yokes, harness, camping outfits, etc. The women would be engaged in preparing the meals, washing or sewing, while the children played merrily with their newly formed acquaintances, and both men and women could be seen carefully placing the packages in the wagon beds in such a way that they would take up the least possible room, and at the same time nothing would be damaged.

Gradually a "social group" of neighbors, friends and acquaintances would form themselves into an immigrant company, which might consist of anywhere from one hundred to one thousand wagons. Early in May this human hive moved out to "Immigrant Grove" where they became a distinct and separate group, with constitution and by-laws and officers to enforce them, all being framed and selected by the immigrants themselves. Then early some morning breakfast was eaten, the oxen yoked and hitched to the wagon, the driver cracked his great whip, the huge beasts put their shoulders to the yoke, the wheels of the heavily laden wagons began to move and the immigrant train was off for Oregon.

An Immigrant's Outfit.—The following is taken from the description of one of the early immigrants:

"The pioneer who came to the Pacific Coast in the 'forties' was not essentially different from the pioneers who had for more than a hundred years been pushing westward, first across the Alleghenies and next across the Mississippi. He was acquainted with pioneer conditions of living and travel.

"Heretofore he had traveled only a few hundred miles at most and he had wood and water always in sight. If his wagon tongue or axle or other part of his wagon were broken there was always plenty of hard wood growing near by with which to mend it. The general geography of the country was more or less well known to him.

"Now he must go across a trackless journey of two thousand miles, six or eight hundred of which were treeless plains or deserts; not a stick of hard wood except what he took with him. But the pioneer was resourceful and acquainted with conditions and doubtless foresaw many of the obstacles to be met with, providing himself with those things necessary to meet them.

"In the beginning each individual would 'outfit' himself in accordance with his own ideas yet as the number increased and 'immigrant trains' were formed he would naturally be more or less guided by the rules and regulations of the 'train' of which he was a party.

"The wagon should be light and well built. Extra tongues, axles, coupling poles, hounds and bolsters should be carried as the strain on the wagon is very great. The crossing of streams when fords are not known, and the jerking, jarring, and wrenching of desert travel will finally cause the parts to wear out and break. There should be good strong bows and heavy sheets of brown cotton drilling.

"The load should not exceed 300 or 400 pounds to the animal used in hauling it and should consist of only absolute necessities.

"The provisions should consist of 150 pounds of flour and 50 pounds of bacon for each person, dried parched corn meal, dried peas and beans as well as rice, sugar, coffee, yeast powder, and vinegar. These things together with buffalo meat and other wild game and the milk from the cows brought along supplied the necessary food.

"Glass, queensware and crockery were not brought but instead tin cups, tin plates, a few knives and forks, a dutch oven, skillet and frying pan, pot hooks and a butcher knife, kettles and cans that fitted one into the other, and a keg or can for water.

"The clothing should be that usually worn and enough to last for a year, except of shoes and of these there should be taken several extra pairs as much walking and rough roads were very hard on them. The bedding should consist largely of quilts, comforts, sheets and blankets as feathers for beds were as cheap on the Columbia as on the Mississippi River.

"Of furniture the least possible, as it takes up space, is heavy, and in the way when the immigrant arrives at his destination where he has no house until he builds a one-room log cabin, and he has abundant time to make his own furniture.

"But of tools there should be as many as possible as they are needed on the way, and when the journey is completed. On the two thousand mile trip there is practically not a place where a horse may be shod or a wagon mended except by the immigrant himself. Tools should consist of saws, axes, chisels, hammers, drawing knives, and augurs; bolts, linchpins, bands, nails, hoop iron, and drills for boring holes.

"The best teams for these trips are oxen. They are more gentle, patient, easily driven; not so easy to stampede nor difficult to catch. They will plunge into the mud, swim rivers, break through thickets and climb mountains a great deal more readily than horses or mules. They require no feed except grass and rarely need shoes, can pull more than a horse or mule, require less harness and are far more reliable in every way."

The following tribute by George L. Curry to the Ox Whip might more appropriately be ascribed to the ox himself:

> "My task is to call from dust and dark forgetfulness that advance banner of Americanism and progress—the ox whip. Its crack was the command 'Forward to the Nation.' Its sharp, keen accent proclaimed that obstacles to prayers must be overcome. It waved aloft on the prairies of the 'Old West' and pointing to the new a vast throng took up the westward march, which keeping step to the music of destiny, dashed across the broad Missouri, rolled a living tide up the grassy slope of the Platte, scaled the imperial heights of the Rocky Mountains, and with 'the tread of a giant and shout of a conqueror' defied the heat, dust, thirst and hunger, the desert heart of the continent, leaped the Blue Mountains, paused but quailed not on the banks of the deep, wide Columbia where again the potential crack is heard and the mighty 'rock-

ribbed' walls of the Cascades are stormed, and as the line rolls bravely over the giddy summit the exultant driver gives a grand triumphant crack into the stolid face of grand old Hood, the storm-clad sentinel of the mountain fastness. The people have reached their goal. The spell is broken. The errand has lost its magic, its mission has been accomplished. A state, with freedom's diadem effulgent on its brow salutes the eye, and dipping its young hand in the Pacific completes the baptism of human liberty and proclaims an 'ocean-bound republic.' All hail and honor to the ox-whip, the symbol of the grand, achieving force of its age."—*Oregon Historical Quarterly.*

The Immigrant Train.—The Oregon Trail was the route usually selected by the immigrants coming to the Northwest, and the place of assembling would be somewhere in western Missouri, St. Joe, Independence, or Westport, now Kansas City. Various methods were adopted for assembling those who desired to migrate to the West. Sometimes it would be published in papers that in a certain month an immigrant train would start west, or some one having returned from the far Northwest would go through the country speaking at various places and conversing with everybody with whom he met in regard to the Northwest Country. By this method families as well as individuals were gradually congregated at the appointed town, prepared for the westward migration at the opening of spring.

Every man over eighteen was required to equip himself with a wagon, oxen, and supplies, which consisted of flour, meal, bacon, dried fruits, etc.

When a sufficient number had assembled, supplied with the necessities for the journey, an organization was effected. Rules were adopted for the government of the party. Officers were chosen for the enforcement of the rules and regulations. The route of march was selected, and everything made ready for starting on an appointed day. A typical emigrant train was that of 1843. It consisted of over one thousand people with one hundred and twenty wagons, each drawn by six yoke of oxen. Besides there were several thousand loose horses and cattle. This company was broken up into smaller groups when they got beyond the danger of the Sioux Indians, as it was more convenient both on account of the pasture and also for the control of the immigrants themselves. The women and children usually rode in the wagons, the men rode horseback and drove the loose stock, or walked. Each division had a guide who knew the country well. The location of the water, the fords, the best places for camping, the richest pasture, as well as the dangers from the Indians, quicksands, etc., were all problems that had to be coped with.

The day opened at four o'clock, when the sentinels fired their guns, indicating that it was time to begin the day's work. The women rose and prepared the morning's meal. The night herders rounded up the stock, first circling round the herd to see that none had strayed away and that no lurking Indians had crossed over. The oxen were then driven into the corral, which was formed by arranging the wagons in the form of a circle, the tongue of each wagon being passed under the back of the other. Each man then crossed within the corral, selected his stock and yoked them. From six to seven was breakfast hour. Promptly at seven every wagon fell into its proper place or was left to trail in the rear. The train broke up into parts of four wagons each, and each wagon took its turn in the lead and in the rear. The guide and the guards led the wing. The hunters deviated to the right and to the left of the trail in quest of game. The loose horses soon learned to follow close to the wagons. Not so with the loose cattle, which never seemed to get enough to eat or to learn what was expected of them. The women and children usually rode in the wagons, but got out and walked at pleasure to rest themselves. The journey was continued until one o'clock, when a stop was made for lunch, to rest, and to graze the stock. After the lunch the journey was resumed, and continued as in the morning. When the appointed hour arrived for camping, and a place was chosen by the guide, the wagons took their places in a circle forming a stockade for protection

The Bateau.

The Raft. Both Used by the Immigrants on the Columbia After Reaching The Dalles.

against the Indians, and a corral for yoking the oxen in the morning.

The average day's journey was about twenty miles. The evenings were spent much as a company of picnickers. Every musical instrument was brought out and its owner used it in his own way. The little children improvised games of their own. The young men and women selected a smooth place and danced. The older people talked over the day's happenings and planned for the morrow, or the men sometimes constituted a court before which a trial was held to settle some dispute between individuals, or parties, or to judge the punishment in case of some rule having been violated.

Sickness and sorrow, accident and death, courtship and marriage, exciting chase after game, the rounding up of stampeded stock, the repulse of Indians, were all incidents of the journey. Some grew tired and discouraged and turned back after the first few miles. The teams grew thin and footsore. The wagons broke down and were abandoned. Loads had to be lightened, and article after article of furniture was thrown along the roadside. The dreary monotony of sagebrush and sand hills, prickly pears and prairie dogs, barren plains and impassable mountains, burning heat by day and biting cold by night, and ever the urgent command to go on, on, on, so as to reach the end of the journey before the coming of winter, and at last the scarcity of food, all tended to make the journey a memorable one.

The Buffalo.—For a half century or more after the purchase of Louisiana, all of that territory was roamed over by vast herds of buffaloes. They, like the migratory birds, started from the far south in the spring working their way northward until the frost began to reappear, when they again turned southward, going as

The Buffalo.

they had come. They traveled in herds which numbered from a few score to several thousand and had their regular watering places on the various streams which they crossed, and to which they came regularly to drink. In their travels they broke up into smaller herds, perhaps because of the convenience of grazing and water, and also because of more freedom from the dust. Whether grazing or traveling, the cows and the calves were gradually forced to the center, while the bulls stood on the outer edge to guard against the attacks of wild animals. When lying down resting, the herd also had guards which were continually on the lookout for danger, real or imaginary, and when frightened, just as in travel, the cows and calves were thrown toward the center for protection.

They had their wallows, that is, mud holes, where they rolled in the mud, plastering themselves with it for protection against insects. They also had "licks," localities where there were certain saline substances in the soil that served them as salt.

The buffaloes were a great source of food supply for the Indian; the hides could be used as robes on which he slept or out of which he constructed his "tepee." The flesh was very fine for food, and represented a great variety, both because of the differences found in the several parts of the animal, and the many ways in which each of these parts might be cooked. When coming across the plain, the Whitmans and Spaldings lived on buffalo meat almost entirely for about two months, and Mrs. Whitman said that her husband never had two meals quite the same; he understood so well the different parts of the animal, and the many ways in which the cooking could be done.

The Indian resorted to various methods of killing the buffalo. He could take the hide of the neck and head of the deer or elk and fix it on his own head securely, and then by walking on his hands and feet could represent the animal so perfectly as to deceive the buffaloes. By this method he could steal up beside the animal and shoot it with bow and arrow or spear it.

For many years Montana was the famous buffalo grazing section, and here the Nez Perce and Flathead Indians from west of the mountains used to meet the Sioux from the east, as well as the Blackfeet from the south. The fiercest battles between these tribes were waged while they were collecting their food supply and buffalo hides.

Buffalo meat, like beef, may be jerked, that is, cut in thin strips and dried; by this means it may be preserved for a long time. Or this dry meat may be ground to pieces with tallow, making what was termed pemmican, which could be placed in baskets and sacks and stored.

The passing of the buffalo came with the building of the trans-continental railways and the coming of the western immigrant. William F. Cody, "Buffalo Bill," was one of the most famous hunters of buffalo known in history. It is said that he killed nearly five thousand buffaloes in 1867 and 1868 to supply the laborers who were constructing the Kansas-Pacific Railway. His famous horse which he rode in hunting buffalo, was named "Brigham." He was so well trained that Cody could ride out without bridle or saddle to a herd of buffalo, and give his horse the command to go, and old Brigham would run up to the side of a buffalo and allow Cody to shoot. If for any reason the buffalo was not killed, Brigham would run up beside it again and give his rider another chance, but if he missed this time Brigham would go on as if to say, "you're no good, and I will not fool away my time by giving you more than two shots." Buffalo Bill, in speaking of his horse said, "Brigham was the best horse I ever saw or owned for buffalo chasing."

The buffaloes frequently gave the western immigrants much trouble by stampeding their stock or causing the cattle to run away from them, thereby leaving the immigrant on the trail with nothing but his wagons. Again the buffaloes might be stampeded, and then an immigrant train was in great danger of being crushed by the hundreds that would break through or run over it. Sometimes wagons were torn to pieces, and the stock scattered in every direction. To guard against this each train had its hunter and guard whose business it was to ward off the herds of buffalo that might be likely to give the train trouble. Today, buffaloes are found only in the national parks, and the zoological gardens of the cities.

Bigfoot's Last Fight.—Many trials, hardships, and dangers beset the immigrant on his two-thousand-mile journey. His wagons often broke down, his stock was sometimes stampeded and lost, and sickness and death in his own family were not uncommon. But he was called upon to endure no trial more nerve-racking than the attack of the lurking, murdering Indian who laid in wait for him in the narrow canyons, or at night when defense was very difficult if not impossible.

Sometimes the Indian's motive was robbery and sometimes it was revenge, but in the case of the subject of this story it was both.

Bigfoot, with a picked body of warriors, ranged along the Oregon Trail from the Grand Ronde Valley in Oregon to the headwaters of the Owyhee and Weiser rivers in Idaho. His favorite field of operation was on the road between Silver City and Boise City, in a narrow canyon a few miles south of the Snake River. Here stages were robbed, lone travelers killed and freighters both robbed and killed, and here, too, the leader of this daring band of highwaymen at last met his fate in the following manner:

"In the spring of 1868," says Wm. T. Anderson, who witnessed the fight and gives an account of it in the *Statesman* of November 1878, "I was going from Silver City to Boise City. This was the last time I saw Wheeler until I met him on the scene where the terrible combat—Bigfoot's last fight—took place. This happened in the latter part of July, 1868. I was going from Silver City to Boise City, traveling alone with a two-horse wagon. When near the dangerous pass where so many had been killed, I, being unarmed, concluded to lay over and let my horses graze until I should have company through the canyon, so I foolishly turned my horses loose and set myself to cooking something to eat. While thus engaged, the horses got frightened at something and ran off, leaving me afoot and alone, and badly frightened. I followed the horses' tracks and found they had gone down Reynolds Creek, in the direction of the massacre ground. As the creek runs through this bluff of rocks within half a mile of where the road does, I followed them and found that they had started through the canyon, and I had just turned back, afraid to go farther, when, to my horror and surprise, I looked across the creek and saw three Indians coming at full speed. They were painted and feathered, and as they were coming directly toward me, I felt certain that they saw me, and I thought that my time had come. The tall and terrible-looking Indian who could be none other than Bigfoot himself was some fifty yards ahead of another Indian, while the third was an equal distance behind the second one. I stood paralyzed with fear. The only chance left me was to hide behind some rocks, and there await my fate, which I felt certain would in a few minutes be death; so I crouched down behind a ledge of rocks, and bade a last farewell to home and friends, as I then thought, expecting that in a few minutes my dripping scalp would be hanging to the belt of the most horrible-looking monster I had ever beheld. It would be useless for me to attempt to describe my feelings at this moment. In less than a minute old Bigfoot came thundering along like an old buffalo bull, within less than thirty yards of me, but did not halt, making straight for the road, which was not far off, and I looked and saw the stage full of passengers, with several females among the number, just coming in sight.

"Somewhat to my relief I now discovered that it was the stage and not myself that was the object of Bigfoot's attention. He had evidently resolved to head off the stage, and murder the driver and rob the passengers. He was destined, however, to do no more scalping on this side of the 'dark river.' When the Indian who was next to the chief was nearly opposite my hiding-place, my blood was chilled by the crack of a rifle, which dropped this Indian dead within twenty yards of me. At the report of the gun old Bigfoot jumped behind a large rock, and the hindmost Indian broke back over the hill and was not seen again. For a moment all was quiet. I saw Charley Barnes throw the silk gracefully to his horses, as was his habit on nearing the canyon, he and his passengers all unconscious of the terrible fate they had just escaped. I afterwards learned that among the passengers were Judge Roseborough, Charley Douglass, the gambler, and Mrs. Record and her daughter. Mr. Record and family were then keeping the stage station at Fifteen-mile House, between Boise City and Snake River. Little did they think that there was one so near them as I was, and in such a terrible plight, who dared not move or ask for aid, and that the most deadly and bloody encounter that had ever been witnessed by any of us was about to take place.

"Those few moments seemed like hours to me. I knew that an Indian had been killed near me, but by whom, or from what direction, I could form no idea. From Bigfoot's action it was evident that he thought the report of the gun came from a tree surrounded by a clump of willows near the creek, some eighty yards from where he stood. The sequel proved that he was right. A few minutes after the stage passed out of sight, Bigfoot commenced practicing a bit of strategy that was new to me. All I could do was to lie still and in dead silence watch his movements. First he would crawl to one side of the large rock behind which he was hiding, then crawl back to the other side and cautiously peep around the side of the rock; but no one shot at him. All was dead quietude. He would then put his ear to the ground and listen, but could not hear the slightest noise. At last he tried another plan of escape. He tied a large bunch of sage brush to his back and tried to crawl away; and to my great horror he was advancing directly toward the spot where I lay hidden behind a ledge of rock. He came slowly and gently toward me. I was undecided whether to remain where I was a while longer, or jump and run toward the clump of willows which Bigfoot had been watching so long, and take the chances of finding a white man. If I remained where I was much longer, Bigfoot, who had not yet seen me, could not fail to find me; but this terrible state of suspense was soon brought to an end.

Bigfoot Meets An Equal.—"When Bigfoot had crawled over about half the distance that separated his hiding-place from mine, I heard a clear voice ring out on the mountain air, in cool, deliberate tones, saying: 'Get up from there, Bigfoot, you old feather-headed, leather-bellied coward. I can see you crawling off like a snake. This is one time that you did not even get a woman's scalp. Here is a scalp; come down and take mine, you coward.' At this Bigfoot sprang to his feet, and leveled a large, double-barreled rifle at the willows, and said: 'You coward; me no coward. You come out; I'll scalp you, too.' At this Wheeler sprang out from among the bushes in plain view, saying: 'Here I am, now sail in, old rooster.' Both men fired almost at the same instant. Bigfoot staggered, but recovered and fired again, then threw his gun down and started to run toward the dead Indian. He ran but a few yards, when another shot caused him to reel again, but he succeeded in reaching the spot where the dead Indian lay, and, picking up the gun left by the latter where he had fallen, he leveled it toward Wheeler and fired again, just at the moment that Wheeler's gun sent another unerring bullet into his powerful frame. Bigfoot again staggered and came very near falling, but again recovered, and, drawing a knife, gave an unearthly whoop, which almost froze my blood, and then started toward Wheeler. He had gone but a few yards when another shot staggered him, and then another. I was dumb with fear, apprehending that after all the Indian might succeed in reaching Wheeler and then grasp him in his powerful clutches. Wheeler never moved from the spot where he stood, but, handling his gun with extraordinary skill, continued to fire, until at last, when within thirty yards of him, the huge red demon fell with a broken leg to rise no more. Wheeler, however, emptied the balance of the sixteen shots into him, and then, without moving out of his tracks, reloaded his rifle and said: 'How do you like the way my gun shoots, old hoss? I'll bet my scalp against yours that you don't scalp any more white men in this canyon very soon.' Bigfoot cried out in plain English, 'Don't shoot me any more, you have killed me.' Wheeler walked up near the Indian, and, pulling out an ivory-handled revolver, gazed a moment at his fallen foes, then shouted out to me, 'Come down, whoever you are; there is no danger now.' I went to the spot and found Bigfoot bleeding from twelve wounds, both legs and one arm broken. The Indian asked for water, and Wheeler said: 'Hold on till I break the other arm; then I'll give you a drink.' Bigfoot said: 'Well, do it quick, and give me a drink and let me die.' Wheeler leveled his pistol, and at the report the arm fell useless to the ground. This to some may seem cruel, but I was yet afraid to go near this powerful and desperate savage monster. Wheeler went down to the creek and brought up his canteen full of water, and placed it on the mouth of the Indian, who drank it all. Bigfoot then said he wished he had some whisky, when Wheeler said he had a small bottle of whisky and ammonia, which he always carried in case of snake bites; that he could have that if he thought it would do him any good. Bigfoot said: 'Give it to me, quick; I'm getting blind.' Wheeler gave him a pint flask, filled with the strong fluid, mixed with a little water. The Indian drank it, every drop, and then said: 'I'm sick and blind,' and then fell back apparently dead.

Bigfoot's Appearance.—"After a few minutes he revived, and said that he was better, and that he wished us to wash the dust and paint from his face, and see what a good-looking man he was. We complied with his request, and to our surprise, we found a fine-looking face, with the handsomest set of teeth we ever beheld. He had large black, but wicked-looking eyes. His complexion had been almost white, but was now of course badly tanned. He had a heavy shock of long black hair, somewhat inclined to be kinky. He was of enormous size, and such hands, and especially feet, I never saw on any mortal before or since. He soon began to be quite talkative, and expressed a wish that we would make him one promise. Wheeler asked him what it was. He asked that we should not scalp him, nor take him to Boise City after he died, but to drag him in among the willows and pile some rocks upon him, and lay his old gun by his side. 'If you will promise me this,' he said, 'I shall die satisfied.' Wheeler told him that if he would tell him who he was, and where he came from, he would perhaps promise, and do what he wished; but that he must answer all the questions he was asked, tell the truth.

"Bigfoot then said, 'I have been a very bad man, and if I tell you all that I have done, I am afraid you will not do what I have asked of you.' Wheeler said: 'I know you have been a bad man, but if you will tell me everything, I will not tell any one that you are dead, nor tell anything about you.' When Wheeler said this, Bigfoot seemed to brighten up and said: 'Now do keep your promise, and I will tell you my whole history, and all that I have gone through, if I can only live long enough to do so.' Wheeler said: 'I have been assured by prominent citizens of Boise City that if any one killed you and brought your feet and your scalp to Fort Boise, at least $1,000 would be paid for them, for you have done a great deal of mischief, killed many white people, and everybody thinks that you were one of the party that killed Mrs. Scott and her husband on Burnt River last fall, as your big tracks were found next day near the scene of the murder, as they have always been found when white people have been killed by Indians in this part of the country. I have now been out here four days waiting for you, and the mosquitoes have nearly eaten me up while hiding in the willows, but now, if it will do you any good, I will hide you, but I will break your gun so that other Indians will not use it again.'

Bigfoot's History and Confession.—"The following is Bigfoot's account of himself and his career, taken down just as it was related to Wheeler and myself:

" 'I was born in the Cherokee nation. My father was a white man named Archer Wilkinson. He was hanged for murder in the Cherokee nation when I was a small boy. My mother was part Cherokee and part negro, so I was told. She was a good Christian woman.

My name is Starr Wilkinson. I was thus named after Thomas Starr*, a noted desperado in the nation. I was always called Bigfoot Wilkinson as long as I can remember. The boys always made fun of me when I was a boy, because I was so large for my age, and had such big feet. I had a bad temper, and got to drinking when quite young, and got to be so strong that when any one would call me a nickname I would fight him. In this way I came near killing several with my fists. I found out that I would soon be killed if I remained in that country, so I ran away from home and went to Tahlequah then capital of the Cherokee nation. There I fell in with some emigrants, who were going to Oregon in 1856, and drove a team across the plains, for my board. The folks I traveled with were kind to me. I fell in love with a young lady of the company, who thought a good deal of me until we fell in with a company from New York. Along with these new people was an artist, who was a smart, good-looking fellow. He soon cut me out. After this the young lady would hardly notice me or speak to me. I knew then that he had told her something bad about me. He made fun of me several times, and while we were camped near the Goose Creek Mountains, he and I went out one morning to hunt up the stock. We went to the bank of Snake River. I asked him what he intended to do when he got to Oregon. He replied "Marry Miss ———." I told him he should not do so, for I thought I had the best right to her. He only laughed and said: "Do you suppose she would marry a big-footed nigger like you, and throw off on a good-looking fellow like me?" This

*There was a family by this name in the Indian Territory, the noted desperado Bell Starr belonged to it.

made me mad, and I told him I was no negro, and that if he called me that again I would kill him. So he drew his gun on me and repeated it. I was unarmed, but started at him. He shot me in the side but did not hurt me much, so I grabbed him and threw him down, and choked him to death, then threw him into Snake River, took his gun, pistol and knife, and ran off into the hills.

" 'The emigrants did not leave camp for a few days. They were, perhaps, hunting for us. Some of them went on to Oregon, but the family that I had been traveling with went back with some others to Salt Lake, where they wintered. I made my way to the Boise River, where I found a French trader and trapper, and a man named Joe Lewis, who had been with the Indians for many years. This Joe Lewis was one who helped massacre Doctor Whitman and many others near old Fort Walla Walla, in 1847. He was a bad man, but he was a good friend to me when I needed a friend. So I went with him and joined the Indians, and have been with them ever since. In 1857 I went with Lewis and some Indians near the emigrant road for the purpose of stealing stock from the emigrants. In one of our raids I found cattle that I knew had belonged to the family I had crossed the plains with the year before. So I determined to go to the train and see if my girl was with them, and try to get her to run off with me. I found her, but she was very mad with me, as were all the rest. They said they thought I had killed Mr. Hart, the artist, and that I ought to hang for it. They told me to leave the camp. I told the girl that if she did not have me she would be sorry for it before she reached Oregon. I had to leave, but was determined to have revenge; so I took Joe Lewis and thirty Indians, and followed down Boise River where it empties into Snake River, and massacred them, and ran off with all their stock, and killed the girl, too. I am sorry for that now for she was a good girl, but it is too late to be sorry now. I was mad and foolish. I have been in several other massacres. I helped to kill the Scott family on Burnt River. We wanted their horses. I also helped to kill an officer, and took his wife prisoner last fall. The officer was on his way to Camp Lyon. His wife got sick, had a child, and could not ride, so some of the Indians killed her. I had a squaw for a wife, and when Jeff Stanford was out with a lot of men fighting us, they killed my wife, and carried off my little boy. Since then I have done all the mischief I could, and am glad of it.'

"Wheeler here asked Bigfoot what became of Joe Lewis. He said that Lewis was shot by a man who carried the express from Auburn to Boise in 1862. While Lewis was trying to steal some horses on the Payette River one night the expressman shot across the river with buckshot, hitting Lewis in the side and wounding Bigfoot in the leg. As it was dark, and neither of the wounded men spoke, the expressman did not know that any one had been hit. 'Joe whispered to me,' continued Bigfoot, 'that he was hurt bad, so I took him upon my back, and started to run with him, but he soon died, and I covered him up in the sand on the bank of the Payette River, where he was never found by the whites; and that was the last of poor Joe, and I hope you will do that much for me.' Mr. Wheeler said: 'All right, Mr. Wilkinson, I guess I will do it; as I am from the Cherokee nation myself, and have a little Cherokee blood in my veins, I will not refuse to grant your dying request.' When Wheeler said this, and assured him that he would not take his body, or any portion of it, to the fort, Bigfoot actually wept, and asked to know Wheeler's name, and said: 'You are a brave man, and I know you will keep your word. I am a brave man, too, but you shot a little too quick for me, and you had the best gun, and you have killed me. Your shot struck me just as I was pulling the trigger, else I think I should have killed you, as I hardly ever missed anything I ever shot at. I got my old gun at the massacre in 1857. I do not know how many men I have killed with it.

" 'Nearly all of our little band of warriors are killed off. There are but five left who have been running with me. You have just killed one of the bravest of the band. He has been one of my head braves ever since the Indians recognized me as the leader of the brave little band. His father is the old medicine man, and he told us when we left not to go on this trip, for he had dreamed about us. He dreamed that there was a large snake secreted in these bluffs that had a white man's head on, and had a medicine gun, that when he pointed it at the Indians they could not see how to shoot, and that after killing them he broke their guns to pieces. He wept when we left camp, and said that he should never see us again until we met in the spirit land. He was right. If I had minded him I would not have been killed.' Wheeler said: 'Well, if you meet the old medicine gentleman in the spirit land, tell him he was a good hand at dreaming, if he did call me a snake.' Wheeler then asked him where the rest of the

Indians were camped. Bigfoot said: 'This is something I cannot tell; but I will tell anything else that you may ask me. There are but few of them left; and now that we are killed the rest will soon go into the fort, and it would do you no good to kill them. The little band I run with call themselves Piutes; the rest call themselves Fish Indians, because they live by fishing on the Malheur and Snake rivers, and do not run with the Lake Piutes and Bannocks. The other Indians are not friendly toward us, and I care nothing about them; but our little band have been brave Indians. They have always treated me well, and I do not wish to betray them as the last act of a bad life.' Wheeler said: 'Bully for you, Wilkinson, I think more of you than I did before, for you are not a traitor, if you have been a bad man otherwise.'

"Wheeler asked him how tall he was, and how much he thought he weighed. Bigfoot said he did not know, for he had grown very much since he joined the Indians; that when he left the whites he was but nineteen years old; that he then measured six feet six inches and a half in height, and weighed 255 pounds. 'But I know,' said he, 'that I must weigh at least 300 pounds and there is not a pound of fat on me,' which was true. He was a model of strength and endurance. I had a tape line and rule in my pocket, with which I took the following exact measurements of this wonderful being: Around the chest, fifty-nine inches; height, six feet eight and a half inches; length of foot, seventeen and one-half inches; around the ball of the foot, eighteen inches; around the widest part of the hand, eighteen inches. I am confident that he must have weighed at least 300 pounds; and all bone and sinew, not a pound of surplus flesh on him.*

"His voice here failed; he fell back, saying, 'Everything is getting dark,' and lay silent for a while, then spoke in husky, rapid tones, 'Look! look! the soldiers are after me! I must go, quick! quick!' He then died without a struggle.

"We then got my horses, put a rope around Bigfoot's body, to which we hitched the horses, and dragged the body 150 yards to the creek, and put Bigfoot's old broken gun by his side. We then threw some brush and rocks upon him, hid the other broken gun, threw away what little ammunition the dead Indians had left, and left the other Indian where he had fallen. Wheeler said the other Indians would probably come and find what was left if they were not afraid.

"We then started for Boise City, where we arrived the next day. Wheeler made me promise to say nothing about the affair, as he had given his word to Bigfoot, and was resolved not to break the promise he had made."

This story ran as a serial during the late seventies in the *Globe Democrat* of St. Louis, Missouri. It is also found in *History of Idaho Territory,* published in 1884 by W. W. Elliott & Co. Bancroft, in his history, also alludes to Wheeler so it would seem to be based on more or less accurate historical facts. The author, too, was at one time a resident of Tahlequah, Indian Ter-

*The Morning *Oregonian* of June 23, 1919, gives the following measurements of Jess Willard—Neck, 17½ in.; right biceps, 16¼ in.; left biceps, 16¾ in.; wrist 9¼ in.; chest, 45 in., expanded 49½ in. Waist 40 in.; thigh, 25½ in.; calf, 17 in.; ankle, 11 in.; height 6 ft. 6½ in.; weight, 248 pounds.

Pony Express Station at Fort Bridger, Built 1860. Old Oregon Trail Passed by the Station about Ten Feet in Front of Door—or Two-Hinged Window on North Side of Fort Bridger.

ritory, the place alluded to and knew of the Wilkinson and Starr families.

James Bridger.—"Due to an innate modesty, James Bridger has left no written record of his long life spent in the plains and mountains where he performed deeds of unusual daring and rendered inestimable service to our government. Major General Grenville M. Dodge bequeathed to posterity a bulletin containing much of the intimate history of Bridger observed and obtained while the soldier and frontiersman were companions in danger and hardship through a long series of years, years which represent one of the most turbulent and dangerous periods of the Oregon Trail, as a fore-runner of the Union Pacific railroad.

"Bridger was illiterate and did not even attempt to sign his name to contracts and documents; he wrote no letters; he kept no diaries, no journals. 'He neither exploited himself nor encouraged others seriously to do so; hence the paucity of original material,' quoting from Cecil Alter's *James Bridger, Trapper, Frontiersman, Scout and Guide.*

"Because of the fact that Major Bridger (as he ultimately became known to the frontier) dwelt in 'the tepees of tangled traditions' and in the open air of the fading memories of friends; and his character and activities have thus been exposed to the 'hoodlumism' of disregard and unjust designations of braggart, drunkard, polygamist or prevaricator, this article is penned, the challenge is accepted and his defense, if needed, is both a duty and pleasure.

"James Bridger, born in Richmond, Va., started to be a bread-winner for himself and sister at the age of thirteen years, first running a ferry at St. Louis. When eighteen, he enlisted with the Ashley-Henry Trapping Company, which was en route for the Rocky Mountains. In this company were men who were destined to write their names into the history of the Great West, of which Montana and Wyoming were so great a part, men of fearlessness, alertness and adaptability to the varied conditions of uncharted rivers, and untrailed plains and mountain passes. In this exceptional group among others were William Ashley, Andrew Henry, Bridger, Provot, Fitzpatrick, Milton and William Sublette, David Jackson, Jedediah Smith, Hugh Glass, who in 1822 were initiated into the fur business 'which they helped make great.' It was a small group of these men under the management of Henry, who, with the help of Bridger, in the fall of 1822 pushed up the Missouri to the mouth of the Yellowstone, where near the junction of the two streams several log cabins and a high stockade were raised to be known in history as Fort Union, near the present day boundary line between North Dakota and Montana.

"In 1823, Henry and his men and Bridger moved farther up the Missouri from the mouth of the Yellowstone to the Powder River (Montana). Journeying up the Powder now with Etienne Provot as captain, the small band of men marched southward to the headwaters of the stream, hunting, exploring and trapping, the group crossing the Continental Divide through which the Oregon Trail was to wind its way to the Oregon Country. In the year following (1824) in the late autumn Bridger discovered Great Salt Lake, reporting, when he returned to the winter quarters of his companions, his belief that he had reached an arm of the Pacific Ocean. To the record of discovery by

Bridger is added the finding of Two Ocean Pass (1825) through the Rocky Mountains at the southeast boundary of the Yellowstone National Park. The summer of 1826 finds a new fur company formed from members of the Ashley Company, with William Sublette, David Jackson and Jedediah Smith the new partners. On the plains these three men were known among their intimate group as 'Bill,' 'Davy' and 'Jed.' When this fur company 'had drunk of success in the fur business to satiety,' it sold, in August, 1830, its interest to Fitzpatrick, 'Broken Hand'; James Bridger, 'Old Gabe'; and Milton Sublette, 'Milt.' From this date, Bridger had established himself as a hunter and trader and Indian fighter. Counting from this period, his fortunes are easily traced.

"At the urgent recommendation of General John Charles Fremont, there were established along the Oregon Trail, four military posts, observations made during his expeditions along this trail during the years of 1842 and 1843 convincing the military explorer that some governmental protection to the homeseekers on their way to the Oregon Country was a necessity if our northwestern country was to be developed by the man of family and his offspring. These proposed forts were not designed to be built to protect the settlers who were living along this road of the homeseeker, for there were no such hardy people along the trail, but the forts were to render assistance by military force to those Americans who were on their way to the 'sea of the West,' in search of homes and agricultural lands.

"Of the four fur posts, or 'forts,' finally taken over by our government and garrisoned by regular soldiers who safeguarded the lives of these venturesome and daring settlers on their way to fortunes in the West, Fort Bridger occupies an important, if not strategic, place. Here the fur-traders and trappers carried on their commerce in the precious skins of beaver and other fur-bearing animals.

"In the valley of the Black-Fork, Southwestern Wyoming, Bridger in 1843 had built a blacksmith and repair shop for the Oregon trailers, this being purchased in 1849 by the government and known then, as now, as Fort Bridger. This was the home of the old trapper for many years, and it is here that Emerson Hough has pictured in his *Covered Wagon* the 'polygamous' Bridger. While Jim Bridger was a much married individual, there is nothing in his history to show that his wives were numerous at one and the same time. 'Blanket Chief,' as Bridger was called, lived in one of the huts of his post, with his second adventure in matrimony, who was a member of the Ute nation. To the couple was born a daughter, Virginia, who was nourished through her earliest childhood on buffalo milk. At the daughter's birth, the mother died, July 4, 1849. Venture number one (or should one say 'adventure?') was a Flathead who died in 1846. A daughter of this union was sent to the Oregon mission managed by Dr. and Mrs. Marcus Whitman. In 1847 when the Indian uprising occurred at Waiilatpu, 'Mary Ann' was rescued when most of the other inmates of the mission were massacred.

"The third and last marriage was in 1850, when Bridger selected a wife from the Snake or Shoshone tribe. This wife lived at Fort Bridger, records showing that if not a relative, she was at least a connection of the Lewis and Clark guide, Sacajawea.

"When 'The Covered Wagon' first appeared on the screen, Bridger's daughter, Virginia, brought suit against the makers of the picture, claiming heavy damages for the defaming of her father's name. This was the daughter who 'ministered to the broken old scout, her father, in his declining years, the buffalo milk he fed her being repaid in the milk of human kindness when all other friends had apparently forgotten him.'

"The courts ruled in Bridger's daughter's protest that a picture such as 'The Covered Wagon' could not defame a character as well known and so highly respected as that of her father, James Bridger.

"The attempt to belittle the wilderness life of so honored an individual as Major Bridger should not go unchallenged. No scout and guide, as was Bridger, for our government could long have remained in the service if he was a drunkard. Only men of unmuddled minds, steady nerves and clear, searching eyes could, for an extended period, be of value in the honored positions occupied by James Bridger. Just before Mr. Hough died, the author of this article wrote him, he having been one of her college acquaintances at the State University of Iowa, asking him for some revisions of the screened 'Covered Wagon,' but it was too late. the playrights of the book had been sold, need it be said for the insignificant sum of $8,000! Fancy!

"In the attempt to place James Bridger in his proper historical place as a man fearless, competent, faithful and sober, the evidence following has been collected, signed by trustworthy associates of this grizzly-headed frontiersman, fur-trader and friend of the white man.

"From the pen of Mr. J. C. Cooper of McMinnville, Oregon, the following is vindicating:

" 'In July of that year (1866) Hugh Kirkendall took a freight train from Leavenworth, Kansas, to Helena, Montana, by the way of Julesburg on the South Platte, Colorado, Bridger's ferry on the North Platte, Powder River, Cheyenne River, Wyoming and Tongue, Big Horn, Little Big Horn and the Yellowstone rivers. Jim Bridger was our pilot from Bridger's Ferry to the Yellowstone. I saw him frequently on that trip. He was a quiet, familiar figure about the camp. . . . . He would ride ahead across the untraveled country and return to the train at noon, or sometimes not until nightfall, when we had made camp. He rode a quiet, old flea-bitten gray mare, with a musket laid across his saddle in front of him and wore an old-fashioned blue army overcoat and an ordinary slouch hat. . . . . He was very quiet in camp and I never saw him ride as fast as a slow trot.

" 'We had liquors on the train, but I never knew of his taking a drink. One thing that got on our nerves was his absence from the train when we would be fighting with the Indians, which was a daily occurrence some of the time. Some days old Sitting Bull would make it so hot for us that we thought we would not see old Jim any more, but he always returned, riding quietly into camp.'

"Dean of our Wyoming pioneers, Honorable John Hunton, resident of old Fort Laramie for over sixty years, gave the author an interesting interview as follows:

" 'This is a condition that could not have been, that of being intoxicated, because he was a trader and trapper (referring to Bridger) and his life would not have been worth much if he were a drunkard. A trader and trapper had to be keen and alert all the time in order to avoid the Indians, and when he became a scout and guide for our government, as he did in 1865 for Connor and in 1866 and 1867 for Carrington in the Powder River country, and in guiding the United States army in the Yellowstone district, he would not have been tolerated for a moment if he had been such a man as was pictured in "The Covered Wagon." He could not have afforded to have done so.'

"Mr Hunton and Bridger 'bunked' together at Fort Laramie during the entire winter of 1867 and 1868, seeing each other daily. In speaking of 'The Covered Wagon' Mr. Hunton concluded the interview, saying:

" 'That is a vilification of one of the finest men that I have ever known who scouted on the Laramie Plains. I never, in all my connection and intimate association with Jim Bridger, ever knew him to be under the slightest influence of liquor.'

"From Mr. Fin G. Burnett, now living at Fort Washakie, Wyoming, who was with Bridger in 1866 when he piloted Colonel Carrington over the Bozeman Trail, was obtained the following statement:

" 'I knew Bridger well and saw him not only every day but many times in every day during '66 and '67 when I was associated with Col. Carrington on the Bozeman Trail, and I never saw him drunk and I never saw anybody who ever said that he was drunk.'

"In the summer of 1926 at Sheridan, Wyoming, near the Montana line, in an interview with Mr. Oliver P. Hanna, an old timer along the Trail and in the Powder River district, was obtained additional testimony:

" 'That,' said Mr. Hanna, 'is a wrong statement; it is a falsification of a splendid character as that of Jim Bridger; to say that he was a drunkard. It is true that we drank on the plains, particularly at night when we gambled for the drinks, a universal custom, but he never, to my knowledge, was drunk and he had the reputation of being a man of great sobriety. In 1865 when he and I were together in the Connor Expedition, I saw him many times every day and never was there the slightest indication that he was in the "cups." '

"In an interview held November 21, 1926, at Laramie, Wyoming, with Mr. Charles William Becker, who came into what is Uinta County, Wyoming, in 1857, that which follows was obtained:

" 'I knew Jim Bridger well. I never saw Jim Bridger drunk. I did know him well and saw him daily for four or five years. At that time at Fort Bridger, then in Utah, where I knew Jim Bridger, the scout had a squaw wife and daughter. Jim was well liked and trusted, old Jim Bridger was.'

"Mr. Becker furnishes the information relative to the relationship of Bridger's Shoshone wife to Sacajawea, both of whom he knew and frequently conversed with in the sign language of the Shoshone Indians while at old Fort Bridger."—*Grace Raymond Hebard*, University of Wyoming.

CHAPTER VII.

THE OREGON COUNTRY.

Captain Gray Who Discovered a River and Thereby Added Three States to the Union.—At the close of the Revolutionary War coin was very scarce in the colonies. Trade had to be carried on by barter. The Chinese were quite ready to accept furs in lieu of coin, and the colonies desired to take advantage of this fact. In 1787 some Boston merchants fitted out the first fur-trading expedition to the Pacific Coast. There were two ships, one, of 220 tons burden, was in command of Captain John Kendrick; the other, the *Lady Washington,* of 90 tons burden, was in command of Captain Robert Gray.

Captain Gray, the Discoverer of the Columbia River.

Nootka was the objective point and here Captain Gray arrived on September 16th. The other boat under Kendrick arrived six or seven days later. On his way from the Atlantic to the Pacific Northwest, Captain Gray had touched at a number of points on the Pacific Coast.

Upon his arrival he found two English boats, in command of Meares and Douglas, anchored there. Captain Meares, while apparently very courteous to the Americans, did all he could to discourage their remaining there. He claimed that he had not obtained over fifty hides that season. While the Englishmen remained no trade of any kind could be brought about with the natives. Some claim that this was because of the Englishmen's harsh treatment of the Indians whom they robbed and otherwise mistreated.

Captain Kendrick decided to spend the winter there, and on October 26th the English ships departed for China. The Americans remained until the following March, spending the winter in hunting and fishing.

But when spring arrived Gray cruised along the coast as far north as 55 degrees and 42 minutes, going in and out and around the various islands found along the coast. Commercially the trip was a very successful one, as they secured many pelts. At one place 200 sea otter skins, worth about $8,000, were obtained for an old chisel. Gray was now put in command of the *Columbia*, a larger ship, on which was placed all of the furs, and he departed for China, arriving in Canton in December.

The following spring and summer he continued his journey around the world, his being the first American ship to circumnavigate the globe. He arrived at Boston in August. Commercially the voyage of Gray was not considered very successful, but the possibilities were very encouraging. A new voyage was immediately planned for the *Columbia,* Gray being in command, and after a little more than a month's rest he again sailed for the Pacific, reaching the coast in the spring of 1791. Here he cruised up and down until the fall, when he went into winter quarters at Clayoqwot.

A house was erected on shore for the men and work was begun on a new boat, materials for which had been brought from Boston. The Indians had been so friendly on the preceding voyage that there was little fear of them; but in February a plot was discovered whereby they intended to kill the whole crew, except a Hawaiian boy whom they attempted to bribe to help them, in return for which they agreed to spare his life. But the plot was discovered and Gray moved his ship to a less exposed point, strengthened his defense, discharged his cannon into the woods, and took other precautions which prevented the Indians from doing any harm.

On February 23, 1792 his new boat named the *Adventurer,* was launched, and on April 1st, Gray, in command of the *Columbia,* sailed south, while the other boat, in command of Captain Hoswell, went north in search of furs.

The commander of every ship must keep a record of all the important happenings of his ship. These are recorded in a book called a "log," which is a history of the ship's voyage.

The "log" of the ship in which Gray discovered the Columbia River was lost, except that including the happenings from May 7th to May 21st, but fortunately the Columbia was discovered between these dates, Captain Gray having entered the river on May 11th, ascending for 25 or 30 miles and naming it in honor of his ship.

A Spaniard and an Englishman had each seen this river previous to Gray's discovery, but neither had entered it and hence could not lay claim to its discovery.

The nation that discovers the mouth of a river establishes a right to all of the country drained by it, so by Gray's discovery, the United States claimed all of what now constitutes Oregon, Washington, and Idaho.

In addition to his discovery of the Columbia River, Gray had also been in the navy during the American Revolution, but his nation did not reward him in any way during his life, nor did it reward his family after his death. A bill was introduced in congress in 1846 to give his widow a pension of $500 and a township of land in the country which her husband had discovered, but the bill did not pass. The old chest in which he kept his papers on the *Columbia*, is now in the rooms of the State Historical Society at Portland, Oregon, but beyond this there is little to remind any one in the Oregon Country of its discoverer.

Claims to the Oregon Country.—This territory was bounded on the north by 54 degrees, 40 minutes, or the boundary of the Russian possessions, on the east by the Rocky Mountains, on the west by the Pacific Ocean, and on the south by 42 degrees or the boundary of the Spanish possessions, and was claimed by Russia, Spain, Great Britain and the United States.

Russia's Claim.—This was based on discovery and occupation by fur-traders. The Emperor exercised authority on the Asiatic Coast as far south as 45 degrees north latitude, and he claimed the right of sovereignty on the American coast as far south as 51 degrees and from these points on both sides for one hundred Italian miles out into the sea, treating the northern part of the Pacific as a closed sea. In 1824 a treaty was concluded with the United States and in 1825 one with Great Britain whereby Russia agreed not to make any settlement south of 54 degrees 40 minutes.

Spain's Claim.—The right of this country was established on the following discoveries: The voyages of Cabrillo and Ferrelo in 1543 to latitude 43 degrees; Juan de Fuca in 1592 to parallel 49 degrees, and the strait which bears his name; Vizcano in 1603 to latitude 43 degrees; Perez in 1774 to latitude 54 degrees; Heceta in 1775 to latitude 48 degrees, discovering but not entering the River St. Roque now the Columbia, and a few minor voyages as far north as latitude 59 degrees.

Spanish settlement was begun by Cortez in 1535 and gradually pushed west and north through Mexico and California, but never extending farther than the southern boundary of Oregon, although the country much farther north was claimed by Spain. By the treaty of 1763 Spain had a still further right to this country, gaining the French claims, but she lost this when the territory was receded to France.

Great Britain's Claim.—Great Britain had little claim to this country by discovery, Drake saw the coast in 1580, Cook examined it slightly in 1778 and Van Couver more thoroughly in 1783, but none of these could be termed original discoverers.

Fur-traders established posts in this country in 1793, 1806, 1811, and 1824, but no attempts at permanent settlement were made south of the 49th degree of latitude, their chief aim being trading.

The Claim of the United States.—The claim of this nation to the Oregon Country is based on discovery, exploration, settlement, and treaties.

(a) On May 11, 1792, Captain Robert Gray discovered the Columbia River, sailing up the stream for several miles. There had been a custom, or understanding among nations, that the nation that discovered the mouth of the river was entitled to all the country drained by its tributaries.

(b) In 1805-06 Lewis and Clark, by authority of the United States government, explored most of the country south of 49th degree of latitude, and in 1811 settlements were made at Astoria; on the Willamette by the Lees in 1832-33; by Whitman near Walla Walla, Washington, and by Spalding at Lapwai, Idaho, in 1836-37.

Treaties.—By treaty with France in 1803 the United States gained all of the French title to the Oregon Country, and by treaty with Spain in 1819 that country surrendered all its right to the same section. In 1818 the United States and Great Britain entered into what is termed the "joint occupancy" treaty, by the terms of which all the land claimed by both powers west of the Rocky Mountains should be "free and open" to the subjects of both, for the next ten years. This treaty was renewed in 1827 and was to continue indefinitely; either nation could terminate it by giving the other twelve months' notice.

In 1844 a popular demand arose for the "re-occupation of Oregon and the reannexation of Texas." The convention which nominated Polk asserted that "our title to the whole of the territory of Oregon is clear and unquestionable," and in his inaugural address, Polk made the same claim, omitting the word, "whole," however.

A bill passed the house in February 1845 providing a territorial government for Oregon with a boundary of 54 degrees and 40 minutes as the northern limit. The Senate defeated this bill because it prohibited slavery; Buchanan, Polk's Secretary of State, proposed in July, to compromise by offering the line of 49 as a boundary, this offer was declined by the English and withdrawn by the President in his annual message in the fall of 1845. There followed, the next spring a joint resolution of the two houses authorizing the President, at his discretion, to give Great Britain the required notice of withdrawal from the agreement of 1827; but before the President acted in the matter, England offered to

Dr. John McLoughlin.

accept 49 degrees as the boundary, and Polk dodged all responsibility by referring the proposition to the Senate which in June, 1846, ratified the treaty proposed.

Old Oregon, Its Boundaries, Its First Capital, Its First and Only King.—Alaska, or the Russian possessions on the north, California, or the Mexican possessions on the south, the Pacific Ocean on the west, the United States, or the Rocky Mountains on the east, constituted the boundary of this vast empire, which was about one thousand miles in length and about half as many in width.

Vancouver.—This fort or fur-trading post was located on the north bank of the Columbia, near the mouth of the Cowlitz River, which rises near the Puget Sound on the north, and the Willamette, whose source was almost to the Mexican boundary, on the south, while the Columbia, with its fan-shaped tributaries, reached far back into the interior. The location was strategical and ideal, as it commanded the Columbia which controlled the only route to the sea on the west, and the rivers of the interior which controlled the fur trade clear back to the Rocky Mountains. Fine land and pasture were abundant and the climate was mild, all of which were necessary for developing agriculture and stock raising.

Here was the typical fur-trading post on a large scale. It represented an inclosure of 150 by 250 yards, surrounded by palisades—trees split in two and cut into lengths of twenty feet, both ends of which were sharpened, one end being stuck into the ground and standing upright. These were fastened so close together as to make a solid fence. This inclosure was surrounded by woods, full of game of every description, and through the woods ran streams well stocked with mountain trout and salmon.

On three sides of the inclosure were the houses for the company's employes. At other places were warehouses, shops, store rooms, and buildings necessary for the company's business. In the center and facing the main entrance was the residence of Dr. McLoughlin, the governor. "It was a French-Canadian structure, painted white, with a piazza and flower beds in front, and grape vines trained along a rude trellis." The steps leading to the residence were horseshoe shaped and in the center was mounted a cannon with a mortar gun on either side. These commanded the gate through which all must enter who came within, and which was in charge of a keeper day and night.

Life in this forest castle was very regular and formal. A large bell was rung at five in the morning, when the day's work began, and at eight, twelve, and six when meals were served, at nine and one, when work was resumed, and at six, when the day closed. When McLoughlin gave a dinner, and he gave many, all were seated according to rank, he at the head and others at the places to which their station entitled them. The dining hall was in the center of his residence and attached was a kitchen where were prepared canvas-backed ducks, baked salmon, rare parts of venison, and, after the orchards and the gardens began bearing, fruits and vegetables of all kinds. The bread was baked in a great oven of fire brick; great quantities were baked not only for the families within the fort but also for those who went into the woods or onto the sea as well. The table was richly set with fine English glass. Mc-

Loughlin led the conversation, and if guests were present and they frequently were, he saw to it that they were very considerately treated. While sufficient time was allowed for the meal, needless time was not consumed. Equal consideration was shown the laborer. Every Saturday evening at five o'clock, his week's rations were given him. In winter this consisted of eight gallons of potatoes, and eight salt salmon, and in summer, peas and tallow. No bread or meat other than salmon was allowed except periodically.

The departure and return of the trapper were days of great interest. Beads and blankets, guns, powder and lead, knives and hatchets, bright ribbons and gay colored kerchiefs, trinkets and other things for trade with the Indians, and everything needed by the trapper himself were supplied. His destination might be a point anywhere between Mexico and Alaska or between the Rocky Mountains and the Pacific. Dangers dogged his footsteps every inch of the way. A lurking Indian might rob or murder him, he might be attacked by the wild animals, or his canoe might be turned over in midriver, his trapping competitors might get into the field before him and catch or frighten away all the game or fur-bearing animals, or turn the Indians against him. But such things were not to be considered. He kissed his little boy or girl or baby whom he might never again see, jumped into the boat, and was off. But he realized that his "great white chief," a term applied by the Indians to McLoughlin, had anticipated his every need, and would follow to the ends of the earth anyone who dared molest or interfere with him. This chief stood by the river bank to cheer him when he departed and to welcome him when he returned. No prodigal ever received a heartier reception on his arrival home than that received from his chief by the returning trapper. For days McLoughlin stood with glass in hand looking up or down the river, according to the direction taken by the trapper, and had scouts stationed beyond where he could see. Upon the first news of the approach of a returning crew, the British flag was unfurled and allowed to flutter from the flag staff. The kitchen, where the homecoming feast was in preparation, was the busiest place at the fort. A warm fire burned on every hearth stone, and when the voyagers, decked with the brightest colors and singing a gay song, approached the landings, their king was there to meet and welcome them.

McLoughlin was not only a strong executive and fine administrator, but he was a great diplomat as well. If the Indians plotted the destruction of his fort, he always discovered it in time to prevent their success. Sometimes when they came bent on mischief, he invited their leaders within and royally entertained them with music and feast, and they went away forgetting that they had ever intended trouble and with such pleasant recollections that the attempt was never repeated. Yet if an Indian dared defy his edict, the fiery eyes and the stern visage of the old king literally consumed him with a passionate temper which he never again wanted to encounter. He might take him by the shoulder and shake him as a dog does a rat, or use his cane with such fierceness that he never wanted to repeat the experience. But after all is said and done, McLoughlin was at the head of a great trust that could not tolerate a competitor. If someone came into his territory with goods to exchange with the Indians for furs, McLoughlin would buy him out, but would not allow him to trade. Yet if one of his fur-trading competitors was robbed, he was just as vigilant in running down the robber as though his own man had been robbed. It was his proud boast that no Indian could commit robbery within his empire—no matter whom he robbed—and escape punishment.

But McLoughlin's sympathies were too broad to be limited by geographical boundaries. While loyal to his company, he regarded his first loyalty to humanity in general. When the immigrants began to find their way down the Columbia or from the sea to the Willamette Valley, they always found a welcome at Vancouver. The wives of Whitman and Spalding stopped there until their husbands selected sites for their missions. Here Lee met his future bride, and here, later, came the immigrants by hundreds and thousands from the Middle West. But, regardless of numbers, McLoughlin ever held out a helping hand. He loaned stock, furnished seed grain, supplied ragged and starving immigrants with food and clothing, and oftentimes took them into the fort and kept them. These broad human sympathies, however, were his undoing with his company, who claimed that $50,000 or $60,000 had been lost by such misplaced philanthropy, and there is abundant evidence to show that hundreds who were assisted by him, not only did not repay but afterwards turned against him.

McLoughlin was dismissed as manager of the company and retired to Oregon City, and took out his papers to become a naturalized citizen of America. The country of his adoption allowed him to be deprived of the homestead which he took up for his old age and he died almost in poverty. Today he lies buried in the city where he spent his declining years, with no marble shaft to proclaim to the present generation his great and good deeds.*

The Settlement.—A social group or settlement was easily formed, as relatives or former neighbors or acquaintances made on the trip west united to establish one. If they were farmers, they selected a locality where plenty of good land, wood, water, and pasture could be obtained. The choice was an arbitrary one, as the land was yet unsurveyed, and each took up such land as he wished.

The men then built crude log houses which could be finished within a few days. These buildings usually had but one room, with one door and sometimes a window. The floor consisted of puncheons—logs split in two with the flat side turned up. The cracks between the logs were "chinked," that is, filled with mud, moss, and sometimes small bits of wood. A chimney was made of sticks, the inside of which was plastered with mud, and the opening between the sticks filled in the same way. The house was covered with "shakes," that is, homemade shingles, which were usually held on by a ridge pole that ran from one end of the house to the other, and rested on the shakes. The buildings were, as a rule, one story, although most of them were high enough to contain what was termed a "loft," which was reached by a ladder or by pins driven into the walls. This loft might be a storeroom for what usually finds its way into an ordinary closet. Jerked meat, dried pumpkins, and other articles of food were also stored here.

* The author is indebted to the writings of Eva Emery Dye for much of the material in this article.

The cooking utensils included a frying pan, skillet, and stewkettle. The skillet was a small oven from twelve to eighteen inches in diameter and about four to six inches deep. It rested on three legs and had a lid fitting tight on the top. Live coals could be placed under the skillet as well as on the lid. The housewife could use it for the baking of bread as well as for frying meat. It had a long handle projecting from one side, and by means of this she could move the skillet from place to place. The stewkettle was eight or ten inches in diameter, and from ten to fourteen inches in depth, with a bail attached as well as legs on the bottom. This could be set on live coals or hung on a crane and pushed over the fire in the fireplace. The frying pan did not differ materially from that which is used today. The

Typical Home of the Pioneer.

The Dirt Roof House, Salmon, Idaho.

kitchen furniture consisted of a water-bucket, churn, a cupboard in which were kept the dishes, a few stools, perhaps, and a table. The pioneer early fenced off a plot of ground for his garden. In this were planted many of the seeds which the housewife had brought from her eastern home.

Reminiscences of Some Pioneer Ladies on Life in the Immigrant Train and in the Pioneer Homes of Oregon. —"On the first of November, 1845, after a journey of eight months of inconceivable hardships, a small party of pioneers first stepped on the banks of the grand Willamette River, near where Morrison Street, Portland, is now located. The rays of the setting sun casting their light and shade over the beautiful landscape, filled the beholders with a deep feeling of thankfulness that they were permitted to reach the new land, and to stand on the shore of the 'wonderful river of the West.' The wind murmuring through the branches of the stately firs bade them welcome, and the old trees served as shelter for the next two months. With the aid of flint, steel, and powder, a large camp fire was soon burning brightly, casting a rich glow over the magnificent wall of forest trees. It was a picturesque scene. The soft moonlight, the sparkle of the water, the lurid light from the resinous fire, formed a scene worthy of a painter's skill. They arrived destitute of all save character, determination, and self-reliance, but with such sterling qualities failure was impossible.

Building of Houses.—"With the first rosy blushes of the dawn the men began to rise, and before the sun was fairly over the horizon the sound and echoes of their axes brought cheer to our mothers' hearts, for they knew that ere long homes would shelter them from the winter's storms. Weeks of hard labor were required to fell the trees, and clear away the brush, and prepare the site on which to build. Trees were cut the proper length, one side of the log hewed smooth with a broadax, and fitted so they would join at the corners and lie compact. It was no easy task, but our loved pioneers, with only a saw, auger and ax, broadax and adz would put to shame some of the more modern workmen. Logs for the puncheon floors were split and smoothed with an adz, and fitted close together, making a warm and solid floor. The structure was raised to a proper height, and poles were used for rafters; some of the logs were cut three feet in length, and shakes were made and used in place of shingles.

The Interior.—"The fireplace and chimney were built with sticks, and plastered inside and out with a thick coating of clay. Some had a stout iron bar se-

Pioneer Household Scene.

curely fastened on one side of the large fireplace; on this bar, which was called a crane, iron hooks were placed, on which the teakettle and other cooking utensils were hung; all cooking and baking was done before the open fire and on the broad clay hearth. Windows were sliding doors in the wall, without glass. The furniture was extremely simple, being split out of fir or cedar trees, and, if not elegant, was substantial; doors were also made of shakes, and hung on wooden hinges. Wooden pegs were used in place of nails.

Bedroom Furniture.—"Rough bedsteads were placed in one corner of the large room, and the trundle beds pushed under them during the day, and drawn out at night ready for the little ones. Large quantities of moss stripped from the trees made good mattresses, and with buffalo robes and blankets they had comfortable beds.

"When their primitive cabins were completed and ready for occupancy, with heartfelt thankfulness they left the shelter of the trees for their first Oregon home.

Food and Household Duties.—"Deer and other game were plentiful, and easily brought down by the trusty rifle; salmon was bought of the Indians; ducks, geese, and swans were numerous. All winter, the women were kept busy cutting and making clothing for the entire household, and teaching their daughters how to sew, knit, and attend to general housework; and if the mothers were sick the daughters did the work with willing hands.

Amusements.—"Occasionally neighbors would surprise each other by bringing their violins, and spending the evening talking and dancing. The large room would be cleared of all furniture, which was placed in the loft where the small children were put to bed, and soon the merry sound of tripping feet keeping time to Money Musk, and other old-time music was heard. The old men talked over the possibilities of Oregon.

"The canoe and bateaux were their only means of transportation.

Dress.—"Our pioneer mothers made their dresses with plain skirts; waists were sewed onto the skirt; sleeves were made much like those worn by the women of today. Their hair was combed smooth from their foreheads and wound in a coil high on their heads; many wore side combs, and a high back comb held their coil of glossy hair. Hairpins were an unknown luxury. White handkerchiefs were worn in place of collars, and they looked very pretty crossed or tied in a bow at the throat. All were deft with the needle, and at weaving; those who have the rare old blue and gray counterpanes, manufactured by their willing hands, possess heirlooms of great value."—By *Mrs. C. M. Cartwright,* in the *Oregon Historical Quarterly,* Vol. 4, pp. 55-58.

The Character of the Early Pioneer.—The Pacific Coast pioneers usually came from the Middle West. They represented men and women who were pioneers in their own states, and whose ancestors were pioneers before them. They were hearty, self-reliant, and acquainted with the wilderness, and more than that, they loved it. They were accustomed to the Indians, and to the use of the gun. They led the simple life and could live independent of others or with them. They raised and manufactured everything they ate and wore or needed in their daily life. Their household furniture, farm implements, and their clothing, were all hand-

Pioneer Quilts.

made. The pioneer was his own carpenter, blacksmith, wheelwright, shoemaker, and cabinet maker. He represented the middle class.

From such a people were chosen the immigrants to the West. Only the young, those in the prime of life, could be taken, nor were those not in robust health to be thought of for the long journey. Neither could those of little means be considered. Every man had to supply himself with an outfit, and have the means necessary to make the journey to the coast. Such an enterprise did not attract capital, as it did not represent an investment that promised large and immediate returns. Unless one were willing to make use of the natural resources and develop them by his own labor, the early West offered little. In brief, a home was the chief goal to be attained by the early pioneer.

This attracted the best class of citizens, both men and women, and the conditions favored keeping them as such. Someone said: "They were all honest because there was nothing to steal; they were all sober because there was no liquor to drink; there were no misers because there was no money to hoard; and they were all industrious, because it was work or starve."

The people had the true American spirit of self-government and of organization. They cooperated in the building of their homes and the opening up of their farms. They aided each other in the planting and harvesting of crops. They united for protection against the Indians and later for the forming of organized governments.

The Pioneers.—The Honorable Franklin K. Lane, Secretary of the Interior, paid the following tribute to the pioneer in his speech at the opening of the exercises at the Panama-Pacific Exposition February 20, 1915.

"The sculptors who have ennobled these buildings with their work have surely given full swing to their fancy in seeking to symbolize the tale which this exposition tells. And among these figures I have sought for one which would represent to me the significance of this great enterprise.

"Prophets, priests and kings are here, conquerors and mystical figures of ancient legend, but these do not speak the word I hear. My eye is drawn to the least conspicuous figure of all—the modest figure of a man standing beside two oxen, which looks down upon the Court of Nations, when East and West come face to face.

"Towering above his gaunt figure is the canopy of his prairie schooner. Gay conquistadores ride beside him, and one must look hard to see this simple, plodding figure. Yet that man is to me the one hero of this day.

"Without him, we would not be here. Without him, banners would not fly, nor bands play. Without him, San Francisco would not be today the gayest city of the globe. Shall I tell you who he is, this key figure in the arch of our enterprise? That slender, dauntless, plodding, modest figure is the American pioneer. To me he is far more. He is the adventuresome spirit of a restless race.

"Long ago he set sail with Ulysses. But Ulysses turned back. He sailed again with Columbus for the Indies and heard with joy the quick command, 'Sail on, sail on and on.' But their westward way was barred.

"He landed at Plymouth Rock and with his dull-eyed oxen made the long, long journey across the continent. Here he stands at last, beside this western sea, incarnate soul of his insatiable race—the American pioneer.

"Pity? He scorns it. Glory? He does not ask it. His sons and daughters are scattered along the path he has come. Here on this stretch of shore he has built the outermost campfire of his race, and he has gathered his sons that they may tell each other of the progress they have made."

* * * * *

Honorable Joseph N. Teal, the donor of this statue, speaks as follows of his purpose in its erection:

"It has long been my earnest desire to express my admiration and respect for the Oregon pioneer. He represents all that is noblest and best in our history. The men and women who saved the West for this country were animated by the highest motives. They made untold sacrifices and endured hardships of every kind in order that their children might enjoy the fruits of their labor. Their courage, foresight, endurance, and industry should ever be an inspiration to the youth of the country. I have, therefore, erected this memorial, which it seems to me should very appropriately stand on the campus of our great institution of learning, the University of Oregon, where for years to come the rising generations of Oregon will have before them a reminder of those to whom they owe every opportunity they enjoy.

"The reasons for selecting the University of Oregon as the home of this memorial are many. It is sufficient to say that here the Willamette and McKenzie rivers

The Pioneer.
(Courtesy of the Sculptor, A. Phimister Proctor.)

join their waters into one grand channel to create this beautiful valley—the paradise to which the pioneer struggled over great mountains and across desert plains, to which he first came in numbers, and in which he first made his home. Here, too, the state which he created has founded its great institution to train its young men and women. No more fitting place than the campus of the University of Oregon could be found for the memorial. Here, amid these beautiful surroundings, in this institution of learning, acting as an inspiration to Oregon's young manhood and womanhood, this pioneer in bronze will find a hospitable home in the land he loved so well. I am happy in the thought that I have had the opportunity thus to show my love and admiration for those whose lives were largely spent in a work whose greatness and value will be better understood when viewed down the perspective of time.

"This statue is erected and dedicated to the memory of all Oregon pioneers. It is in no sense personal or individual, and it is my earnest wish and hope that this fact may ever be kept in mind."

CHAPTER VIII.

The Development Of The Oregon Country.

Live Stock.—Civilized man differs from uncivilized man in many ways, chief among which is his domestication of many of the wild animals which minister to his needs. Cattle furnish him his supply of milk, butter, and cheese; oxen hauled his first loads; from the hides, he makes leather for shoes; from the tallow, candles; their flesh furnish him his best food. From hogs he secures bacon, hams, lard, etc., which may be cured and kept indefinitely. The horse first carried man and his packs, later displacing the ox and becoming the chief draft animal; while from the sheep man derives the wool which, spun into thread and woven into cloth, furnishes him with clothing.

Supplied with these animals the pioneer could go anywhere he pleased, with his living assured, being inde-

Razor-Back Hog.

Long Horn Cattle.

pendent of wild game, fruits, nuts, or other wild food products.

The first live stock introduced into the Northwest was at Astoria by the Astor party, in 1811. The Hawaiian Islands represent a much older civilization than is found here in the Northwest, and ships crossing the the Pacific or sailing along the coast of North America were accustomed to stop there for all kinds of supplies. In accordance with this custom the boat, *Tonquin,* carrying provisions to the colonies established at the mouth of the Columbia River, went by these islands and, among other things, secured two sheep, two goats, some poultry, and a hundred head of hogs, which they brought to Astoria. To these were added a few head of Spanish cattle brought from California in 1814 by the Northwest Fur Company, which had succeeded Astor.

In 1821 the Northwest Company and the Hudson's Bay Company were united, and three years later the headquarters of the new company were transferred to Fort Vancouver, where a fine farm, surrounded by an abundance of range, was soon opened up. The company added horses to their other live stock, and by 1828 there were 200 head of cattle, fourteen goats, fifty horses, and 300 hogs.

In 1833, at the southern end of Puget Sound, a fort called the Nisqually House, was established on a bay of the same name. Here were brought four oxen and four horses. A few years later a farm of 4,000 acres was opened up on the Cowlitz Prairie, and live stock was brought over from Vancouver as well as from California. Here fur-trading was made secondary to agriculture and a new company, termed the Puget Sound Agricultural Company, was formed. The business thrived and by 1841 shipments of butter, cheese, and beef were being made to Alaska, and the Company was offering to the head of each family the use and service of fifteen cows, fifteen mules, the necessary work oxen and horses, as an inducement to immigrate thither from the Red River country. From these two companies, from Fort Vancouver and the Cowlitz farm, the early settlers in western Oregon and Washington obtained live stock.

The Indians in the Oregon Country were sometimes divided into the canoe and the horse Indians. The former lived largely by fishing and the latter were hunters and used horses. The Indians of eastern Oregon and northern Idaho got their horses from California and from the Indians east of the Rocky Mountains, where they went annually to hunt the buffalo.

When Whitman and Spalding, and, a little later, Eells and Walker came, they brought live stock. Aside from pack and saddle horses the Whitman party had sixteen cows, and to these were added, soon after their arrival, sheep, goats, and hogs from the Hawaiian Islands. The flocks and herds were not only shared among the missionaries themselves, but also among the Indians. It is recorded that by 1841 the Nez Perces owned thirty-two head of cattle, ten sheep and forty hogs, while the Cayuses had 70 head of cattle, mostly cows, and a few sheep. The Catholic missions also had live stock which they shared with the Indians. The St. Mary's Mission must have had a considerable number of stock, for Mullan, when building his road, got much of his meat supply from this mission. When the Methodist mission was established they obtained their start of live stock from the Hudson's Bay Company at Vancouver. The settlers who took up homes near the missions secured their stock in the same way, but the company supplied only work animals. Breeding stock could not be had.

By 1837 the American settlers in the Willamette Valley were so numerous and the demand for live stock was so great that the Willamette Cattle Company was organized for the purpose of bringing live stock from California, where cattle were slaughtered chiefly for the hides and tallow, and hence were cheap. Several thousand dollars were subscribed by the settlers, the missions and the Hudson's Bay Company. Eight hundred head of cattle were purchased in California at $3 per head, and forty horses at $12 apiece. These were driven to the Oregon Country where they were sold at cost. A second drove was brought to the valley in

1843, consisting of 1,250 head of cattle, 600 head of horses and 3,000 sheep. These drives were very dangerous and exciting, as the entire distance was through unsettled country, inhabited by hostile Indians. The stock was wild and had to be driven through a country which was without roads. The stock had to swim the rivers, and sometimes when part or nearly all of the herd had crossed over they would suddenly become frightened; a stampede would occur, and all would swim back and scatter in every direction. Little lambs had to be carried on pack horses. One of the drivers said they fought Indians every foot of the way from the start to the crossing of the Rogue River.

By the date of the last drive of the cattle companies mentioned, the immigrants had begun to arrive in large numbers. They brought stock of all kinds. Sometimes these were left at Whitman Station, being exchanged for fresh stock. By this method the herds in the Northwest were greatly increased.

Trappers of the Hudson's Bay Company, when they became too old to stand the hardships of the trapper's life, frequently retired and engaged in farming and stock raising.

When gold was discovered in eastern Washington, northern Idaho, and Montana, the demand for pack horses and mules, as well as cattle for beef, became very great. The former were needed for packing and staging while the cattle were needed for food. To meet this demand live stock was brought across the Cascades on the west and the Rocky Mountains on the east into the Walla Walla and Yakima valleys in southeastern Washington, the Umatilla, Grand Ronde and Powder River valleys in eastern Oregon, the St. Joe and Clearwater valleys in northern Idaho, and the Payette and Boise valleys in southern Idaho; and western and southern Montana acquired large herds of live stock.

It was estimated that the miners purchased 1,500 head of horses at Walla Walla in the year 1866 and that 5,000 head of cattle and 6,000 pack mules went to Montana from the same place.

From this time on to the present there has never been any scarcity of live stock.

But the Mexican sheep of doubtful ancestry is no more. The little dun cow and her longhorn brother are now seen only with the circus. The razor-backed, slab-sided hog, indicative of shiftlessness, exists only as a figure of speech, and the cayuse is largely used at roundups in wild west stunts.

In their stead there are the Rambouillet, Shropshire Downs, Hampshires, and Cotswolds that will shear annually eight to ten pounds of wool and will sell for $10 per head; the Shorthorns, Holsteins, Herefords, Guernseys, and Jerseys from which may be obtained steers that will weigh 1,200 pounds at two years of age, or cows that will give 27,000 pounds of milk annually; the Poland Chinas, Duroc Jerseys, and Berkshires, that have to be killed at the age of six or eight months or be docked for overweight; the Percheron, Belgian, Shire, and Clydesdale draft horses that can move any load, and the chanticleer that wakes us in the morning and resembles his ancestors little except that he has feathers, while his sister, the hen will lay as many eggs within the year as a whole flock of the former tribe.

Where Our First Vegetables Came from.—"In a private paper, found after Dr. McLoughlin's death, September 3, 1857, the following appears: 'In 1824 I came to this country to superintend the management of the Hudson's Bay Company's trade on the coast, and we came to the determination to abandon Astoria and go to Fort Vancouver, as it was a place where we could cultivate the soil and raise our own provisions. In March, 1825, we moved there and that spring planted potatoes and sowed two bushels of peas, the only grain we had, and all we had. In the fall I received from the York Factory (on Nelson River, near its mouth as it enters Hudson Bay) a bushel of spring wheat, a bushel of oats, a bushel of barley, a bushel of Indian corn and a quart of timothy (seed), all of which was sown in proper time, and produced well, except the Indian corn, for which the ground was too poor and the nights rather cool; and we continued extending our improvements. In 1828 the crop was sufficient to enable us to dispense with the importation of flour, etc.'

"In this connection it is interesting to note that the potatoes alluded to by Dr. McLoughlin were taken to Fort Vancouver from Astoria, where the first potatoes, turnips, radishes, etc., were planted in May, 1811. The potatoes were taken from New York in October, 1810, but they were so shrivelled up that only twelve were planted, and these gave but little sign of life. However, they produced 190 potatoes the first season, five bushels the second season, and in 1813 there was a crop of fifty bushels. Seeds of different kinds of fruit were brought to Fort Vancouver from London in 1825-26, so that in a few years there was an abundance. Mrs. Narcissa Prentiss Whitman, one of the two first white women to cross the plains to Oregon, who arrived there September 12, 1836, in writing to her mother, alludes to 'apples, peaches, pears, grapes, plums, fig trees, melons, cucumbers, beans, cabbage, tomatoes,' etc.

"Vegetables grow from seeds which are frequently small and easily taken from place to place; so every immigrant to the west doubtless brought many seeds with him. These he planted on his arrival and as new settlements were established the settlers could always secure seeds from the older settlements."—*George H. Himes.*

"One of the original Lewelling trees still stands near Olympia, Washington. As a two-year-old tree this was brought across the plains from Henry County, Iowa, in 1847, by Henderson Lewelling, and with about eight hundred other trees of different varieties includ-

A Black Heart Cherry Tree.

ing apples, pears, peaches, crab-apples, plums, etc., was planted about half a mile north of the present town of Milwaukie, Oregon. This aggregation of fruit trees was known as 'The Traveling Nursery,' and were the first grafted fruit trees on the Pacific Coast. About 1852, early in the spring, Mr. David J. Chambers, an Oregon Pioneer of 1845, but then living four miles east of Olympia, on Puget Sound, then known as 'Northern Oregon,' visited Mr. Lewelling and bought this tree, the last of the Black Heart variety he had, paying $5.00 therefor. He returned to his northern home, first by steamer to Monticello near Kelso of the present day, then by canoe propelled by Indians to Cowlitz Landing near Toledo of the present time, and from that point to his home the tree was carried on horseback. This photograph is copied from one that was taken in April, 1905, when the tree was in full bloom. That year the crop was over forty bushels. Beginning in 1853 this tree has borne a crop of fruit every year up to 1916, and the prospects for a crop in 1917 are good. At present it is more than ten feet in circumference three feet above the ground, and the spread of the limbs is more than sixty feet."—*George H. Himes,* Portland, Oregon, May 24, 1917.

The Traveling Nursery.—Few people, as they eat the luscious Crawford peach, the Bartlett pear or the big red apple, know who made it possible for them to enjoy this privilege, or what it cost to provide it.

The honor belongs to Henderson Lewelling and his son, Alford, a boy of 16, of Henry County, Iowa.

The elder Lewelling was an experienced nurseryman whose attention had been attracted to Oregon by the reports of Lewis and Clark, the missionaries, the immigrants, and the agitation which led up to the "54°-40' or fight" political campaign.

But the Lewellings and the nursery business were "one and inseparable" and they had no thought of going to Oregon without fruit trees. Mr. Lewelling prepared about 700 fruit trees, "embracing most if not all the best varieties then in that country," together with some shrubs. The trees doubtless represented choice varieties and plants were from 20 inches to 4 feet in height in the spring of 1847 when the start to Oregon was made.

Two stout immigrant wagons were secured. Into these were fitted the full length of the bed, two boxes about 12 inches deep, filled with earth and charcoal, and the trees were set in this mixture. That the hungry stock might not browse on the green trees, when they reached the barren plains, the trees were protected by long strips of hickory fastened securely to posts bolted to the sides of the wagon boxes.

In the spring of 1847 the Lewelling family together with that of a neighbor, Mr. John Fisher, started for Oregon. They went down into northern Missouri and soon were on the Oregon Trail. Here they joined the Whitcomb's (Immigration Company). This party soon broke up, and they then became a part of Captain John Bonser's party. Mr. Fisher died soon after and the entire responsibility of caring for the trees fell on Mr. Lewelling and his son.

Mr. "Faint Heart" like the poor, is ever with us and he tried to discourage Mr. Lewelling by telling him that the taking of these trees to Oregon was a most hazardous undertaking, that he could not cross the Rocky Mountains, that he would endanger the lives of his family, that the undertaking was impossible. Mr. Lewelling invariably replied that until they did endanger the lives of his family he would "stick to them."

As always happens, the world got out of the way of the man with ideas and allowed him to proceed. The trees needed water continually and they got it. Soon the wagons carrying provisions were lightened of their load and some of the stock attached to these wagons could be used for those carrying the trees. Not only this but the Lewelling party traveled either alone or in small companies, thus hastening the progress of the journey.

At the close of a day's journey the cattle were all belled and turned loose and herded until they had sufficient feed, and at the tinkle of the first bell in the morning, Mr. Lewelling was up and after them. His management was so successful that he lost only two oxen, one from poison and one from inflammation caused from a sore foot.

The party arrived at The Dalles the sixth of October; here travel by wagons came to an end temporarily. Boats were built to get by the rapids. "The fruit trees were taken out of the boxes and wrapped in cloths to protect them from the various handlings and from the frosty nights."

On November 17th, just seven months from the day of starting, the party arrived at Fort Vancouver.

From there Mr. Lewelling moved in early December to a point opposite Portland, Oregon. About the fifth day of February he moved his family to a farm, afterwards owned by J. H. Lambert, and adjoining Milwaukie. About one half of the trees survived and were set out.

Next year William Meek, a neighbor of Mr. Lewelling's in Iowa, followed him to Oregon, bringing a few grafted trees. He settled near Mr. Lewelling, later marrying his daughter. While Mr. Lewelling and Mr. Meek were both engaged in the nursery business they do not seem to have been partners.

Others joined the nurserymen at Milwaukie. Mr. Ralph C. Greer came the same year as Henderson Lewelling, and brought one bushel of apple seeds and a half bushel of pear seeds. Seth, a younger brother of Mr. Henderson, joined them in 1850. He, too, brought seeds, so the community using seeds for seedling trees and the buds from the grafted trees soon had a big business not only of trees but of fruit as well.

The April 3, 1851 issue of the *Western Star*, a paper published at Milwaukie, states that peach trees were in full bloom and that Lewelling and Meek had 10,000 trees and 100,000 scions. Two years later, according to one authority, the first shipment of Oregon apples were sold in San Francisco at $2.00 per pound, or $80 per box.

In 1854 Henderson Lewelling sold out his nursery to his brother Seth, under whose management it was continued until his death in 1896. From these nurseries originated many new varieties, as the Lewellings, especially, were continually experimenting with seedlings.

The Black Republican grew from a Black Eagle Cherry in 1860; the Lewelling from the Black Tartarian in 1870-72; and the most famous of all, the Bing, named for the Chinese foreman, came from the seed of the Black Republican in 1890. The Lambert cherry, another famous cherry of the Northwest was developed in the orchard of a neighbor of Mr. Lewelling's, Joseph Hamilton Lambert.

One of the original trees—a Black Heart cherry—still stands near Olympia, Washington, and yields large crops. It is ten feet in circumference three feet above the ground and the spread of its limbs is more than 60 feet in diameter.

The Royal Anne cherry was one of those brought by Lewellings from Iowa, the original name, it is claimed, being Napoleon Bigairi, but for some reason changed by Mr. Lewelling to the present name.

Other varities of fruit in the original nursery that Mr. Lewelling brought along the Oregon Trail were:

Apples: Yellow Newtowns, Spitzenberg, Northern Spy, Baldwin, Winesap, Red Astrachan, Gravenstein, Bellflower, Golden Russett, Red Cheek Pippen, Rambo, Blue Pearmain, White Winter Pearmain, Rhode Island Greening, Gloria Mundi, King of Tompkins County, Seek-No-Further, Early Harvest.

Pears: Bartlett, Fall Butter, Winter Nellis, Seckel, Pound, Vicar of Wakefield, Clapps Favorite, and a few others.

Peaches: Early Crawford, Golden Cling, and others.

The Beginning of Agriculture.—Wheat was the first grain grown in the Northwest. It was introduced by the Hudson's Bay Company and the early missionaries. As the soil was rich, it needed only to be broken with some sort of crude plow, and the grain sown broadcast; frequently a tough hawthorne tree or some other tree that had bushy tops, would be dragged over the plowed ground, and thus the grain was covered.

The harvesting was done with an ordinary reaping hook, an instrument much the shape of the grass hook used in connection with lawns, but considerably larger. A little later all of the grain was cut with a scythe and cradle.

Threshing the Grain.—At first the sheaves were thrown down in a corral, where wild horses could be turned in and driven around and around, thereby tramping the grain out. It was then gathered up in buckets or baskets, the grain, chaff, and smaller particles of straw being all together. Then a man took a bucketful of this and, standing on a stump, slowly poured it out, the wind blowing away everything except the grain, which fell on a sheet beneath. Or, if the wind were not blowing, two men would take hold of two corners of a sheet and by using it as a fan separ-

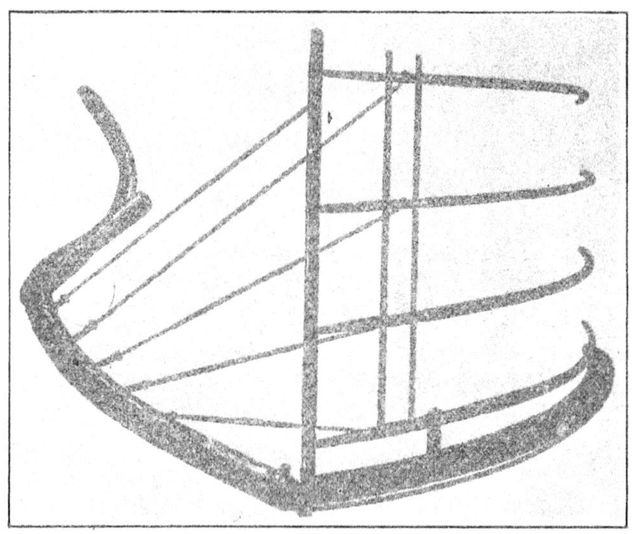

Scythe and Cradle.

The Combine Harvester.

ate the chaff and straw from the grain as it dropped from the bucket or basket.

The Story of the Crickets and the Sea Gulls.—"No event in western history awakens more interest than the episode of the crickets and the gulls. It occurred in 1848, when Salt Lake City—the earliest settlement in the Rocky Mountain region—was less than one year old. The so-called 'City' was not even a village at that time; it was little more than a camp, consisting of a log-and-mud fort, enclosing huts, tents, and wagons, with about eighteen hundred inhabitants. Most of these had followed immediately after the pioneers, who, with Brigham Young, their leader, arrived on the shores of the Great Salt Lake in July, 1847. President Young and others had returned to the Missouri River to bring more of their migrating people to their new home among the mountains, and those who remained here were anxiously awaiting the results of their first labors to redeem the desert and make the wilderness to blossom.

"Some plowing and planting had been done by pioneers upon their arrival, but the seeds then put in, such as potatoes, corn, wheat, oats, peas, and beans, though well irrigated, did not mature owing to the lateness of the season. The nearest approach to a harvest, that year, was a few small potatoes, which served as seed for another planting. It was, therefore, their first real harvest in this region that the settlers of these solitudes were looking forward to at the time of the episode mentioned.

"Much depended upon that harvest, not only for the people already here, but for twenty-five hundred additional immigrants who were about to join them from the far-away frontier. The supplies brought by those who came the first season had been designed to last only about twelve months. They were gradually getting low, and these settlers, be it borne in mind, were well nigh isolated from the rest of humanity. 'A thousand miles from anywhere,' was a phrase used by them to describe their location. They had little communication with the outside world, and that little was by means of the ox team and the pack mule. If their harvest failed, what would become of them?

"In the spring of 1848 five thousand acres of land were under cultivation in Salt Lake Valley. Nine hundred acres had been sown with winter wheat, which was just beginning to sprout.

"Then came an event as unlooked-for as it was terrible—the cricket plague! In May and June these destructive pests rolled in black legions down the mountain sides, and attacked the fields of growing grain.

The tender crops fell an easy prey to their fierce voracity. The ground over which they had passed looked as if scorched by fire.

"Thoroughly alarmed, the community, men, women, and children, marshalled themselves to fight the ravenous foe. Some went through the fields, killing the crickets, but crushing much of the tender grain. Some dug ditches around their farms, turned water into the trenches and drove and drowned therein the black devourers. Others beat them back with clubs and brooms or burned them in fires. Still the crickets prevailed. Despite all that could be done by the settlers, their hope of a harvest was fast vanishing—a harvest upon which life itself seemed to depend.

"They were rescued, as they believed, by a miracle—a greater miracle than is said to have saved Rome, when the cackling of geese roused the slumbering city in time to beat back the invading Gauls. In the midst of the work of ruin, when it seemed as if nothing could stay the destruction, great flocks of gulls appeared, filling the air with their white wings and plaintive cries. They settled down upon the half-ruined fields. At first it looked as if they came but to help the crickets destroy. But their real purpose was soon apparent. They came to prey upon the destroyers. All day long they gorged themselves, disgorged and feasted again, the white gulls fell upon the black crickets like hosts of heaven and hell contending, until the pests were vanquished and the people saved. The birds then returned to the lake islands, leaving the grateful settlers to shed tears of joy over their timely deliverance.

"A season of scarcity followed but no fatal famine; and before the worst came, the glad people celebrated with a public feast their harvest home.

"The gull is still to be seen in the vicinity of the Great Salt Lake. The wanton killing of these birds was made punishable by law. Rome had her sacred geese; Utah would have her sacred gulls, forever to be held in honor as the Heaven-sent messengers that saved the pioneers.

The Sea Gull Monument.—"To commemorate the above historic incident, a sea gull monument has been completed and unveiled upon Temple Block.

"For several years the erection of such a monument has been contemplated, and about two years ago, Mahonri M. Young, a grandson of the great pioneer leader, Brigham Young, submitted a design which was accepted by the First Presidency and he was authorized to proceed with the work.

"The granite base, weighing twenty tons, rests upon a concrete foundation. From the base rises a round column of granite fifteen feet high, surmounted by a granite globe.

"Two sea gulls of bronze rest upon the granite ball. The birds weigh about 500 pounds and the stretch of the wings, from tip to tip, is eight feet.

"The unveiling ceremony took place on Wednesday, October 1st, 1913."—*Orson F. Whitney,* in *The New West Magazine.*

Pioneer Grist Mill.—The Indian used a mortar and pestle to pulverize roots and berries or anything which he wished to break into very small particles. He at first found a depression in a rock to use as a mortar, but later shaped one from a rock which he could carry with him. For a pestle he used another rock a few inches in diameter and six or eight inches long. The objects to be crushed were placed in the mortar and the pestle used to pound and rub the food into meal.

The pioneer of the Northwest adopted the same method, or boiled his wheat—he had no corn—and made bread from this. This made a very wholesome food, yet since it contained all of the grain, flour, shorts, and bran, the people soon tired of it, as there was little chance for variety.

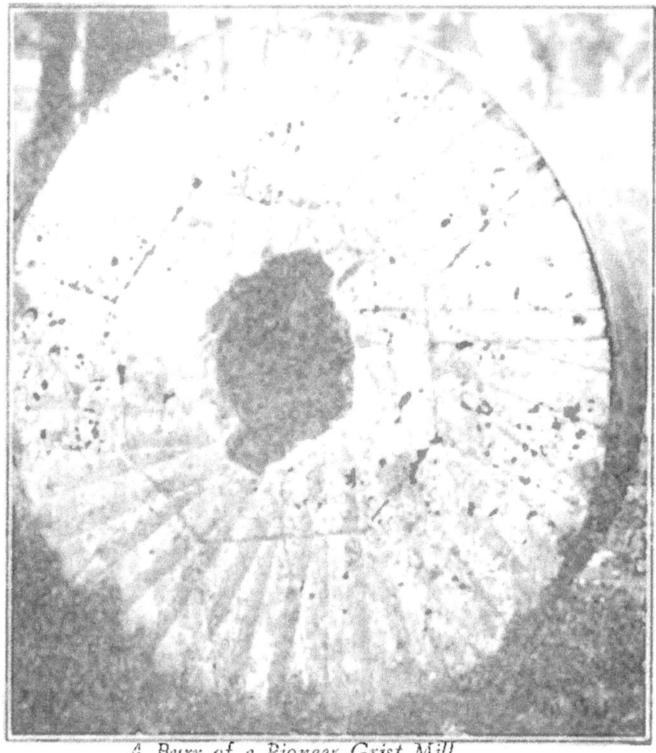

A Burr of a Pioneer Grist Mill.

The Burr Mill.—This method of grinding grain is almost as old as the human race and was well known to the early missionaries and pioneers. The mill is simple, requires little machinery, is easily constructed, and very satisfactory. It consists of two cylindrical stones, about three or four feet in diameter, and twelve to sixteen inches thick. The flat surfaces are made smooth and divided into triangular spaces extending from the center to the circumference. By means of a steel pick the surface of each of the triangular spaces is gradually ground down from one side to the other. These burrs are made from granite or other hard stone, so that no small particles will be ground into the flour.

The stones are placed one above the other, the flat surfaces together. Holes are drilled through the center, and through these extends an upright rod or beam; this is securely fastened to one or the other of them which it turns around as it is made to revolve. Above the upper burr is a "hopper" or box, in which is placed the grain to be ground. This is made of four triangular boards which form a box, sloping downward and toward the center. The grain being placed in this hopper trickles down through the hole in the center of the upper stone, and when this revolves the grain is gradually thrown toward the outer rim. The miller, by means of machinery, can adjust the two burrs so as to bring the flat surfaces as close together as he desires. The revolution of these whirls the grain toward the circumference, and as the burrs are surrounded by an inclosure in which there is only one hole, the current of air escaping through this hole carries the ground grain with it. A spout is fixed at this opening, over which a sack may be fastened and into which the ground grain is forced.

The grain was brought to the mill in sacks much like those used by the farmers today. Sometimes a sack was placed on a horse and a boy sat on top of it, going to the mill in this way. Henry Clay, as you remember, was called "the mill boy of the slashes." Sometimes several sacks were brought in a wagon. The miller arranged the sacks in a row in the order of their arrival, each customer's grain being ground in the order in which it was received. The miller took a sack of grain, poured it into the hopper, and when it was ground he took another sack, and so on until all were finished.

The first of these mills in the Oregon Country was built in 1821, by the Northwest Company, on the Colville River, four miles above its junction with the Columbia. Later, when this company was combined with the Hudson's Bay Company, they erected another mill at Vancouver, as well as others at some of the more important forts. Each of the missions had its grist mill, where its own grain, as well as that of the Indians, was ground.

In the early sixties the government surveyed three quarters of a million acres of land in the Inland Empire and threw it open to settlement. The land was soon taken by settlers and within a few years there were 52 threshing, heading, and reaping machines, and six flour mills within that country. About the same time flour mills were erected in the Grand Ronde and Powder River valleys in eastern Oregon, and in the Boise and Payette valleys in southern Idaho, while Lewiston, in northern Idaho, had its own mill. A grist mill was also erected on the Sound in Western Washington, at Tumwater.

The old mill built in 1821 on the Colville River, was rebuilt by the Hudson's Bay Company in 1843, and a third mill was erected by L. W. Meyers on the same site in 1872. These mills supplied the settlers of the Colville Valley for many years. Another mill, on the little Pend d'Oreille, known as the Oppenhimer mill, was built in the early sixties. It did not have a single iron shaft, pulley, connecting rod, or gearing of any kind. Everything was made of wood, the timber necessary for the mill being found near by. This machinery was all handmade and ran so smoothly that not the least noise was heard. The capacity of the mill was about thirty barrels per day. Perhaps the first flour mill built in the Umpqua Valley was that of Dr. Baker, a pioneer railroad builder, and erected on Calopaola Creek in about 1855. The place was called Oakland. In the early days the mills mentioned, in the main, supplied all of what was known as the Oregon Country.

Early Saw Mills.—The pioneer who lived in a log cabin had little use for lumber except for doors and floors for his cabin and the few tables which he needed; and the miner needed little except a few boards for sluice boxes. These boards could be whipsawed. The whipsaw is in some respects like the ordinary cut-off saw used by a logger, except that the handle is set perpendicular to the saw on an iron extension fastened to the end of it. The saw is about eight feet long and a log must be put upon "horses" or trusses eight or ten feet high. One man stands on top of the log and the other beneath it, and the saw is pulled up and down by the two men, the weight of the saw being almost sufficient to push it down. Thus a board may soon be

The Whip Saw.

sawed off the side of the log; two men are able to saw 150 or 200 feet per day.

Soon after the Hudson's Bay Company established their headquarters at Vancouver, they erected a saw mill, using the circular saw. Water power was used. At first they sawed the lumber only for their own use and an occasional shipment to the Hawaiian Islands.

In 1847 Michael T. Simmonds erected a saw mill on the Deschutes River, where it empties into Puget Sound and has a fall of eighty feet. (This was the first American settlement north of the Columbia River.) The mill had a capacity of 3,000 feet per day. For four years it was the only saw mill north of the Columbia, but after that there were sixteen saw mills on Puget Sound, with a daily capacity of 85,000 feet.

The cause of this remarkable growth was the demand for lumber in California. The population there grew very rapidly. Towns sprang up everywhere and the thousands of miners also needed much lumber. All of these things combined to make the Puget Sound industry very profitable.

The discovery of gold in Idaho, in 1860, and a little later in Montana, and the rush of settlers to that section of the country, created a demand for saw mills in the Inland Empire. To meet this demand six mills were erected in the Walla Walla Valley alone. Lewiston, Idaho, also erected a saw mill early in its history. The settlers, who had stopped in the Grand Ronde Valley in eastern Oregon, had four saw mills by 1846, using water power and sawing the timber on the Blue Mountains.

Practically all of the early mills were run by water power, as rivers with sufficient fall were always available

Site and Shaft of the First Saw Mill Erected in the Northwest at Vancouver on the Columbia.

to furnish such power. And it was easy, if no waterfall were at hand, to take the water out a few hundred feet up stream and bring it down by flume or ditch, and secure sufficient fall.

The saw, as well as the other equipment necessary, was much the same as that found in the little portable mills now seen almost anywhere in the Northwest. These mills could saw only a few thousand feet per day, but enough in the aggregate to meet the demands of that time.

The Country Fiddler.—Proof of Shakespeare's assertion that music hath charms to soothe the savage breast, might be verified in a thousand mining camps and pioneer communities in the Northwest. No form of amusement and entertainment for a mixed gathering of young people has yet been devised which has proved so popular, so satisfying and so lasting as the dance.

It affords an opportunity to expend in a pleasing way the physical energy of which the average young person always seems to have a surplus, and an opportunity for rhythmic expression which satisfies one's physical well-being at any age.

Music has always been an element in the dance. Today it is supplied by a trained orchestra of several pieces, but in pioneer days the lone fiddler was all-sufficient and filled a place in the social world that was indispensable. If he were too pious to play for dances, as in the case of Uncle Lou Southworth, people would come for miles around to his cabin that they might enjoy the sweet music of the old time tunes. But if he were of a professional turn of mind, he could turn his art to good advantage, as in the case of Kelly, the other fiddler here mentioned, whose music was his living. But whichever class it might be, it, nevertheless, remained true that every community had its fiddler and its dance.

Uncle Lou Southworth.—Lou Southworth was born a slave in Kentucky, was taken to Missouri, and then brought to Oregon as a slave in 1851. He purchased his freedom in Oregon with gold which he dug out of the Yreka and Jacksonville mines. He fought in the Rogue River Indian War, in which he was wounded. Subsequently he built a home and married. He became widely known for his hospitality and public spirit, and his happiness would have been complete but for one circumstance—his white brethren dropped his name

Uncle Lou Southworth.

from the church roll for playing the violin. This weighed heavily upon his mind, and in later years he expressed his feelings as follows:

"The brethren wouldn't stand for my violin, which was all the company I had most of the time. They said it was full of all sorts of wicked things and that it belonged to the devil. And it hurt me a good deal when they told me that playin' a fiddle is a proceedin' unbecomin' to a Christian in the sight of the Lord. So I told them to keep me in the church with the fiddle if they could, but to turn me out if they must, for I couldn't think of parting with my old-time friend. They turned me out, and I reckon my name isn't written in their books here any longer, but I somehow hope it is written in the Big Book up yonder in the land of golden harps where they aren't so particular about the old man's fiddle.

"And I know, friends, you won't think hard of me and give me the cold shoulder for loving my fiddle these many years. Every man has his own way of lookin' at things and lovin' them. You have your way, and I have my way; and my way is to love this old friend of mine that always pleased me and never went back on me. And I sometimes think that when you go up yonder and find my name to your surprise in the Big Book, you'll meet many a fellow who remembers the old fiddler who played 'Home, Sweet Home,' 'Dixie Land,' 'Arkansas Traveler,' 'Swanee River,' and other tunes for the boys who were far away from home for the first time. And some of the fellows will tell how the poor, homesick boys listened to the fiddle during the long winter evenings until they forgot their troubles so they could sleep as they had slept under their mothers' roofs at home. And they'll talk over the days when there was no society for men like us out West: when there wasn't any Bible, and hymn books were unknown; when playin' poker and buckin' faro were the only schoolin' a fellow ever got; when whiskey ran like water and made the whites and Indians crazy; when men didn't go by their right names and didn't care what they did, and when there was no law, and the court was the man who carried the best six-shooter. And when they have talked over those early days, the fellows will say:

" 'Where'd we all been and what'd we all done in the mines, but for Uncle Lou's fiddle, which was the most like church of anything we had?' For the boys used to think the good Lord put a heap of old-time religious music into my fiddle; and the old-time religious music is good enough for an old man who's done some mighty hard work in 85 years.

"But I forget the work I've done and the years I've lived when my bow comes down soft and gentle-like and the fiddle seems to sing the songs of slavery days till the air grows mellow with music and the old-time feelin' comes back, and I can hear familiar voices that are no more.

"There are things a plain old man can't tell in words, and there are feelin's that won't fit into common, every-day talk like mine. When there's plenty of rosin on the bow and the player's feelin' fine, and the fiddle pours out great torrents of music that calm down till he hears the bob white's whistle and the rustlin' of the corn, and the whippoorwill and mockin' bird come to sing for him, and he forgets what he ought not to remember and he wants to make everybody glad—then it is that a plain man has feelin's he can't describe. But he knows he's happier and better, and his next day's work is easier. He has a smile and a kind word for every one he meets, and every one has a smile and a kind word for him. The world is heavenly to that man, and his feelin's are nigh on to religious.

"So, my friends, I hope to keep the fiddle a little longer, 'cause it'll make it easier and pleasanter for me the few more days that I can stay. And if you'll be kind to the old man and let him keep his friend, I know your pillow will be softer and your dreams will be sweeter when you lay your head down some day for the last time. For my fiddle is as sweet to me as David's harp was to him; and the good Lord who loved David and the music of his harp I know won't turn down an aged man and his old-time friend, nor will he forsake those who gave him aid in trouble. But he'll have a smile and a kind word for those who made the road smoother for the old pilgrim that traveled footsore and alone with his southern violin, with no one to care for him except the Father, who loves music everywhere—the Father who loves the music of the waters, the music of the woods, the music of the stars and the music of the old man's violin."—*J. B. Horner.*

Kelly, the Fiddler of Idaho City, Idaho, in 1862-3.—"Among the many musicians employed as attractions in the saloons and gambling houses, was a violinist named Kelly, whose proficiency as a fiddler was well known through all the mountain regions of the Pacific slope. He commanded a salary second to none and was engaged in the largest gambling resort in the city. The contract under which he played included the installation of a swinging stage, or platform, swung by iron rods from the upper joists, several feet above the heads of those who might stand on the main floor below. This platform was reached by a movable ladder, which, after he had ascended, he pulled up out of reach of those below. The object was twofold: First, when located upon his aerie, he was removed from the danger of panics which were an almost nightly occurrence, caused by the sportive instincts of some visitor, who, having imbibed too freely of the regulation vest-pocket whisky, or having suffered some real or imaginary grievance, proceeded to distribute the leaden pellets of a Colt's navy revolver, not only into the anatomy of the offender, but quite as frequently to the serious if not fatal injury of some innocent bystander.

"When it is understood that it was not unusual for five hundred men to be present in the room at the time these diversions occurred, it is not difficult to imagine the kind of panic liable to ensue. Hence, the first object of Kelly's lofty perch. His second object was to be above the course of flying missiles and thus preserve his violin, which was a valuable one, from the chance of being perforated by stray bullets.

"It seemed to be an instinct with Kelly to protect it, for he invariably rose to his feet when the first shot was fired and faced the disturbance, holding his instrument behind him, evidently preferring that any stray bullet should find lodgment in his body rather than in his violin.

"As an artist with the bow he had no equal in that day; he could make his pet instrument tell a plaintive tale of home and mother, or of tearful ones who waited, oft in vain, the return of father, brother, or lover; again he would arouse the reckless instincts of his hearers by a rollicking tune which told of wine and song.

He was a big-hearted son of the Emerald Isle and although untoward circumstances had made him the leading attraction of a den of iniquity, he loved best to play those tender chords that awakened the memories of other days and sent some of his hearers back to their lonely cabins up the gulch better men for the hour they had spent under the musician's spell, even in that dreadful haunt. On such occasions he seemed to be inspired by his own music and all unconscious of games and men, with eyes closed to his surroundings, he played on and on, such strains as melt the hardest hearts."—*W. J. McConnell.*

The Story of a Little Girl who Saved Her Scalp and That of Her Mother by Playing on the Melodeon.—"In pioneer days people did not live in cities but on farms which were often far apart. Hired help could not be had. Every family did all of its own work or 'swapped' work with its neighbors. That is, the men would congregate at the home of one farmer and build his house and barn or help him cut or pile logs, fence his land, reap or thresh his grain. Then they would go to another farmer doing likewise until all the neighbors were served.

"On such occasions, as a rule, mothers and children were left at home, and as there were no telephones they had to wait until the men returned for any message. Such a home was that of Mary, whose father owned a farm on the northern part of Gray's Harbor. She could look out through the trees and see the broad waters of the Pacific Ocean. One morning while helping her mother around the cabin she glanced out of the door and caught the flash of the paddles of Indian ca-

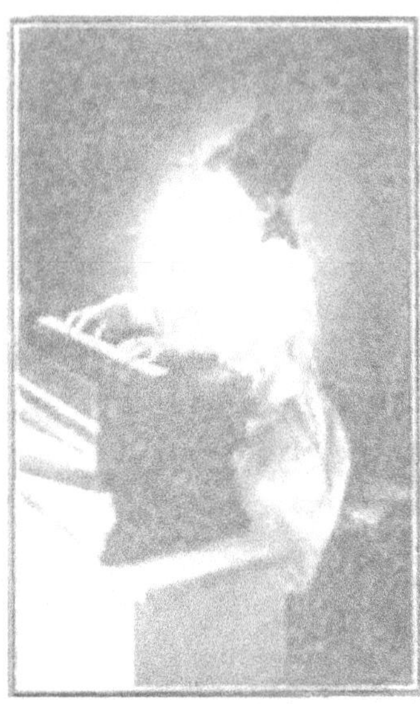

The Melodeon.

noes. She saw the Indians land. 'Mother,' she exclaimed in great fright, 'the Indians are coming.'

"But mother was an English woman and very brave. By the time she got to the door the Indians also had reached it. There were thirty or forty of them, big, strong, bold, daring men.

"An Indian is different from a white man. With him everything is held in common. He does not knock when he wants to come in, and after he is in he pries into every box, cupboard, basket, and bed, or other place just as if it were his own. And they would regard it as an insult if they were denied any of these privileges. So the Indians crowded into the cabin offering no harm to anyone but picking up or handling everything, curious as children.

"After a while one of the Indians using the Chinook language, asked where the men were. The truth was the men were away that day helping another farmer, but Mary's mother answered carelessly, 'Oh, they are just outside. They will be here in a minute.' Mrs. James knew there was no chance at all of the men coming. She also knew that the Indians might steal her and her little girl and take them north in their war canoe.

"Mary was very much frightened. She was very white and the Indians saw it. They began to talk about her and she knew that they were by their looks. Her lips grew white. 'Mary,' said her mother, quickly seeing the danger, 'play on the melodeon. Play something quickly.'

"In pioneer homes there are few musical instruments and those few must be light and easy to carry from place to place. It so happened that this family had a little melodeon which had first been brought from England to Wisconsin and later to this home. Mary's music teacher had been a drummer in Napoleon's army in France. He had taught her many pieces on the melodeon.

"But when Mary sat down and tried to play, her fingers were stiff and cold. Still she could push down a key or two to make a noise. The Indians became interested in the melodeon and forgot Mary. Gradually her fingers lost their stiffness and she played more easily. Where did the music come from? The Indians were amazed and looked everywhere.

"They were so charmed that some of them went to their canoe and brought in their hiaqua (Indian money), mats, baskets, and other treasures. Everything they laid down in the center of the cabin floor. Then they told Mrs. James they wanted to buy Mary for the chief's wife—with the melodeon, of course. Mrs. James was very grave and quiet and she said in a careless sort of way, 'Oh, no, Mary is too young.' She talked to them pleasantly and made them some presents. At last the Indians went away friendly without doing any harm at all."—*Judson* in *Early Days in Old Oregon.* Courtesy of the author and publisher, McClurg & Co.

Oregon's First Piano.—"A piano with a history was sent with the Oregon exhibit from Portland to the Panama-Pacific International Exposition. It was sent by C. Sommer, whose piano factory is just across from the city hall. Inside of the case is the inscription, 'George Astor, Cornhill, London, '79.'

" 'This piano is an historical instrument,' said Mr. Sommer. 'Wait, I will show you its sounding board and the strings. I had to replace them. Otherwise I left the old piano just as it was. You see its original sounding board was of very thin spruce and was broken and mended beyond repair. Its strings also were so far gone I had to replace them. If you will look up the history of the piano you will find that John Jacob Astor brought three pianos of this type from London for sale in New York. One is now in Central Park Art Museum in New York. This is one of them and the other has disappeared. Possibly it has been burned or destroyed.

" 'About six years ago a Polish Jew who had a second hand store on First street near Salmon, came to me to get an estimate on repairing a piano. I told him it would cost $250 or $300 to put it in good condition. He threw up his hands in despair. He thought he could have it fixed for about $10. He asked me if I would buy it from him and said he would have to get $6 out of it to come out even, so I paid him $6. He told me he had traded some second-hand furniture for it to a farmer who had bought it second hand many years ago at Astoria. The Jew had it several years before I got it. I used it for several years as a writing desk. It is solid mahogany, its turned legs are also of solid mahogany. It is inlaid with holly, rosewood, and ebony. Its length is five feet six inches and it is 22 inches deep. There is no iron whatever in it and it weighs about 125 pounds. Compared with the modern piano it looks like a toy. The piano of today has seven and one-third octaves; this has but five. The body and the legs are separate so that the body of the piano can be lifted from the frame. I kept account of my time and material and it cost me $225 to fix it up in perfect condition. It has a beautiful tone, sounding somewhat like a mandolin. As it was made by George Astor in London in 1779 you will readily understand that it is very unlike the modern piano. For example, it has no foot pedals. The pedal action is controlled from the keyboard, being operated by the left hand. The keyboard action is crude. The heaviest wire on the old Astor piano is lighter than the lightest wire in the modern piano. Here are the wires I took from the Astor piano. You see some of them are as fine as silk threads, while the heaviest wire is not much thicker than a good sized pin. They are of brass and steel. In a modern piano the heaviest wire has but 16 vibrations to a second, while the upper C wire vibrates 4,800 times to the second. The old ivory keys were yellow with age and were much heavier than the keys of today. In place of steel springs all of the springs on the old piano were of whalebone. I have sent it to be shown with the Oregon exhibit and I believe it will attract great attention.'

"A rather odd thing in connection with this old piano is the fact that when John Jacob Astor, the founder of Astoria, Oregon's oldest city, brought the three from London he inserted an advertisement in a New York newspaper of January 10, 1789. This was the first advertisement ever inserted for the sale of pianos in the United States. The advertisement read as follows:

" 'John Jacob Astor, at No. 81 Queen Street, next door but one to the Friend's Meeting House, has for sale an assortment of piano fortes of the newest construction made by the best makers in London, which he will sell on reasonable terms. He gives cash on all kinds of fur and has for sale a quantity of Canada beaver and beaver coating as well as racoon skins, racoon blankets, and muskrat skins.'

"The manufacture of piano fortes was not begun in England until 1766, so the old Astor piano bearing the date of 1779, was made about thirteen years after their manufacture started in England. How this old piano came to Astoria is not known but the supposition is that it must have been sent there by Astor before Astoria became Fort George. Crude as is this old piano, it was considered a wonderful improvement on its predecessors.

"Originally the piano was a harp having from two to three strings. As more strings were added the harp took the form of a letter P and was called the cithara. The standard cithara had ten strings and it was some centuries later before some inventive genius discovered that by stretching the strings across an open box a better musical effect could be produced. By 1200 A. D., the cithara had been improved and was called a dulcimer, the strings being struck with hammers held in the hands of the player.

"A century or so later the key board was invented, the hammers being controlled by the keys. This instrument was called a clavicytherium. Further improvement was made and in the time of Queen Elizabeth it was rechristened the virginial. A little later it received a new name, the spinet. Some time between 1700 and 1800 it was again rechristened and was called the harpsichord. In the early part of the eighteenth century Bartholommeo Cristofori, an Italian, evolved the piano forte. A little later Marius, a Frenchman, and Cottlieb Schroeter, a German, made important improvements. Cristofori completed his piano forte in 1749 but it was more than fifty years later before the piano forte came into general use throughout Europe."
—*Fred Lockley.*

"Dick," the Cat, and His Good Friend the Bishop. —When your grandparents came to the Northwest from their eastern homes, they brought with them their faithful dogs. A dog was no trouble, he followed along with the wagons or helped drive the horses and cows through the day, and at night slept near, keeping guard. He was ever watching for the lurking Indian, who wanted to kill his master or steal his stock.

But poor pussy cat had to be left at her eastern home. She would not follow nor would she stay with the wagon unless nailed up in a box. She was a home body, never going anywhere except to the nearest neighbors with whom she fought ofttimes instead of visiting. When the settlers first came to their new homes, if they did not have a dog they could buy one from the Indians who usually had many; not so with cats. Mr. Indian had never seen a pussy cat, and the first one he saw he called "pits-pits," this being the sound conveyed to his mind by the pronunciation of the word "pussy-pussy."

When the miners came, they needed cats more than dogs. The mice and the wood-rats got into their cabins and cut holes in the bags of rice, fruit, and sugar, as well as in the sacks of flour. Provisions were very expensive, so the miner would pay as much as five dollars for a kitten to keep mice and rats out of his cabin.

Miners, however, were not the only men in the country then. There were ministers as well. One of these, a good bishop, came all alone from his eastern home where he had left his wife and little boy. This good man had to live in an old log house covered with poles and dirt, and there was little furniture in the house, but worst of all, there was no one to welcome him when he came home from his hard day's work. How glad he was when some kind friend gave him a furry little kitten, which he named "Dick." The kitten soon grew to be a big cat, and no wood-rat dared to come into his master's cabin. "Dick" was a playful fellow and would run and catch a string or piece of cloth drawn over the floor. Or, he would climb up on the table beside his master and sit quietly while the bishop wrote letters home to his wife and little boy. Sometimes Dick would climb up on the back of the chair and sit on his master's shoulder, watching him write. Or again, when he was very lazy he would lie stretched out by the little sheet iron stove that kept the cabin warm.

Dick was very happy in his new home, where he got plenty to eat and was protected from the dogs which would chase him when they caught him away from home. Then, too, his master was so good to him, bringing him tidbits to eat and preparing him a nice warm bed at night. But Dick was a cunning little rascal, and did not always do as he was told. The bishop prepared a nice rug for him beside the stove where Dick could sleep at night, but as the house was very cold, Dick would sometimes climb up onto the foot of his master's bed, and if he got too cold there, he would crawl in under the cover beside the bishop. So, when the bishop awoke in the morning, he would sometimes find a furry little head sticking up beside his nose. Finally Dick's good friend had to go away, but before leaving, he found Dick another good home where he lived to a good old age, and where his old master sometimes visited him.

Oregon's First Fourth of July, 1846.—The following are excerpts taken from the *Washington Historical Quarterly*. Vol. IV, No. 3, Page 178-9, giving accounts of the first Fourth of July celebration in the Northwest Territory:

"On the Fourth of July, 1846, months before you received the news of the adoption of the treaty of the 15th of June preceding, and while you were yet ignorant of what had taken place in regard to Oregon, you celebrated, in a heavy rain, the Anniversary of American Independence. The Oregon Rangers, a military company organized in May previous, were out in force, and despite the inclemency of the weather, acquitted themselves creditably. There is nothing in rain to deter an Oregonian from pleasure or duty. There may be some of that company here today. This celebration was not for display. It was not mere pomp and parade to gain the applause of men, for this small band embraced a good portion of the settlers; nor was it an idle pastime. It was social in its nature, sincere in its object and eminently patriotic. These pioneers were repeating for the purpose of preserving, the traditions of their fathers in a land which, for aught they knew was still claimed, as it had been, by Great Britain, and liable to fall in part or wholly into her hands, through the skill of diplomacy, or by arbitrament of war. What a Fourth of July that would have been to you, had you but known that your own land—your Oregon—had, like that of your fathers, been conceded to you by the only adverse claimant among the powers of the earth; that the Government of your fathers was now yours, and that the day you were celebrating was legitimately a day for Oregon."

Washington's First Fourth of July, 1852.—"It was a great event; a celebration that would be a credit in older communities. Quite elaborate preparations were made. One of the streets was set apart for the occasion. An arbor was made by setting posts in the ground and putting poles across, on which were placed fir boughs. This arbor was the width of the street and about 150 feet long. One or more oxen were barbecued. The celebration attracted settlers from all parts of Northern Oregon and from the down-Sound settlements.

The late Daniel R. Bigelow of Olympia was the orator of the day. Simpson P. Moses read the Declaration of Independence and Frank Shaw acted as marshal. After the ceremonies of the day had been concluded, an enthusiastic meeting was held and the division of the territory discussed."

Idaho's First Fourth of July, 1861.—The Indian wars of 1854-5 in the inland empire and the desire to find routes to the Northwest from the upper Mississippi induced Congress to appropriate money to build a military road from Fort Benton, which was the headwater of navigation on the Missouri, to Fort Walla Walla (Wallula), the chief fort toward the headwaters of navigation of the Snake and the Columbia. The construction of this work was entrusted to Captain John Mullan, and the road was known as the Mullan Road.

On July 4, 1861, Captain Mullan and his company of road builders, consisting of about two hundred men, were located in what is now known as Fourth of July Canyon. Mullan, being a military man, naturally observed all national holidays, and since the Civil War was raging, no ceremony could be more appropriately observed than that commemorating the birth of our nation. He therefore suspended all construction work and devoted the day to the usual celebration.

They were located in a dense forest of cedars varying in diameter from three to eight feet, so thick that the sun's rays could scarcely penetrate, and surrounded by Indians who lurked along the road. The latter gave some trouble because of their opposition to the work and ill-feeling stirred up by the recent wars.

Mullan turned his men loose and with an abundance of patriotism and gunpowder they made the canyon echo and re-echo with their noise and merriment. The "Old Flag" was hoisted to the top of one of the giant cedars and the patriotic men pledged renewed allegiance to it.

Poor "Lo" was bewildered and terrified at such conduct for which he could see no conceivable reason. He hastened to the old mission at St. Mary's and told the Fathers that the men had all gone crazy and were fighting each other to death in the Big Cedar swamp or were calling down the wrath of their gods on the red men so they could cause no more trouble. The Fathers attempted to explain, but it was impossible—the Indians could not understand. They had never heard of the Fourth of July and knew nothing of its significance or manner of celebration.

On that day the canyon was christened Fourth of July Canyon, a name it has borne ever since. It was famous then because through it ran the first road to the Northwest; it is equally famous now because the state highway passes along the same route.

How a Pig in a Potato Patch Almost Involved the United States and England in War.—The Island of Victoria lies just off the northwestern coast of the state of Washington. In the strait between this island and the mainland are some small islands. In the treaty of 1846, settling the Oregon question between Great Britian and the United States, no disposition was made of these little islands, so both English and American citizens settled on them. An American planted a potato patch, and his neighbor, an Englishman, had a pig which kept breaking into the potato patch. When the American told the Englishman to keep his pig out of the potato patch, the Englishman retorted by saying, "Keep your potatoes out of my pig." The matter was brought to a climax when the American killed the Englishman's pig and each appealed to his government for protection. The details of this droll story are still further related by Mr. Charles Prosch, in his *Reminiscences of Washington Territory*.

"A very exciting episode in the early history of our Territory was the San Juan Island imbroglio. For a

Old Block House erected by the English on San Juan Island in 1859 when they and the Americans almost came to war. It is on Friday Harbor, Washington, the most northwesterly town in the United States.

time it actually bade fair to involve the United States in a third war with Great Britain. Long before an American thought of settling upon this island the Hudson's Bay Company occupied it as a sheep pasture, for which it was admirably adapted, and also cultivated small portions of it. For some time but a single American resided on San Juan, or Bellevue, as it was sometimes called; in 1858 he was joined by others, until the number reached twenty-five or thirty, when discord arose between our people and the Hudson's Bay men. Each group claimed for its government the sovereignty of the island. Meanwhile the sheriff of Whatcom County, of which this island then formed a part, seized and sold for taxes thirty head of Hudson's Bay Sheep. Some time later a man named Cutler, who had taken a claim and was cultivating some land on the island, killed a Hudson's Bay boar for trespassing on his garden patch. For this act the Englishman threatened to take him to Victoria to be tried and punished.

"Complaints were then made on the one side to Governor Douglas, and on the other to the American authorities. In August, 1859, General Harney, then in command of the military department of the Columbia, ordered to San Juan all the available troops stationed on the Sound, which comprised half a dozen companies of fifty or sixty men each. The British had a small detachment on the island and two men-of-war in the harbor, but the American troops were landed without opposition during the night. The Americans immediately commenced fortifying their position, and in a few hours had eight 32-pound guns mounted and ready to do battle with either the ships on the water or the redcoats on the land.

"At this stage the signs were truly warlike, and many people on both sides regarded a collision as unavoidable. But Colonel Casey, who commanded the American troops, united discretion with undoubted courage; while Captain Hornby, the senior British naval officer on the Victoria station, was no less discreet, sensible, and courageous. Had the question of peace or war rested alone with the hot-headed and valorous General Harney and 'His Excellency James Douglas, C. B., Governor of Vancouver's Island, etc., and Vice-Admiral of the same,' it was thought that war certainly would have been the result of this controversy. Harney was absent at Fort Vancouver, on Columbia River, whence he issued the orders for the military occupation of San Juan Island; Governor Douglas remained at

Victoria, fortunately for the issue of this threatening affair.

"The first act of Colonel Casey, after a rigid execution of the orders of General Harney, was to invite Captain Hornby, of the British warship *Tribune,* to a conference in his tent. In the afternoon the two men met and discussed the situation in a sensible and friendly spirit. On the following day Colonel Casey and other officers were invited on board the *Tribune,* where there was an exchange of courtesies that removed all danger of a rupture, so far as these gentlemen had the power to prevent it.

"General Winfield Scott arrived on the scene a few days later and withdrew all the troops except a small detachment, which remained in accordance with a mutual arrangement for the joint occupancy of the island. So scrupulous was General Scott while undoing the work of General Harney that he would not even remain on San Juan while his orders were being carried out, but took up his abode on Fidalgo Island.

"Emperor William of Germany was chosen arbiter by the two governments and decided the controversy in favor of the United States. And thus ended the San Juan imbroglio, greatly to the disappointment of the Hudson's Bay Company, who hoped to have the island awarded to them."

The Early Military Organizations of Old Oregon.— " 'My people came to Oregon with the immigration of 1843,' said Miss Pauline Looney when I interviewed her at her tent at the state fair grounds recently. 'That is, they came as far as Dr. Whitman's mission in '43 and in the spring of '44 came on to the Willamette Valley. In the old days the state fair was a great event among the pioneers. I remember how sixteen young ladies, of whom I was one, competed for the $100 prize saddle just about fifty years ago here on the state fair grounds. I was the fortunate one. As a matter of fact I was sorry to win it, for some of the other girls wanted it so badly and I already had a good saddle.

" 'It is hard to realize how times have changed during the past fifty years. As an instance of the change of conditions, my father, Jesse Looney, paid a man named Buck $500 for two hives of bees which he had brought up from California in his wagon.

" 'I remember in the sixties they held a big Fourth of July celebration at Salem in Bush's grove. War times had made us patriotic. We had organized a military company consisting of 120 young men. We rode in the procession in a column of two's. There were sixty couples of us on our prancing horses. "Sis" Waldo was captain and I was marshal. We wore blue skirts, white waists and red sashes. As "Sis" Waldo carried the flag at the head of the procession we were cheered all along the line. Speaking of flags reminds me that Mrs. Horace Holden, my mother and my sister Susan, made the first flag in Oregon. The red stripes were made from red handkerchiefs, the white was from some white goods my mother had at the house and the blue cloth they bought at the store. They presented it to the Oregon Rangers at the first Fourth of July celebration ever held in Oregon. That was on July 4, 1846, at Salem. A celebration was also held the same day at Oregon City. The flag was presented to the Oregon Rangers commanded by Captain Bennett, who was later killed by the Indians near Walla Walla. W. C. T'Vault delivered the oration. After his talk a barbecue and public dinner was held and this was followed by a sermon by Reverend Harvey Clarke.'

"The Oregon Rangers, of Salem, commanded by Captain Bennett, to which Miss Looney refers, are often spoken of as the first American military company organized in old Oregon. This is a mistake, however. Another company was organized a year or two prior to the formation of this company. It came about as follows: In the spring of 1844 there was a camp of Molalla Indians on the west side of the Willamette from Oregon City. They were really a wandering branch of the Cayuse tribe, called Molallas from the Molalla district where they made their home. Cockstock, a Molalla Indian, had been cheated by a negro named Winslow. Cockstock took the negro's horse to get even. Another negro, named Soules, reported the matter to Elijah White, the Indian agent, and Dr. White offered a reward of $100 for Cockstock. The Molalla Indian heard that a reward had been offered for his capture, so he put on his war paint and on March 4, 1844, paraded through the main streets of Oregon City. He was unmolested and went back across the river. Soon he returned with several other Indians. The white men then decided to capture him and secure the reward. In the melee Cockstock was killed and George W. Le Breton, who had been secretary of the Wolf meeting when the provisional government was organized, was wounded by an arrow; so also was a man named Rogers. Both died, presumably from the poison on the arrow points.

"A public meeting was called at Champoeg to organize a military company. The meeting took place on March 9, 1844, at La Chapelle's house. W. H. Wilson was chosen chairman and T. D. Kaiser, secretary. A company was formed and christened 'The Oregon Rangers.' Commissions were issued to the officers by D. Hill, J. Gale, and A. Beers, the executive committee of the provisional government.

"No need for the services of the company of rangers occurring, they ceased to meet. Two years later, in the spring of 1846, a meeting was called at the home of Daniel Waldo and a new company was organized to take the place of the disbanded one. Charles Bennett, later a discoverer of gold at Marshall's millrace, at Sutter mill, was made captain. A. A. Robinson was first lieutenant; Isaac Hutchins, second lieutenant; Hiram English, third lieutenant; Thomas Holt, orderly sergeant; Thomas Howell, second sergeant; S. C. Morris, third sergeant; William Herring, fourth sergeant; P. C. Kaiser, first corporal; Robert Walker, second corporal; B. Frost, third corporal; John Rowe, fourth corporal. Thirty-three were enrolled as privates. It was this latter company, also known as the Oregon Rangers, to whom the flag was presented."—*Fred Lockley.*

CHAPTER IX.

Indian Wars.

From the Coming of Columbus, Until the Last Outbreak of the Sioux Indians in the Nineties.—The causes, methods, and results of the Indian wars have been largely the same—ignorance, clash of ideals, greed of the whites, murder of the defenseless and the final defeat and extinction of the Indian.

Prior to the great Indian wars in the Northwest there were three well-known stages or epochs: (1) The fur-trading period, when the Indian came to know the white man as a friend and a helper, reaching its height during the reign of the Hudson's Bay Co. (2) The missionary era, when the white man attempted to change the Indian's mode of life. (3) The age of the immigrant when the white men came in large numbers to occupy the land heretofore occupied by the Indian, who was now forced to reside on reservations in accordance with treaty stipulations.

The Indian got along well with the fur-trader who bought his furs, furnished him with needed supplies, kept peace between warring tribes, inter-married and, to some extent, became a member of a tribe.

The missionary was not so acceptable as the fur-trader, as he interfered with the Indian's standards of life, insisting on higher ideals; besides some of the missionaries later became traders and were more interested in secular affairs than in religious. Yet the influence of the missionary in changing the wild nature of the Indian, eliminating his harsh, cruel customs and immoral practices can be hardly overestimated.

The immigrant came with no thought of trade with the Indian or of missionary benefit to him but with the sole idea of securing a home. This meant taking possession of the land heretofore held by the Indian who was now deprived of his hunting grounds.

The Indian did not understand very well the meaning of the treaties which he made with the whites and he protested against leaving the lands where he had hunted and fished, where his tepees had been set for generations, and where his ancestors were buried. Heretofore no limitations were placed upon the boundaries over which he might roam. His brothers in the East had told him how the coming of the white man meant his own extinction, so through misunderstandings, fear, and sometimes hatred, he waged war.

The Indians of the Inland Empire. (1855-6).—Mr. James M. Kelly, a former senator of Oregon, in speaking of the inland empire, meaning all of the country east of the Cascades and west of the Rockies, said:

"From the Des Chutes River to Fort Hall there was not an inhabited dwelling house occupied by the white man. The same was true of eastern Washington, with one single exception—from the Cascade Mountains to the Rocky Mountains the only white man left was Major John Owens, then living in the Bitter Root Valley. There had been a number of white families living in the Walla Walla and Touchet valleys, and at the Hudson's Bay Company's fort at Walla Walla, but these were removed, for safety, in the fall of 1855, to western Oregon and Washington by Nathan Olney, who was then the United States Indian agent in that country. There had been a number of Canadian half-breed families who had gone from French Prairie in the Willamette Valley to the Walla Walla country.

These people had all left their habitations, and for safety had gone to the Nez Perces, who were friendly to the whites. Their homes, which were not destroyed, were left tenantless, and their household goods removed. This was the condition of the country in the late fall of 1855. These Indian tribes were the Indians of eastern Washington, numbering about twelve thousand. The Nez Perces occupied the country between the Clearwater and the Snake. North of them lived the Coeur-d'Alenes, Spokanes, Pend d'Oreilles and Flatheads. South of the Nez Perces were the Walla Wallas, Cayuses and Umatillas, while over the mountains in the desert country were the Shoshones and west of the Yakima River were the Yakima Indians. This was the general location of the Indians about 1855 when the treaty was concluded with them by Governor Stevens of Washington. In this treaty the Nez Perces were to receive the country lying between the Snake River and the Bitter Root Mountains. The Yakimas were to retain their home on the river of that name, while the Indians to the south were assigned to tracts in eastern Washington.

"To enforce the laws of the United States in connection with these Indians a Fort was established at Walla Walla in 1855."

I. I. Stevens, Governor of Washington, Reservationizes the Indians of the Northwest.—The Whitman massacre, the Mexican Cession and the discovery of gold in California attracted renewed attention to the Pacific Coast and especially to the Northwest.

On March 17, 1853, Washington Territory was organized, embracing all of the Oregon Country north of the Columbia and the 46th parallel of latitude, extending east to the crest of the Rocky Mountains, a distance of six hundred miles.

Isaac Ingalls Stevens was appointed the first Territorial governor. He was a man of great natural ability, graduating from West Point in 1839, at the head of his class; a man of ripe experience, having served in the Mexican War and in many official positions connected with his military profession. "He was thirty-four years old—in the prime of life and of his mental and physical powers." His appointment carried with it the superintendency of Indian affairs. He seemed almost intuitively to have grasped the real problems of the Pacific Coast, viz.: a practical route to reach it, and the pacification of the Indians.

On March 3, 1853, Congress had appropriated $150,000 for the exploration and survey of railroad routes from the Mississippi to the Pacific. On March 21st, Governor Stevens writes the Secretary of War, Jefferson Davis, proposing to conduct all expeditions to determine the most feasible routes for railroads and immigrants from the source of the Mississippi to Puget Sound.

His proposal was immediately accepted. The expedition was at once organized. This work was to be effected by two parties, one under Stevens' supervision starting from St. Paul, the other under George B. McClellan starting from the West, the two meeting somewhere on the upper Columbia.

Stevens party, however, started from St. Louis on the 23rd of May, 1853, and proceeded up the Mississippi to St. Paul which is said to have had a population of 1,200. The party numbered 240. Fortunately there were among them many soldiers and army officers, which made discipline easy. One of these was Lieutenant Mullan who afterwards built the Mullan Road from Ft. Benton to Walla Walla.

Governor Stevens "early realized that the establishment of peace among the Indian tribes was indispensable to exploration, immigration, and settlement, and set about accomplishing this. One of the first messages sent out by him to the Indians was one to the powerful tribe of Blackfeet asking them to meet him in council, urging them not to make war upon their neighbors, and assuring them national protection. At these councils he made a liberal distribution of blankets, shirts, calico, knives, beads, paints, powder, shot, tobacco, hard bread, etc."

His route after reaching the Missouri was much the same as that taken by Lewis and Clark until Fort Vancouver was reached. On the 24th of September, 1853, Stevens reached the summit of Cardotte's Pass. This being the eastern boundary of Washington Territory, he issued his proclamation as Territorial Governor and assumed his duties.

He and other members of his party had explored nine passes across the Rocky Mountains and four across the Bitter Root Range. Two of these were afterward traversed by railroads, one by the Great Northern and another by the Northern Pacific.

He had met many Indian chiefs, learned of the extent of their territory, listened to their grievances, etc., broached the subject of future councils and gathered much other useful information. As soon as civil government was established in the territory, the work among the Indians engaged his attention. The Indians on the Sound numbered about 8,500 and included many tribes and remnants of tribes. The Indians on the upper Columbia numbered 14,000 including ten powerful tribes:

1. Yakimas on the Yakima River.
2. Umatillas on the Umatilla River.
3. Cayuses located just east of the Umatillas.
4. Walla Wallas located just north of the Umatillas.
5. Spokanes located just north of the Walla Wallas.
6. Nez Perces located just east of the Spokanes.
7. Coeur d'Alenes located just north of the Nez Perces.
8. Kootenais located just north of the Nez Perces.
9. Pend d'Oreilles located just north of the Kootenais.
10. Flatheads located just east of the Pend d'Oreilles.
11. Blackfeet located just east of the Flatheads.

Each of these Columbia tribes had its own country with more or less well-defined boundaries; had large bands of cattle and horses, and represented a manly and athletic people not yet contaminated by the vices of the white men as were the coast Indians.

The Indians' contact with the whites thus far had been with the fur-traders who supplied them with powder, arms, clothing, etc., and took their furs in exchange. The missionaries taught them how to farm, raise stock, make clothes from cloth, and inculcated in them higher moral ideals. The Indians saw the immigrants taking their land and growing rich in farming and stock-raising. They were now to come in contact with national power which demands implicit obedience to authority.

Stevens began his work among the Sound Indians. They were not strong, numerically or otherwise, and he soon had them assigned to their respective reservations. But the work among the more powerful tribes east of the Cascades was not so easy.

At the Walla Walla council of May 29, 1855, Governor Stevens met these tribes. Lawyer, the able chief and a good friend of the whites, brought 2,500 of his braves to this meeting. Kam-i-ah-kin, the proud chief of the Yakimas, came, but not in friendly mood. Pu-Pu-Mox-Mox, Yellow Serpent, head chief of the Walla Wallas, and Young Chief, head chief of the Cayuses, leaders in the Whitman Massacre, came also.

The council opened by smoking the peace pipe. Two interpreters were chosen for each tribe and secretaries were appointed who kept a record of everything that transpired. All were seated in front of the commissioner's headquarters under a roomy arbor. The conference was long and at times stormy. Governor Stevens explained what the reservations meant. No white man was to come upon the reservations without the Indians' consent. The government would furnish an agent, school teachers, mechanics and farmers who would instruct the Indians in the ways of the whites. The head chiefs were to receive $500 each that they might devote their entire time to their people; clothing and tents were to be given to the Indians for twenty years and finally their lands were to be allotted in severalty.

After days of patient work the chiefs were one by one induced to sign, that is, make an X on the treaty. Governor Stevens then hastened eastward and concluded treaties with the Flatheads in western Montana, and later, with the Blackfeet in the eastern part of the state; he then returned to Olympia.

He held many councils; entered into ten treaties; dealt with over 30,000 Indians, placing them on reservations; made peace between warring tribes, and prepared for settlement by the whites all of that country between Puget Sound and Nebraska, embracing the present states of Washington, northern Idaho and Montana. The main features of his policy were:

1. To put the Indians on reservations and teach them to cultivate the soil and adopt civilized ways.

2. To pay them for their land in the things needed by civilized man, the payment extending over many years.

3. To furnish them with agents, teachers, and others who would assist them in learning the ways of the white man.

4. To stop wars among them.

5. To abolish slavery.

6. To stop the use of liquor.

7. To allow them their old ways of living by fishing, hunting, and gathering herbs and roots, but to encourage farming.

8. To get them to adopt land in severalty.

But the Indian did not understand very well the meaning of the treaty which he had signed, and every where he protested against leaving the lands he had roamed at will.

Many bloody wars were fought before he became reconciled to living on the reservation. But, while these wars were appalling, they were nothing like so terrible as they would have been had not Stevens done his great work among the Indians.

The Coming of the Soldiers.—The Whitman massacre had caused the settlers to appeal to the government for military protection. Now, the heavy migration to the West, the building of the Mullan Road, the discovery of gold which resulted in the exploration of every nook and corner of the country, all excited great fear and suspicion among the Indians lest the white men should seize their country, so they began to manifest their hostility to the whites in various ways. They stole stock, occasionally murdered some lone settler, and assumed a threatening attitude which finally developed into open hostilities with which the settlers, in their scattered condition, could not cope, so they again im-

Fort Walla Walla in 1857.

Site of the present city of Walla Walla. From a pencil drawing by Edward Del Girardin, a friend of Captain O. H. P. Taylor, who visited that officer's home at quarters at the fort in 1857. After Captain Taylor was killed in the Steptoe fight in 1858, the drawing was preserved for his little daughter, now Mrs. Mae Taylor Chapman, and now hangs in her home in Cincinnati.

portuned the government to send soldiers to the Northwest.

The army is composed of two general classes, the soldiers who fight on foot, termed infantry, and those who fight on horseback, termed cavalry. It is also divided into companies of a hundred men, each in command of a captain. Twelve companies constitute a regiment which is in command of a colonel. Sometimes, however, neither the captain nor the colonel has his full quota of men.

GEN'L GEO. WRIGHT, U.S.A.

When the soldiers came they had to be provided with homes. This was done by establishing at some central location what is termed a fort, consisting of several acres of enclosed ground on which were erected buildings for housing the men and the horses. There were also parade grounds, pastures for the stock, etc. Here the soldiers, officers, and their families lived when not engaged in fighting. From the sound of the reveille in the morning until taps at night, when all lights must be put out and all noise cease, the soldier's life is one continual round of duties. He must keep his guns and other implements of war in first class condition, and he must drill continually. His hours for eating and sleeping must be regular. He is taught habits of cleanliness and hygiene, as well as what to do for himself and his companions when wounded. He must learn the various signs and commands which will enable him at all times to act in perfect unison with other members of his company.

FORTS IN THE NORTHWEST.

Location	*Date*	*Name of Troop*	*Commanding Officer*
Vancouver	1849	Rifles of 4th U. S. Infantry	Col. Bonneville
The Dalles	1855	9th U. S. Infantry	Col. Wright
Lower Cascades	1855	3rd Artillery	Major Wise
Simcoe-North Yakima	1856	3rd Infantry	Major Garnett
Walla Walla	1857-8	9th U. S. Infantry	Col. Steptoe
Colville	1859	9th U. S. Infantry	Col. Lugenbell
Lapwai	1863	Oregon Volunteers	
Boise	1863	1st Oregon Cavalry	Major Rinearson

Campaign of Colonel Wright.

The Soldier on the March. Campaign Against the Indians of Eastern Washington, 1858. Colonel Wright in Charge.—"Our transportation consists of six mules to a company, a mule to each officer, besides 325 mules which the quartermaster has in his train. Our entire train, therefore, consists of about 400 mules. Baggage wagons cannot go beyond Snake River, only light vehicles will be taken.

The Fighting Force.—"The Dragoons number 190, the Artillery, 400, the Infantry (as Rifle Brigade), 90. Total, about 680 soldiers besides attachés, as packers, wagon masters, etc.

Rules to be Observed Upon the March.—

I. The residue of the troops for the northern expedition will march from Fort Walla Walla tomorrow, and unite with the advance at the Snake River.

II. Marching from Snake River, the order will be as follows:

1st. The Dragoons.
2d. The Mountain Howitzer Company.
3d. The Battalion of Artillery, serving as Infantry.
4th. The Rifle Battalion of the 9th Infantry.
5th. Pack train of the corps of Headquarters.
6th. One company of Infantry as rearguard.
7th. General train of Quartermaster and Commissary.
8th. One troop of Dragoons as rear guard.

III. The mounted troop will not precede the Howitzer Company more than four hundred yards; and on approaching canyons or defiles, where Dragoons cannot operate on the flanks, they will be halted and the rifles advanced.

IV. No firearms of any description will be discharged, either on the march or in camp, except in the line of duty, without the special authority of the commanding officer.

V. No person, excepting the employe of the Staff Department and the officer's servants, will be allowed to accompany the troops or to encamp with them, without the written authority of the commanding officer.

VI. Habitually the Guard will consist of one company, and mount at retreat.

VII. Whether in camp or on the march the companies will parade with arms, at retreat and reveille roll calls, and the arms and ammunition will be inspected. The men will habitually wear and sleep in their belts.

Other Instructions.—

1st. The mules with ammunition will be led, and follow close in rear of the column, in compact order under a guard.

2d. The baggage mules and supply train will be kept in close order in rear of the ammunition, and under the special orders of the Quartermaster.

3d. The ammunition for the Mountain Howitzers will follow close in rear of the guns.

4th. The animals for the Hospital Department will move with the ammunition.

5th. Particular attention will be given by the company and battalion commanders, to see that the men, *at all times,* by day and by night wear their belts; that their rifles are always at hand

and in order; and that, on the march, the men keep in the ranks and in proper order.

6th. The camp signals will be sounded at the proper times, by the buglers of the Artillery and Battalion, and repeated by the other corps. At retreat inspection, the last roll call for the day will be made at 8:00 p. m., and signal will be given for extinguishing lights, after which no noise or loud talking will be allowed.

7th. When the troops are to march, the company cooks will be called up in season to have breakfast ready immediately after reveille.

8th. Should the enemy be met while on the march, and a combat ensue, the entire pack train will be closed up, and either picketed or the animals tied together, and the whole enveloped by the rearguard. In case of alarm at night, the companies on rearguard the previous day will protect the train. The detachment of friendly Nez Perces, as well as the guides and interpreters, are placed under the special direction of Lieutenant Mullan, acting engineer, who will receive instruction in relation to their positions, etc."

The Battle of Four Lakes, September 1, 1858.—"On the plain below us we saw the enemy. Every spot seemed alive with the wild warriors we had come so far to meet. They were in the pines, on the edge of the lakes, in ravines and gullies, on the opposite hillside, and swarming over the plain. They seemed to cover the country for some two miles. Mounted on their fleet, hardy horses, the crowd swayed back and forth, brandishing their weapons, shouting their war cries and keeping up their song of defiance. Most of them were armed with Hudson's Bay muskets; others had bows and arrows and long lances. They were in all the finery of their war array, gaudily painted and decorated with their wild trappings. Their plumes fluttered above them while below skins and trinkets and all kinds of fantastic embellishments flaunted in the sunshine. Their horses, too, were arrayed in the most glary finery. Some were even painted and with colors to form the greatest contrast, the white horses being smeared with crimson in fantastic figures and the dark colored streaked with white clay. Beads and fringes of gaudy colors were hanging from their bridles, while plumes of eagle feathers, interwoven with the mane and tail, fluttered as the breeze swept over them, and completed their wild and fantastic appearance.

By heavens! it was a glorious sight to see
The gay array of their wild chivalry.'

"But we had no time for mere admiration for other work was at hand. The companies moved down the hill with all the precision of a parade; and as we rode along the line it was pleasant to see the enthusiasm of the men to get in reach of the enemy. As soon as they were within some six hundred yards, they opened their fire and delivered it steadily as they advanced. Our soldiers aimed regularly, though it was no easy task to hit their shifting marks. The Indians acted as skirmishers, advancing rapidly and delivering their fire, and then retreating again with a quickness and irregularity that rendered it difficult to reach them. They were wheeling and dashing about, always on the run, apparently each fighting on his own account. . . . . As the line advanced, first we saw one Indian reel in his saddle and fall, then, two, or three, then, half a dozen. Then some horses went dashing madly forward, showing that the balls were telling upon them. The instant, however, that the 'braves' fell, they were seized by their companions and dragged to the rear to be borne off. We saw one Indian leading off a horse with two of his dead companions tied on it.

"But in a few minutes, as the line drew in, the fire became too heavy, and the whole array broke and fled toward the plains. This was the chance for which the Dragoons had been impatiently waiting. As the line advanced they had followed on behind it, leading their horses. Now the order was given to mount, and they rode through the company intervals to the front. In an instant was heard the voice of Major Grier ringing over the plain, as he shouted; 'Charge the rascals!' and on the Dragoons went at headlong speed. Taylor's and Gaston's companies were there burning for revenge, and soon they were on them. We saw the flash of their sabres as they cut them down. Lieutenant Davidson shot one warrior from his saddle as they charged up, and Lieutenant Gregg clove the skull of another. Yells and shrieks and uplifted hands were of no avail as they rode over them. A number were left dead upon the ground when once more the crowd broke and dashed forward toward the hills. It was a race for life, as the flying warriors streamed out of the glens and ravines and over the plain and took refuge in clumps of woods or on the rising ground. Here they were secure from the Dragoons. . . . . What the Indians' loss was, we cannot exactly say as they carry off their dead. Some seventeen, however, were seen to be killed while there must have been between forty and fifty wounded. Among those killed we subsequently ascertained were a brother and brother-in-law of Garry, the head chief of the Spokanes. Strange to say not one of our men was injured. One Dragoon's horse alone was injured."—*Army Life on the Pacific, Laurence Kipp, page 59.*

The newspapers of the times, speaking of the Battle of Four Lakes, said: "No event has ever done so much to secure the safety of our settlers as this victory. The people of this territory owe a debt of gratitude to the officers and soldiers under Colonel Wright."

The Hanging of Qualchien, Chief of the Yakimas. —"How sharply and swiftly justice was meted out by Colonel Wright in his campaign against the Indians is illustrated by one, Chief Qualchien. Kamiaken was a a noted Yakima chief. Another chief of the same tribe was Owhi. He and his son Qualchien, were probably two of the worst Indians west of the Rocky Mountains, the son being even more notorious than the father. In all the battles, forays, and disturbances in Washington Territory, Qualchien was one of the leading spirits. The influence which he exercised was probably greater than that of either of the Yakima chiefs. He was directly charged with the murder of nine white men. In the action of March 1856, on White River, in the Puget Sound country, Qualchien was present with fifty warriors, seven of whom were killed. He went over the mountains, he said, to learn to fight at night. On the 24th of September, at about twelve o'clock, says Lieutenant Kipp, who was present, there trotted out from the canyon near our camp, two Indian braves and a fine looking squaw. The three rode abreast and a little behind rode an Indian hunchback whom we had before seen in camp. The three principal personages were gaily dressed and had a most dashing air. They all had on a great deal of scarlet, and the squaw wore two ornamental scarfs fastened over the right shoulder and under the right arm. She also carried, resting across in front of her saddle, a long lance, the handle of which was completely wound with various colored beads, and from the end of which depended two long tippets of beaver skins. The two braves had rifles, and one who was evidently the leader of the party carried an ornamental tomahawk. With the utmost boldness they rode directly up to Colonel Wright's tent.

"Captain Keyes, who was standing in front of the tent, pulled aside the opening, remarking as he did so: 'Colonel, we have distinguished visitors here!' The Colonel came out, and after a short conversation, to his surprise, recognized the leader of the party, Qualchien. For a few moments the Indian stood talking with Colonel Wright, with his rifle standing by his side. His bearing was so defiant, that Captain Keyes, thinking he might meditate some desperate act, placed himself on his right, a little in the rear, with his eye fixed on Qualchien's rifle, ready to spring upon him on the slightest demonstration. In a short time, Colonel Wright mentioned Owhi's name. At that Qualchien started, and exclaimed, 'Car? Where?' The Colonel answered, 'Owhi, mittite yawa.' When this was communicated, I was standing near him, and he seemed to be paralyzed. His whole expression changed as though he had been stunned. He gazed about him and repeated mechanically, 'Owhi, mittite yawa! Owhi, mittite yawa!' In a moment he made a motion as if he would use the rifle he held in his hand and advanced toward his horse. He evidently saw at once that he had run into the toils of his enemies. The guard, however, had by this time arrived, and he was at once disarmed. On him was found a fine pistol, capped and loaded, and plenty of ammunition. Colonel Wright told him to go with the guard, to which he consented with silent reluctance, hanging back as he was pulled along, but evidently undecided what to do.

"Qualchien was finely shaped, with a broad chest and muscular limbs and small hands and feet. When taken to the guard tent, it required six men to tie his hands and feet, so violent were his struggles, notwithstanding he had at the time an unhealed wound through the lower part of his body.

"Fifteen minutes after his capture the officer of the day received an order from Colonel Wright to have him hanged immediately. When his fate was made known to him he began cursing Kamiaken. A file of the guard marched him at once to a neighboring tree, where, on attempting to put the rope around his neck, the contest was again renewed. Bound as his arms were, he fought and struggled until they were obliged to throw him down on his back to fix the noose, he shrieking the while: 'Copet six, stop, my friends; Wake mameloose nika, do not kill me; nika potlatch hiyou chickamen, hiyou knitan, I will give much money, and great many horses; spore nika mamaloose, nika hiyou siwashe silex, —if you kill me, a great many Indians will be angry; copet six,—stop, my friends.' The rope was thrown over the limb of a tree and he was hung up. Among those who assisted with great alacrity in hauling him up, were two miners who had been with the party which was attacked by him and his band some months before. His last words, as the noose tightened, were a curse upon Karniaken."—*Kipp's Army Life on the Pacific.*

A Scalp Dance.—"The chiefs and braves, in full war paint and adorned with all their savage finery, formed a large circle, standing several ranks deep. Within this arena a chosen body of warriors performed the war dance while the densely massed ranks of braves circled around them, keeping time in measured tread, and accompanying it with their wild and barbaric war song. The ferocious and often hideous mien of these stalwart savages, their frenzied attitudes and shrill and startling yells, formed a subject worthy the pen of Dante and the pencil of Dore. The missionary still had work to do.

"Peo," Chief of the Umatillas.

The War Dance.

"Presently an old hag, the very picture of squalor and woe, burst into the circle bearing aloft on a pole one of the fresh scalps so recently taken by Looking Glass, and, dancing and jumping about with wild and extravagant action, heaped upon the poor relic of a fallen foe every mark of indignity and contempt. Shaking it aloft, she vociferously abused it; she beat it; she spat upon it; she bestrode the pole and rushed around the ring, trailing it in the dust again and again, while the warriors, with grim satisfaction, kept up their measured tread, chanted their war songs, and uttered, if possible, yet more ear-piercing yells.

"A softer and more pleasing scene succeeded. The old hag retired with her bedraggled trophy, and a long line of Indian maidens stepped within the circle, and, forming an inner rank, moved slowly round and round, chanting a mild and plaintive air. A number of the stylish young braves, real Indian beaux in the height of paint and feathers, next took post within the circle near the rank of moving maidens, and each one, as the object of his adoration passed him, placed a gaily decorated token upon her shoulder. If she allowed it to remain, his affection was returned and he was accepted, but if she shook it off, he knew that he was a rejected suitor. Coquetry evidently is not confined to the civilized fair, for, without exception, the maidens as if indignant at such public wooing, threw off the token with disdain, while every new victim of delusive hopes was greeted with shouts of laughter from the spectators.—*N. W. Durham* in *History of the City of Spokane and Spokane County, Washington.*

The Medicine Men.—"The Indians have what they term medicine men, in whom they place great confidence, and suppose that they possess the power by means of charms to counteract the influence of evil spirits, and to drive them away. They are called to exercise their charms in every case of sickness. They blow their breath upon the body, rub it, and press upon the stomach. After continuing this for some time, they pretend to have drawn something from the patient; they press it in their hands, and appear to hold it with the greatest difficulty; immerse it in the water, and continue alternately to rub and immerse it, until the evil spirit is overpowered. Then, holding the clinched hands above the head, several loud shouts are uttered in as frightful a manner as they are able. They then open their fingers gradually, to allow the terrified Scocum, (evil sprit), to make his escape—blow through their hands—continue to utter fearful cries, and to make threatening gestures—until they have driven the agent of evil entirely away. They go through the same operation until they have drawn the last devil from the body of the patient and driven it away. All the time these incantations are going on a number of persons, sitting in a row beside the sick, chanting their savage song, beat constantly and loudly with sticks upon a large dry board. These medicine men are supposed to be invulnerable, and lead the van to battle. They frequently exhibit proofs of their magic powers, at their dances and celebrations, by holding live coals of fire between their fingers for several minutes at a time. They are held accountable for the success of anything which they undertake, and if a person dies in their hands, or if they lose an engagement, they are tried for their lives. —*The Oregon Historical Quarterly,* Vol. VII; 181.

Timothy, the Noted Nez Perce Chief Who Aided the Whites on so Many Occasions.—Timothy's achievements group themselves into a life drama of four acts. The first revealed the Timothy of 1836, a stalwart young Indian of a fine type. The Reverend Mr. H. H. Spalding had been preaching to the redskins of the Palouse for three years, hoping always that some one among them would come to an understanding and belief in Christianity. Though discouraged, he had no more idea of quitting than Mohammed had after preaching his fortieth year with only three converts. But the waiting was long. At last Spalding was to taste the sweetness of first fruits. Timothy, far-sighted and thoughtful, was the first to glimpse the meaning of the strange new word. He declared himself for the unpopular cause, and so the way was opened to others.

Timothy came again to the foreground in the awful days of the Whitman massacre, when the Spaldings were at Lapwai. Eliza, their ten-year-old daughter, had fallen into the hands of the Cayuse tribe and was carried away. Timothy learned that she was alive. He rode to the Cayuse camp. By persuasion first, and then by threat of an exterminating war, he drew from them the promise that Eliza would be sent back to the Spaldings at once. Then he rode to Lapwai to tell her anxious parents and to reassure them of her safety.

One of the outstanding events in the history of the Indians in the Northwest is the great council at Walla Walla, when it was finally arranged to place each of the Indian tribes on a reservation.

The Nez Perces were the strongest and the dominant tribe in that council and Timothy was their preacher. His influence did much to cause his fellow tribesmen to shape their policies in accordance with Christian principles and ideals rather than those of primitive man. He held morning and evening worship. His preaching on Sundays kept ever uppermost in the minds of the Nez Perces the Golden Rule and the Ten Commandments and the brotherhood of man.

In the year 1859 Timothy was wearing the crest of a chief. The Steptoe expedition was on its way north in response to an appeal from forty unprotected miners of the Colville region. The Snake River, they knew, crawled along just ahead of them, and must be crossed. But was not Timothy encamped on the Snake with his Nez Perces? And Timothy lived up to their trust. Men and ordnance of the Steptoe force were ferried across by silently paddling redskins. But the Palouses and their allies were hostile and alert. When Colonel Steptoe had advanced into the Palouse country as far as to the butte which now bears his name, his men were outnumbered and defeated. At bay in a ravine, with a horde of savages guarding it, they waited for morning. There was still the one resource of appeal to Timothy. And he, chief of the Nez Perces, again stood in defense of the hated minority. By keen scouting of the ravine and guidance to a weak point in the patrol, he effected their secret escape.

The last scene remains to be enacted. The foot of the dominant race had been firmly established on the soil of old Oregon before Timothy's days ended. He returned to his government grant at the mouth of the Alpowai, Washington. He was ever true to his Christian faith. His blindness and old age made it difficult for him to secure a living but he was known and respected by all the whites in that locality, and in the fall when they brought their grain to the warehouses, Timothy visited much with them. They knew his condition and frequently divided their lunch with him, but he would never eat his share until he had returned thanks.

He died and was buried on his old homestead and today his last resting place is marked by a memorial bridge across the little creek before mentioned.

The Sign Language.—An Indian once told the author that if he could grunt and make signs he could speak any Indian language, and it is true that if one can utter the right grunts and make the right kinds of signs he will be able to make his wants known anywhere among the Indians. In our early history many tribes lived in the country between the Mississippi River and the Pacific, and Mexico and Canada. They spoke different dialects or languages. That they might converse with each other the "sign language" was gradually developed and was later employed with the trapper, the trader, the missionary and the army officers. This contains about eight hundred different signs and while all of them were known to only a few, many of the more common signs were generally known. It was possible to ask for food, the direction, the tribe to which an Indian belonged, the price of anything, the number of men, whether friends or enemies, the distance, and many other things if one understood a few simple signs.

The following may serve as illustrations:

1. Pass the right hand from left to right across the face. Ask the question, "To what tribe do you belong?" and the answer is the tribal sign.
2. The first two fingers on the right hand, separated from the mouth, signify "You lie."
3. One finger on the right hand, pointing directly from the mouth, signifies "You tell the truth."
4. Hold the left arm across the breast and with the right hand seize an imaginary object under the left fist. This signifies "To steal," while to represent the cutting of a lariat, indicates "A horse thief."
5. To describe a circle on the ground and point to some place in it, then with the hand describe another circle, indicates a day, and to point to the place indicated, signifies "A day's journey from where you are to that place."

The sign language was very helpful in many ways. If an Indian stripped and offered to meet a white man between the two companies, this signified a willingness to treat with him; while if the Indians lay down their arms and approached, this signified friendship.

When Meek and Sublette at one time were captured by the Indians, they understood the discourse carried on in the sign language as to what was to be done with them. The decision was that they were to be put to death after dark. They expressed no fear, but planned to get away, which they did.

The use of sign language exists to a greater or less degree among Idaho Indians as among most tribes. Thus the tribal sign of the Pend d'Oreilles is made by holding both fists as if grasping a paddle, vertically downward and working a canoe. Two strokes are made on each side of the body from the side backward. The tribal sign of the Nez Perces is made by closing the right hand, leaving the index finger straight, but flexed at right angles with the palm, then passing it horizontally to the left, by and under the nose. That of the Shoshone or Snake Indians is made by holding the right hand horizontal, flat, palm downward, and advancing it to the front by a motion representing the crawling of a snake. For that of the Bannocks, a whistling sound "phew" (beginning at a high note and ending about an octave lower); then drawing the extended index finger across the throat from left to right and out to nearly arm's length. They used to cut the throats of their prisoners.

Major Haworth states that the Bannocks made the following sign for themselves: brush the flat hand backward over the forehead as if forcing back the hair. This represents the manner of wearing the tuft of hair backward from the forehead. He also states that the Shoshones made the same sign for the Bannocks as for themselves.

It is not difficult to understand how readily ideas may be conveyed by signs and gestures. Thus, the Shoshone sign for "rain" is made by holding the hand or hands at the height of and before the shoulder, fingers pendent, palm down, then pushing it downward a short distance. The sign for "to weep" is made by holding the hand as in "rain," and the gesture made from the eye downward over the cheek, back of the fingers nearly touching the face.

"Brave" or "strong-hearted" is made by the Shoshone and Bannock Indians by merely placing the clenched fist to the breast, the latter having allusion to the heart, the clenching of the hand to strength, vigor, or force.

As a good example illustrative of the universality of sign language, may be mentioned the conversation which took place in the presence of Dr. W. J. Hoffman at Washington in 1880 between Tendoy, chief of the Shoshone and Bannock Indians of Lemhi Reservation, Idaho, and Huerito, one of the Apache chiefs from Mexico. Neither of these Indians spoke any language known to the other; had lived over a thousand miles apart, and had never met or heard of one another before.

HUERITO—"Who are you?"

TENDOY—"Shoshone Chief."

HUERITO—"How old are you?"

TENDOY—"Fifty-six."

HUERITO—"Very well. Are there any buffalo in your country?"

TENDOY—"Yes; many black buffalo. Did you hear anything from the Secretary? If so, tell me."

HUERITO—"He told me that in four days I would go to country."

TENDOY—"In two days I go to my country just as you go to yours. I go to mine where there is a great deal of snow, and we shall see each other no more."

Here was an intelligent dialogue carried on by two savages, strangers to each other, without a word spoken on either side. To make the last answer as Tendoy did, place the flat hands horizontally, about two feet apart, move them quickly in an upward curve toward one another until the right lies across the left, meaning "night." repeat this sign, "two nights," literally, "two sleeps hence"; point toward the individual addressed with the right hand, "you"; and in a continuous movement pass the hand to the right, i. e., toward the south, nearly to arm's length, "go"; then throw the fist edgewise toward the ground at that distance, "your country"; then touch the breast with the tips of the left fingers, "I"; move the hand slowly toward the left, i. e., toward the north to arm's length, "go to"; and throw the clenched hand toward the ground, "my country." Make the sign of "rain" as already described, then place the flat hands to the left of the body about two feet from the ground, "deep", literally, "deep rain, snow." Raise the hands about a foot, "very deep, much"; place the hands before the body, about twelve inches apart, palms down, with forefingers only extended and pointing toward one another; push toward and from one another several times, "see each other"; then hold the flat right hand in front of the breast pointing forward, palm to the left and throw it once on its back toward the right, "not," "no more."—*Onderdonk's Idaho. p. 138.*

Spokane Garry Who Built the First Schoolhouse and Taught the First School in the Oregon Country.—In 1821 the Hudson's Bay Company and the Northwest Company were united and George Simpson was appointed governor. He conceived the idea of selecting a number of Indian boys from the various Indian tribes of the Northwest and having them educated in the Red River mission schools.

Alexander Ross was delegated to make the selection of two boys from the Spokane and Kootenai tribes. Councils were held and the decision reached by the Indians to grant the request. In the formality of turning over the boys, the father of the Spokane boy spoke as follows:

"You see, we have given you our children, not our servants, or our slaves, but our own," and striking at

Spokane Garry.

the same time one hand on his left breast, while pointing with the other to his wife, the mother of the boy, he continued, "We have given you our hearts—our children are our hearts—but bring them back again to us before they become white men. We wish to see them once more Indians, and after that you can make them white men if you like. But let them not get sick or die. If they get sick, we shall be sick; if they die, we shall die. Take them, they are now yours." When the old chief sat down, all present broke out in lamentations, after which the two chiefs again rose and placing their boys' hands in Ross's hand, silently departed.

These two Indian boys with six others were sent to the schools as planned. Before their departure, the son of the Spokane chief was renamed, being given the name of Spokane for his tribe, and Garry, one of the directors of the Hudson's Bay Company, for his second name. Garry spent five years in the schools where he learned to read and to speak the English and the French languages. He also learned something of agriculture and stock-raising, as well as gardening. He returned home in about 1830, and was henceforth prominently connected with all matters relating to Indian affairs in his section of the country. He rapidly acquired influence, not only among the Indians of his own tribe, but the neighboring Indians as well, and was for sixty years the leading Indian character in the Spokane country, and the champion of his people in councils with the whites, with whom he ever maintained a friendship.

One of his first acts upon his return was to build a schoolhouse for the benefit of his countrymen. This schoolhouse was twenty by fifty feet in size and was built with a framework of poles covered with tulle mats. The reeds were woven and sewed together by the squaws, and were stretched over the framework of the building. It was located about two miles north of the Falls of Spokane, at the foot of the gravel terrace or bench, near a large spring, afterwards called Drumheller's Springs, west of Monroe Street, and now well inside the limits of the city of Spokane. One of the principal Indian trails passed this spot in the early days, and the site was a favorite camping ground of the Indians.

His daughter Nellie, in speaking of her father's work as a teacher, says, "Garry read the Bible to the Indians. I have read Garry's Bible. My father taught me how to pray; taught me a morning and an evening prayer; taught me my first religion." After Garry had begun his work, people from other tribes came to hear him. He first taught the Indians the Ten Commandments, and then proceeded to teach them from his little book *(Minor Historical Catechism)*. Garry's method was first to show the Indians the pictures at the commencement of each lesson, and then read and explain to them the accompanying lesson. If he were absent, some of the older Indians familiar with the lessons took his place. Religious services were held at least every Sunday, this work beginning several years before the arrival of either Protestant or Catholic missionaries to the Northwest. He taught not only the Bible, but he taught them things of a practical nature as well. He encouraged them to raise gardens and fields of grain, and instructed them as to the best methods of agriculture, productive gardening, etc., which he learned during his residence at the Red River settlement.

But Garry's greatest work was that of a peacemaker between the Indians and the Whites. His efforts to prevent the disastrous Steptoe campaign and the punitive campaign of Colonel Wright which followed, both failed at least in part, but his efforts were none the less praiseworthy.

His letter to General Clark, commander of the Department of the Columbia, to avert the Wright campaign, is a masterly appeal, and is as follows:

"You, General Clark, you are my friend. I am very much sorry for the battle which took place. I think that you have fought for nothing. The blood of your soldiers and the Indians has been spilled. If there should have been a just cause of fighting, I would not regret it; though there should be killed on both sides, I would not then be much sorry for it.

"Now, I am at a loss what to think of it, for you say, you white people, this is my country; you Americans and English claim the land, and the Indians, each on his side of the line you have drawn. Then you make a useless war with Indians; you cause trouble to the whites living hereabout, and you have nothing to gain from the war.

"Now I hear that somebody—you perhaps, General Clarke—want to make peace. I would be very glad no enmity should be left. I, Indian, am unacquainted with your ways, as you with mine. When you meet me, you Americans, you are ignorant of the uses of the Indians. When you meet me, we talk friendly; we shake hands.

"Two years after you met me, you American, I heard words from white people, whence I concluded you wanted to kill me for my land. I did not believe it. Every year I have heard the same.

"Now you arrived; you my friend; you Stevens, in Whiteman Valley; you called the Indians to that place. I went there to listen to what should be said. You had a speech you, my friend Stevens, to the Indians. You spoke for the land of the Indian. You told them all what you should pay they for their land.

"I was much pleased when I heard how much you offered: annual money, houses, schools, blacksmiths, farms, etc. And then you said, all the Cayuses, Walla Walla and Spokanes should emigrate to Layer's (Lawyer's) country; and from Colville and below all Indians should go and stay to Camayaken's country; and by saying so you broke the hearts of all the Indians; and, hearing that, I thought that you missed it.

"Should you have given the Indians time to think on it, and to tell you what portion of their land they wanted to give, it would have been right. Then the Indians got mad and began to kill you whites. I was very sorry all the time.

"Then you began to war against the Indians.

"When you began this war all the upper country was very quiet. Then every year we heard something from the lower Indians. I told the people hereabouts not to listen to such talk. The governor will come up, you will hear from his own mouth; then believe it.

"Now this spring I heard of the coming of Colonel Steptoe. I did my best to persuade my people not to shoot him. He goes to Colville, I said, to speak to the whites and to the Indians. We will go there and listen to what he shall say.

"They would not listen to me, but the boys shot at him; I was very sorry. When the fight was over, I was thinking all the time to make peace, until I was told that Colonel Steptoe had said, 'I won't make peace now with the Coeur d'Alenes and Spokanes. I will first shoot them (he said) and then, when they shall be very sorry, I will grant them peace.' Hearing that, I thought it was useless for me to try to make peace; and when I hear now what you say, what you write here to the Indians, there is one word which you won't do.

"Until now you never came to an understanding with the Indians to let them know your laws. You ask some to be delivered up. Poor Indians can't come to that. But this one word, and sure you will make peace. Then calling a meeting of the chiefs, you will let them know your law, and the law being known, all those who shall continue to misbehave, red and white, may be hung. The Indians will have no objection to that.

"I am very sorry the war has begun. Like the fire in a dry prairie it will spread all over the country until now so peaceful. I hear already from different parts rumors of other Indians ready to take in. Make peace, and then American soldiers may go about; we won't care. That's my own private opinion.

"Peace being made, it won't be difficult to come to a good understanding with these Indians. You, General Clarke, if you think proper to withdraw the sword, peace will be easy.

"Please answer us, for we want it.

GARRY."

Sad to relate the old Indian chief who had done so much for his own people as well as for the whites, died

Tendoy, Chief of the Bannocks. *His Wife.*
The Peace Pipe.

homeless and in poverty. "A crude wigwam which had been his last shelter from the winter's snow and cold became his mortuary on death. Crowded from their lands, disease and poverty had decimated his tribe, and his title of chieftain was in melancholy contrast with his impoverishment of body and the departure of his temporary power. About the only thing that Spokane Garry possessed when he died was a childish faith that the white men would eventually do the square thing and compensate him and his people for the land they had taken."—*William S. Lewis.*

The Post Trader.—"At every point, where the fur trade was carried on, the white people erected forts for

Home of Chief Joseph, Nespelim, Washington, 1902. Here the Great Chief, on September 21st, 1904, "Passed Peacefully Away While Sitting Before His Campfire."

their own safety and protection, this being the reason for the many forts established throughout the West. They were usually built at the most central points and at places which were surrounded with plenty of grass, game, fuel, water, and in proximity to all other natural resources of that particular part of the country. After the purchase of the Louisiana Territory, in 1803, and the adjustment of the Northwest boundary, in 1846, all these forts came into the possession of the United States, and were at times garrisoned with soldiers by our government, making them military posts. The sutlers of these military posts became known as post traders, and their business as such merchants, was regulated by means of licenses issued by the government. A considerable part of the business carried on by these post traders was with the Indians, and in time, as the soldiers were removed from the posts, such trade became their sole business. Congress has power to regulate the commerce with Indian tribes and under this power certain rules were prescribed by the Indian Department for the regulation of trade and traffic among the red men. Therefore, any Indian trader who was properly appointed and licensed by the government became known as a post trader.

"It was natural that the army would be the first part of our administrative system to come in contact with the aborigines and, therefore, all business connected with Indian affairs was, in the beginning, conducted by and through the War Department of the government. The agents first appointed to look after the welfare of the Indians were military officers and were given the rank of Major in the army. In 1849, matters pertaining to Indian affairs were transferred to the Interior Department and thereafter was administered by civil officers. However, the empty title of Major still adheres to Indian agents.

"After 1849, each governor of a territory was made the superintendent of Indian affairs for all redskins coming under his jurisdiction, but in 1869 this was changed by President Grant, who assigned to the various religious denominations of the country the appointment of agents from the different churches. This method, however, proved unsatisfactory and was soon abandoned, after which bonded agents appointed from civil life by the President for a term of four years was inaugurated. These appointments were political according to the spoils system and continued so until the advent of civil service reform, after which the Indian agent became designated a 'Superintendent,' and held his position under rules and regulations of the Civil Service Commission.

"Post traders were appointed in the same manner as were the agents and under the same system of political preferment and, while the laws regulating their business continue in force and govern those that are still in existence, yet no more post traders have been allowed since 1890. Upon the change of an administration they were as much at the mercy of the victors as were the agents or other civil officers and in addition they were generally burdened with a stock of merchandise which they must get rid of in case they failed to receive a reappointment. However, they were usually able to sell out to their incoming successor. The conduct of their business was regulated by the Indian agent who might be in charge at the time of their appointment, and he could, if he so desired, restrict them in the kind and amount of trade they carried on and could set the prices by which they must sell their goods to the Indians. This method simply fostered the grafting system, making it necessary that the Indian trading business should be conducted for 'all the traffic would bear,' as the trader was usually forced to 'cough up' quite often to continue in favor with his agent.

"In Lewis and Clark's account of their expedition of 1804-6 is found the first authentic information concerning trading between white people and the Lemhi Indians. This exploring party had reached the head of the Missouri River in boats, but as their route lay across the Rocky Mountains, horses were needed to transport their baggage and equipment over the divide. It is doubtful if the journey of those captains would have been as brilliant and successful as it proved to be, had not the Lemhis aided by trading them ponies with which they were enabled to pass through the rough canyons, up the steep divides and over the rugged mountains which lay between the headwaters of the Missouri and Columbia rivers. Capt. Lewis, with three companions, left the main party of his command on the Beaverhead River in Montana, crossed the divide into Lemhi and persuaded the Indians to return with him to what is now Armstead, Montana, with ponies sufficient to remove their camp from there over the mountains into Lemhi Valley. While Capt. Lewis was employed in the task of moving the camp across the mountains, Capt. Clark with a few members of the expedition, started on to explore the Salmon River region. In their Journal of August 18, 1805, we read: 'In order to relieve the men of Captain Clark's party of the heavy weight of their arms, provisions, and tools, we exposed a few articles to barter for horses, and soon obtained three very good ones, in exchange for which we gave a uniform coat, a pair of leggings, a few handkerchiefs, three knives, and some other small articles, the whole of which did not cost in the United States more than twenty dollars; a fourth was purchased by the men for an old checked shirt, a pair of leggings, and a knife. The Indians seemed to be quite as well pleased as ourselves with the bargains they had made.' Lewis continued to barter for horses with which to move their baggage over the mountains. The Journal of August 22nd, says, 'We began our purchase of horses. We soon obtained five good ones on very reasonable terms: that is, by giving for each, merchandise which cost us originally about six dollars.' Again on August 24th, the Journal says, 'As the Indians who arrived the day before had a number of spare horses, we thought it probable they might be willing to dispose of them, and desired the chief to speak to them in relation to it. They declined to give any positive answer, but requested to see the goods which we proposed to exchange. We then produced some battle-axes which we had made at Fort Mandan and a quantity of knives, with both of which they appeared very much pleased; and we were soon able to purchase three horses, by giving for each, an ax, a knife, a handkerchief, and a little paint. To this we were obliged to add a second knife, a handkerchief, a shirt, and a pair of leggings before we could obtain a mule; and such is the estimation in which those animals were held, that even at this price, which was double that for a horse, the fellow who sold him took to himself great merit, in having given away, as he said, one of them to us. They now declared they had no more horses for sale; and as we had already nine of our own, two hired ones, and a mule, we began loading them as heavily as was prudent, and placing the rest of the baggage on the shoulders of the Indian women, left our camp at twelve o'clock.' They then passed over the mountains into Lemhi Valley and camped on the Lemhi River near the Seventeen-Mile-House. The Journal of August 28th, says, 'The purchase of horses was resumed and our stock raised to twenty-two,' and on August 29th, 'Capt. Clark joined us this morning, and we continued bargaining for horses. The late misfortune of the Shoshones have made the price higher than common, so that one horse cost us a pistol, one hundred balls, some powder, and a knife; another was purchased with a musket; and in this way we finally obtained twenty-nine,' and on August 30th, 'Having now made all our purchases, we loaded our horses and prepared to start. . . . . We now took our leave of the Shoshones, who set out on their visit to the Missouri at the same time we, accompanied by the old guide, his four sons, and another Indian, began the descent of the river.'

"In 1868 the government made a temporary agreement with these Indians relative to establishing a reservation for them. By order of the government Nathan T. Hall furnished these Indians some supplies and rations, as part of this agreement. He established a small store consisting principally of Indian goods, on the south side of Patee Creek opposite Fort Lemhi, but in 1870, after selling his ranch to N. I. Andrews and his store to Joseph B. Patee, he left the country. The store was soon closed out by Patee.

"Finally, in 1875 the Lemhi Reservation was created by Executive Order, the first Agency buildings being erected on Agency Creek near the site where now stands the present residence of Seth A. Ball; but in 1877 were removed to their present site near Lemhi, Idaho. The first party to make application for the position of post trader upon this reservation was Smith & Boxwell, a firm composed of George A. Smith, a carpenter in the employ of the government at the Agency and William F. Boxwell Sr. of Baltimore, Md. They formed a partnership and were licensed as post traders upon this reservation, in 1882, while John Harris, President Garfield's appointee, was agent. They erected their establishment about one-half mile south of the Agency buildings at the base of the hill to the west of the public highway, near the junction of the Lemhi and Hayden Creek wagon roads.

"In the early history of Indian trading, owing to the ready sale and immense profit in handling the goods, the great Indian destructive "fire" items were the chief articles of merchandise dealt in. They were firewater, firearms and finery and these constituted the main articles of early trading with the aborigines. Alcohol typifies Indian character, as it stimulates those basal faculties which predominate in his brain. He takes to whisky greedily and his passion for it is a species of madness, for he will usually give up anything he has, gun, horse, wife, family, or all to procure it. It produces his idea of happiness, that of being dead drunk, and he will get in that condition as soon as it is possible for him to do so after obtaining the liquor. In a short time the effect of intoxicating liquors became so prostrating upon the natives, that the great fur companies forbade its traffic among them. Its use curtailed the Indian's ability to gather in the furs and its prohibition became necessary to preserve this immense business. The United States put a stop to the sale of intoxicating liquors among the Indians by statute. Nothing that contains alcohol can legally be sold to them, and in our trade we were always careful to keep out of sight all extracts, bitters and liniments for fear that some depredation would be committed by the redskins to procure them, if they knew such was carried in stock.

"Firearms were sold to the Indians by the fur companies as they could be used by them to advantage in the fur business, although traps, snares, and deadfalls were the usual and better instruments for capturing fur-bearing animals. After the subsidence of the fur industry, firearms proved to be more harmful and dangerous to them than of any benefit. This possession of firearms usually got them into more trouble than it helped them out of, just as do firearms that are constantly and habitually carried around by white men. It was also a menace and constant source of trouble and aided the Indians to go upon the war path and murder the early settlers, who came into the country immediately after the fur-traders. And once the war whoop was sounded, the Indian became unable to discriminate, but waged a relentless war of extermination upon all whites without regard to condition, age, or sex. So the government, by statute, prohibited the sale of firearms and ammunition among all Indian tribes. These laws regarding the sale of intoxicants and firearms are ofttimes violated regardless of the severe prosecutions that have been made and the heavy penalties that have been placed upon the breach of those laws.

"The love of finery was another Indian weakness, so highly colored and gaudy articles were always staple goods in an Indian store. The varied and highly colored beads which he demanded could only be procured by importation from Germany, Austria, and Italy. Cardinal was always a favorite shade, and calicoes, robes, handkerchiefs and other garments had to be of the most brilliant and fast colors, as they were always worn in strong sunlight. Vermilion and lemon were the predominant colors for face paint. Coffee was the Indian's great stimulant, tobacco his narcotic, and no transaction could be completed until he had a supply of candy. In my trade with them, I handled so much candy that I usually purchased it in ton lots. Their tastes gradually changed as the government educated them, being quite different when I ceased trading with them from what it was at first. Salt or anything with salt in it, could not be sold to them. Bacon and vegetables were not used by them to any extent, and so accustomed were they to eating most things raw, that any foods sold to them by the whites must be most thoroughly cooked; otherwise they were readily carried off by disease.

"The goods sold by the Indians were furs, buckskins, gloves, trinkets, and bead work. These were taken in trade for other goods which they desired, and in early days the trader who had the monopoly of such traffic, enjoyed an immense profit from such exchanges, just as all other monopolists do. But, in later days, as the country was settled and other businesses established nearby, the Indian became as wise as any one concerning prices and quality of goods. However, the traffic among Indians has always been considered a more precarious business than trade with white men, because they are not supposed to be controlled in their actions by as upright virtues as the white man and for these reasons goods were always sold to them at a shade higher price than to whites. It is true that one man's money is as good as another's in a mercantile way, and should purchase as much, but with Indians, when two-thirds of the business is done on credit, goods must always be sold them at credit prices. It never could be explained to an Indian how a merchant could sell cheaper for cash than on credit, and as to the payment of interest for the use of money, he knew nothing about it and it was beyond his comprehension. His idea of such things came from his communistic mode of life. With him all things were common property. This proves the fallacy of that theory of the origin of the Indian being from the Lost Ten Tribes of Israel.

"There is a certain fascination about Indian trading. There are no conventionalities, but all traffic is carried on in that simple and naturalistic mode which characterizes the primitive life which all are prone to relapse into, especially in younger days. And the average person, after learning the business, desires to trade with them rather than with the white man. He must learn their language, especially that used by the tribe with which he is trading, and as the Indian sign language is a universal one, it is well that he learn that also, as Indians from other tribes are occasionally coming in to trade.

"The fur company furnished the Indians with supplies and sent them out into the mountains to catch furs, upon their promise to bring them in to them at certain intervals of perhaps several months. This was the Indians' only method of getting help in their business and the practice developed inveterate creditors. The habit stayed with them and they always insisted on being allowed credit and at any time money became due them they were always ready to hypothecate it. As there was no statute by which the trader could collect his money from an Indian by law, he usually exacted a larger profit for waiting until the Indian made good his promise to pay. The Lemhi Indian proved to be a good payer of his accounts. Every one had a limit of credit beyond which he was not allowed to go. This limit ranged from one to fifty dollars according to their power, ability, and willingness to pay. A few were allowed more. There were from five to eight hundred Indians upon the Lemhi Reservation during the time the store which I owned was in operation. In 1907, when they were removed from Lemhi and I made final settlement with them, there was just fifty dollars that could not be collected and that amount was struck from the ledger as the books were closed. The loss of fifty dollars was the result of twenty-five years' trading with them, in which a business approximating one-half million of dollars was transacted.

"It might seem that more money would be lost by reason of some dying, leaving debts unpaid, but usually the trader had no fear of losing an account in this way. His relatives or friends always paid the dead man's account and especially if he had mentioned it before death, which he usually did, for while he had no scruples in making debts, he had a dread and horror of dying with them unpaid. While a relative of a dead person might be shiftless and his own credit utterly worthless, yet he would see that the dead man's account was paid even should it be the last act he ever did. When allowed credit the Indian always wanted to know the amount, after each and every purchase, and the final amount he carried in his head, for he had no method of accounts. The amount of his total credit he always remembered and that exactly, too, to the end of his life. The books, containing Indian accounts, were ruled with three columns, for in addition to the debit and credit columns there was a third column which showed the sum total of the account to date, which was always kept added up in order to inform the Indian at once of his total credit. Too much figuring aroused his suspicion and he never would accept such results. Sums must be demonstrated by actual count upon the fingers.

"When trading with money he demanded the change due him at the end of each transaction. A white man purchases a bill, and when finished will add up the total and pay it in one sum. Not so with the Indian. He buys but one thing at a time. This caused silver money to be their chief medium of exchange and they knew little about the other kinds. He demanded his change because he did not know what he desired to buy until the notion "struck him." Stop an Indian going into a store and ask him what he intends to buy, he would perhaps be unable to tell you. At least this would be the result obtained in nine out of ten cases. He knew simply he had some money to spend and was just as liable to buy a lantern as a pair of overalls, or a sack of flour in preference to an Indian robe. He bought what happened to "strike him," or his fancy at that immediate moment.

"The last trading done by the Lemhis, in Lemhi County, was in 1907, when they sold their earthly holdings consisting of farms, homes and improvements upon the Lemhi Reservation to the various white parties who purchased them at that time. They were removed from hence and the Indian trading business was no more. Thus passed away an institution, which was quite familiar to the old timer of pioneer days but the like of which will be seen no more in Lemhi County."—*John E. Rees*, Salmon, Idaho, December 2, 1916.

The Modern Indian.—The average person acquires his idea of the Indian from the school histories—beads and braided hair, plaited ropes and painted faces, feathers and furbelows of all kinds, war paint and scalp locks, bows and arrows, tepees and tomahawks, peace pipes and spears, mortars and pestles, stolid countenances and studied reticence, lying in ambush to pounce down upon an unsuspecting victim, who, when captured, is tortured in all sorts of horrible ways, but this no more represents the modern Indian than do the coonskin cap, the homemade clothes, the log cabin, the muzzle loading gun, and the three-legged skillet represent the modern American.

An examination of an "Annual" of the Chemawa Indian School near Salem, Oregon, gives one an accurate idea of the modern Indian. Here we see depicted groups of young men and women representing various societies, basket ball teams for both boys and girls, football and baseball teams, glee clubs, bands and orchestras, military companies, and first-aid and home

United States Indian School, Chemawa, Oregon.

The Kappa Alphas.

The Sigma Phi Deltas.

economics exhibits. These are all most convincing and visual proof that there is a modern Indian. A study of the physiques and intelligent faces is a still further proof of this.

There are few high schools in the Northwest that make a better showing along all lines of advancement than does this institution. In this year's graduating class are representatives not only from the various reservations of Idaho, Oregon, and Washington, but also from the Dakotas, Montana, California, Alaska, Wyoming, and Minnesota. It may be claimed that these young people are a superior group in that they are so promising and enterprising; but they merely represent Indian possibilities in civilization.

We are especially concerned with the Indians of the three northwestern states: Idaho, Oregon, and Washington.

Indian Reservations—

Coeur d'Alene in Benewah County; Nez Perce in Nez Perce, Clearwater and Lewis Counties; Fort Hall in Bingham, Bannock, and Power Counties, and Kalispel on the Pend d' Oreille Reservation in Washington. These Indians have 783,107 acres of land.

There are nineteen schools on Idaho Reservations, four government schools and two missions. Two of the government schools are located at Fort Hall and Fort Lapwai. The latter is largely a sanitarium for children in the incipient stages of tuberculosis. It was opened in 1909 and has about 150 patients. It is one of the best equipped hospitals in the United States Indian service. Thirty-six Indian tribes are represented among the patients treated.

Other government schools are for the Kootenais and Kalispels.

The Catholics have a boarding school near Fort Lapwai and the Episcopalians another at Fort Hall.

Besides these schools the Indian child nearly everywhere is allowed to attend the regular public schools.

There are eight Protestant churches on these reservations, besides some Catholic. The Protestants own their own church buildings and have a membership of 592.

The Indian population of Washington comprises about 10,000 and they live on a score of reservations on the coast and in the Inland Empire. These reservations with their populations are located as follows: Queniult, 265; Chehalis, 120; Spokane, 639; Yakima, 2,933; Ozette, 10; Jamestown, 298; Quileute, 209; Neah Bay (Makah Indians), 428; Hoh, 38; Muckelshoot, 186; Colville, 2,518; Tulalip, 376; Nisqualli, 78; Fort Madison, (Susquamish Tribe), 201; Lummi, 500; Port Gamble, 281; Swinomish, 226; Equaxon Island, 66; Skokomish, 250; Queets River, 43. They own 2,700,000 acres of land.

The Indians on the Sound are engaged in fishing, berry picking, and dairying, while those of the Inland Empire, especially the Spokanes and Yakimas, devote their time to stock-raising and farming. They, for the most part, observe the customs of the whites in their dress, worship, and marriage relations. On the Spokane, Colville, and Yakima Reservations the government maintains a doctor and two field matrons.

Twenty-four schools are maintained for the benefit of the Indians of Washington; one government boarding school, eighteen government day schools and two missions; and many of the Indian children are attending the regular public schools. Illiteracy varies from fifty per cent on some reservations to as low as one-half per cent on others. The Tulalip training school located on Puget Sound maintains the first nine grades and has a staff of twenty-one teachers, matrons, etc. The enrollment is about two hundred, and comes from seven different tribes.

There are eight Protestant and eight Catholic mission churches among the Indians of Washington, but the church attendance, membership or support is not nearly so large as that in Idaho.

Oregon has the largest area devoted to Indians of any state in the Northwest, 1,719,376 acres being included in this area. It is occupied by about 4,000 Indians belonging to something over 1,200 families.

The five reservations are: Warm Springs, in Wasco County; Klamath, in the southern part of the state at the eastern base of the Cascade Mountains; Siletz, on the Pacific Coast in Lincoln County; Umatilla, in the northeastern part of the state, and Grande Ronde, between Yamhill and Polk counties.

Educational facilities are supplied by 27 schools; of these six are government, two are Catholic and nineteen are public schools.

There are five Protestant churches and a few Catholic. Four of the former hold weekly services.

The family life is much like that of the whites; their homes are frame or log dwellings. Home conditions are improving more and more as the children, well-educated, return and demand more comforts and conveniences.

According to the revised statutes of the United States, Indian citizenship is based on the following acts:

1. *Allotment under the Act of February, 8, 1887.* In the Act of February 8, 1887, (24 Stat. L., 388), Congress provided for the allotment of land to the Indians in severalty and in Section 6 thereof declared that Indians so alloted should become citizens of the United States and of the state in which they reside.

2. *Issuance of Patent in Fee Simple.*—In the Act of May 8, 1906 (34 Stat. L., 182), Congress amended the Act of February 8, 1887, so as to postpone citizenship of Indians thereafter allotted until after a patent in fee had been issued to said Indians. Provision was also made whereby patent in fee might be issued by the Secretary of the Interior to competent Indians before the expiration of the twenty-five-year trust period. Therefore, Indians whose trust patents are dated subsequent to May 8, 1906, and who have also received their patents in fee simple have become citizens under said Act.

3. *Adopting Habits of Civilized Life.*—Section 6 of the Act of February 8, 1887, both before and after its amendment of May 8, 1906, provided "That every Indian born within the territorial limits of the United States who has voluntarily taken up within said limits his residence separate and apart from any tribe of Indians therein, and has adopted the habits of civilized life is hereby declared to be a citizen of the United States and is entitled to all the rights, privileges, and immunities of such citizens, whether said Indian has been or not, by birth or otherwise, a member of any tribe of Indians within the territorial limits of the United States, without in any manner impairing or otherwise affecting the rights of any such Indian to tribal or other property."

Full citizenship was granted the Indians by an Act of Congress approved June 2, 1924. This provided:

4. "That all non-citizen Indians born within the territorial limits of the United States be, and they are hereby declared to be citizens of the United States: *Provided*, That the granting of such citizenship shall not in any manner impair or otherwise affect the right of any Indian to tribal or other property."

It will be seen from the above that the political status of the Indian is subject to the same rules and regulations that govern any other citizen of the United States.

The future of the Indian is either one of annihilation or amalgamation with the white race, with a preponderance of evidence in favor of the latter. There is no instance in history where two different races have lived side by side and maintained their identity; as sooner or later one or the other was obliterated or absorbed.

The Indian, by the allotment of land in severalty where the whites are settled all around him, learns the English language, adopts the ways of the whites, and, to all intents and purposes, in his mode of living becomes standardized in accordance with the rules of measurement of the white man. This being true, he becomes less and less a member of an individual race and his Indian characteristics give place to those of his fairer neighbor. It is yet too early to predict with any degree of certainty just how largely the primitive Indian will be able to bridge the gap between the primitive and the civilized man.

The question is sometimes asked, Why study Indian history? They have painted no great pictures, composed no masterpieces of music, written no great poems nor plays, constructed no great bridges, erected no great buildings, led no great armies. In short, they have made no contribution to civilization. But these things are not all of life. By his truthfulness, his rugged honesty, his willingness to pay his just debts, his strict observance of all conventionalities, his uncomplaining and forbearing disposition, meeting without a whimper whatever the fates had in store for him; his generosity in sharing his last morsel of food; his loyalty to his friends, his splendid poise, and his willingness to sacrifice himself for the good of others, the Indian has left an indelible impression on his white brother, and for this reason, Indian history may be studied profitably. Such were his racial traits before he was contaminated by his contact with the avaricious whites whose vices have served in many instances to degrade him.

An old chief once said in addressing a scout who was seeking game to relieve his starving people: "Let neither cold, hunger, pain, nor the fear of them, neither the bristling teeth of danger nor the fear of the jaws of death itself, prevent you from doing good deeds."

CHAPTER X.

MINING.

Placer Mining.

Prospecting.—Placer gold was the first kind of gold discovered. It consisted of small particles of pure gold, varying in size from mere dust, to pieces as large as beans or even peach stones, and was taken from the beds of rivers and small streams. The prospector supplied himself with clothing, food, and tools sufficient to last several weeks, and then with pack horse and one or two companions, went to the section of the country to be prospected. Here they established a camp from which they worked up and down the streams in their immediate vicinity. With a pan much like the ordinary dish-pan, the prospector takes samples of gravel and sand found along the creek or river banks. By filling the pan with water and shaking or whirling it around and

Pan and Rocker.

The Sluice Box.

around, the water and dirt and lighter particles of sand are thrown out, while the gold sinks to the bottom. If there are sufficient "colors," that is, particles of gold, to pay twenty-five cents or more to the pan, a claim is established.

**Locating Claim.*—This is done by marking off so many feet of water front and so many feet up and down the stream. The miners then begin mining, at first with a pan, but if, after investigation, there seems to be sufficient gold to justify it, a rocker is built.

The Rocker.—This is built on the plan of the old-fashioned baby cradle, and has a flat bottom, two sides

*See Page 307.

that flare upward, with a board at the head; while the foot is open except for a riffle to catch the gold that is washed down from the other end of the rocker. At the head of the rocker, which is eighteen inches or two feet high, is a hopper from one to two feet square. The bottom of this hopper is a perforated piece of sheet iron or wire screen, and under this is sometimes placed a piece of cloth covered with quicksilver. The screen catches the larger particles of gold, while the fine gold is caught by the quicksilver.

A vertical handle is placed at the head of the rocker, which is set near the ground to be mined. One man dips the gravel and sand into the hopper into which he also places the necessary water, while the other man rocks the rocker from side to side, causing the muddy water and the lighter particles of sand to flow over the sides of the rocker, while the gold, which is heavier, drops down below and is caught in the manner previously indicated.

Long Tom.—This was simply an enlarged rocker, and was made in various ways. If lumber could be had, it was made in the shape of a long box with cleats across the bottom. If no lumber were available, it might be a hollow tree split in two with the open side turned up, thereby making a trough. In either case the dirt and water were thrown in just as in the case of the rocker; or the miner could go up the stream in which he was mining and take out a certain amount of water and by means of a ditch run it into the Tom. This washed out all of the dirt, as well as the lighter particles of sand and gravel, while the metal would sink to the bottom and be caught by the cleats, which sometimes had quicksilver lying behind them. This was a much more efficient way of taking up gold than with a rocker.

The Sluice Box.—The sluice box is made of three planks, the bottom plank being about ten inches wide, while those on the sides were about six inches; and just as in the Long Tom, cleats were nailed across the bottom of the sluice box, and the dirt to be mined handled just as in the case of the Long Tom. Time was gained here, in that the sluice box could be made of indefinite length, and any number of men might be shoveling in sand at the same time, while a large stream of water could run through it continually. The sluice box, however, was not used very much until the saw mill arrived, as "whip sawed" lumber cost anywhere from three to five hundred dollars per hundred.

A miner could dig and wash from fifty to seventy-five pans of dirt per day. With a rocker, he could do three times this much, while with a Tom he could do three times as much as with a rocker, and this amount was indefinitely increased when he used sluice boxes. In the early days of California, the richest dirt went five dollars to the pan, while it is claimed that as much as ten thousand dollars could be rocked out in a single day in the mines of Florence, Idaho.

The Discovery of Gold in Oregon.—The large number of people who went to California soon prospected every probable place where gold might be found and made locations of all of the richer mines. As a result there was an overflow of prospectors in the adjoining territories. Oregon being the oldest and nearest to California was invaded first. Miners both from the California and the Oregon side began to prospect in southern Oregon. Gold was found on the Klamath, the Umpqua, and the Rogue rivers. While the mines were not so rich as those in California, they were rich enough to excite a good deal of interest and cause the country to be quite well explored. A little later, mines were discovered in the eastern part of that state.

The Discovery of Gold in Washington.—In the spring of 1855 gold was discovered near Fort Colville. The amount did not equal that found in California or

Arrastra.—Used in Early Days instead of a Stamp Mill.

This crude piece of machinery was the first used in quartz-milling. The power was water and the bottom of the tub was large, smooth stones. The frame in the center turned round and round. A chain was attached to the end of each of the beams in the center and drawn round and round the rocks attached to the other end of the chain. This gradually wore the rock out and the pulverized parts would drop to the bottom where the minerals would be caught by the quicksilver which lay at the bottom of the tub.

Oregon, but it was not difficult to create a great deal of excitement in those days over new discoveries. Thousands of men rushed to these new fields, but they had to pass through a section of country inhabited by strong and warlike Indian tribes who protested against the invasion of their country. By this time, however, Washington had an organized territorial government and was able to furnish a certain amount of protection to the miners, yet the double disadvantage of mines that were not rich, and the hostility of powerful Indian tribes caused the miners to seek other fields.

The Discovery of Gold in Idaho.—Idaho's history, like that of the other Rocky Mountain States, begins with the discovery of gold. In 1852, a French Canadian reported the finding of gold ore on Pend d'Oreille River. Two years later, General Lardner made other discoveries in the southern part of the territory, while Captain Mullan, who built a road from Fort Benton to Fort Walla Walla in 1855, reported gold in paying quantities on the Clearwater and Salmon rivers. None of these discoveries, however, caused much interest.

In the spring of 1860, a trapper, E. D. Pierce, organized a party of a few men for the purpose of prospecting in the Nez Perce country. The party discovered gold on Orofino Creek, a tributary of the Clearwater, but as this was an Indian reservation, whites could not legally enter the territory. Yet as the report of Pierce's discovery found its way to Walla Walla, Portland, and on down the Pacific coast, hundreds of men soon forced their way into the location of the new mines. Every creek, river, and canyon was prospected. Rich mines were discovered, towns were located at

Lewiston, Elk City, and Pierce. Each soon had a population varying from two to ten thousand people living in tents. However, as the numbers grew, there were soon more men than mines, and prospectors began to go in every direction in search of new fields.

The Salmon River District.—In the summer of 1861, rich mines were discovered on the tributaries of the Salmon River. A man with a pan could take out from seventy-five to one hundred and fifty dollars per day, while from two to three thousand were in some cases taken out with a rocker. Some one returning to Walla Walla in the early fall, reported that six hundred miners would winter at the new mines on Salmon River, that he had met 394 packs, and 250 head of beef cattle enroute for these new mines; a week later 250 pack animals, heavily laden, left for the same locality.

The Boise Basin.—It had been reported from time to time that there were rich placer grounds in the Boise Basin, and in July of 1862, a party was made up at Baker, Oregon, for prospecting in that section. This party followed the Oregon Trail until it came to the mouth of the Owyhee River. It then divided, one division going up that river, and the other going up the Boise Basin. The latter party soon discovered gold near the present site of Idaho City. The names of the discoverers were: Grimes, Wilson, and Splawn. The Boise basin is a valley about thirty miles square, easily reached from the Oregon Trail. The climate is mild, and work may easily be carried on throughout the entire year. This is the location of rich placer fields, and there soon sprang up a number of mining towns. Within six months after the discovery had been made, there were from twenty to thirty thousand people in this district. Pack trains from Walla Walla and Salt Lake brought provisions for the miners who continued to work for many years in that locality.

The Owyhee Mines.—In 1845, some immigrants were reported to have discovered gold on the Owyhee River, but the location was lost. A party which came from Baker City in 1862, was successful in the rediscovery of old mines or the discovery of new ones. They crossed the Snake River near where the Boise flows into it, and then followed up the Snake to its union with a creek which they called Reynolds Creek. Here they found gold, and located as much ground as was allowed to that number of men. Soon they were joined by hundreds of men who had gone into the Boise Basin. Mines were located far up on the mountains. Wood and water were scarce, but the mines were rich. Silver City, Ruby City, and Bonneville were soon thriving mining towns, and the mines of both placer and quartz were very rich.

The Materials Used by the Miner and the Prices Paid For Them.— The miner's shirts were made of flannel and purchased from the Hudson's Bay Company at seven dollars each. His trousers in the beginning, were much the same as those worn today, but eventually they were made of all sorts of odds and ends of cloth from a flour sack to a piece of blanket. His boots were much like those worn by the cowboys today, and cost nine dollars per pair. His blankets came from the mission mills in California, or from the mills established in the Willamette Valley. The stove with which he warmed his cabin, and the one on which he cooked his food, were manufactured in New York and shipped around by water. A good cook stove cost one hundred dollars. Guns, pistols, knives, pans, picks, and shovels completed his equipment. As to food, he was supplied at the following prevailing prices:

Bacon, per lb., Portland, 8-9c; Orofino, 35-40c.
Flour, per sack, Portland, $3.75-$4.50; Orofino, $16-$18.
Tea, per lb., Portland, 50c-$1.00; Orofino, $1.25.
Candles, each, Portland, 28-30c; Orofino, $1.00.
Nails, per lb., Portland, 5½-6c; Orofino, 33-37c.
Beans, per lb., Portland, 6c; Orofino, 25c.
Sugar, per lb., Portland, 11c; Orofino, 40c.
Coffee, per lb., Portland, 20-25c; Orofino, 45-50c.

In addition, for a part of the year, if the camp had been established for some time, he would have plenty of fresh vegetables. Droves of cattle were also driven in from the Willamette and Walla Walla country, and slaughtered to furnish provisions for the miners.

The miner paid for his provision with gold dust, at so much per ounce, the amount allowed depending upon the location of the mine. Elk City dust sold for sixteen dollars per ounce, Florence, eleven to thirteen, Warren, fifteen to sixteen, Pierce being the same. Other camps had various prices, according to the purity or baseness of the metal.

The straits to which the miner was sometimes reduced to get the materials necessary for living, is well illustrated by the experience of a minister, who, after he had preached an inspiring sermon on the text, "Godliness is profitable unto all things," dismissed his congregation. He noticed, as the men filed out, that their pants were patched with all the various brands from flour sacks, such as, "Superfine," "IXL," "Superior," "Excelsior," "Gilt Edge," etc.

A Mining Camp.—A mining camp was composed of men from every walk in life, from every state and territory in the Union, and every nation on the globe. There was no legal form of government and they had to form rules for laying out, holding, and working claims, and make regulations for governing themselves in all of their relations. Sometimes they elected an officer whose duty it was to enforce the rules. He was given power to hear complaints, settle disputes, and enforce the laws drawn up for the government of the camp.

The punishment might consist of flogging, fines, or even expulsion from the camp, and in extreme instances, death itself.

Sometimes a court composed of all the men in the camp might meet as a jury to determine the guilt or innocence of the one accused and pronounce the punishment if convicted. The crimes requiring judicial consideration were horse stealing, claim jumping, sluice box robbing, and murder. The accused was usually defended by some attorney who happened to be in the camp who had practiced law before becoming a miner. The chairman of the meeting delivered his charge much as a judge to a jury; the verdict was rendered in accordance with the evidence, and the sentence pronounced.

Questions like quarrels, individual debts, and difficulties between man and man had to be settled by the parties interested. The court took no notice of such things.

The gambler, the whisky peddler, and every other form of evil followed the mining camps. Fights, robberies, and murders were common. Desperadoes and organized bands of thieves held the inhabitants in terror; honest citizens were shot down in cold blood, and highway robbers seized the miner's earnings whenever he came within their power.

Dance halls were conducted, sometimes with many questionable characters of both sexes as participants, and in some instances respectable women were engaged who danced indiscriminately with the men who patronized the halls. But the saloon and the gambling halls were the chief sources of amusement and furnished recreation for the miners when not employed. If the mines were rich and seemed likely to furnish "pay dirt" for a considerable length of time, stores were erected where the miner could get all things necessary for his work and for his living. A blacksmith shop was usually found there, too, where the picks or shovels could be sharpened or repaired. There was always a demand for pack horses, so each mining town usually had a livery stable, where horses, pack saddles, and other things necessary for the packer and the traveler, could be had.

Locating of Mining Claims.—The following is taken from an old record book now in the possession of Reuben McGregor of Elk City, Idaho. It is Book A of the records of mining claims in the district. It is a well-preserved book, 12½ inches wide, 2 inches thick, leather covered, and contains 570 pages.

Written in ink on the title page we find:

1861—RECORDS OF UNION DISTRICT. BOOK A

The first record on page one, written in long hand with pen and ink is as follows:

DREW FOR CLAIMS.

"At a drawing had for certain mining claims situated on American River and numbered from one to ten inclusive for the benefit of the original prospectors of the same the following persons drew the numbers opposite their respective names and are entitled to the corresponding claims:

Moses Wright	No. 3
Charles Silverman	No. 1
Charles Gwin	No. 5
John Jordon	No. 3
Geo. Robertson	No. 4
Mat Craft	No. 10
N. Harris	No. 2
John McKay	No. 9
J. N. Stubbs	No. 7
Frank Prepley	No. 6

"We certify that the above drawing was conducted by us and that it is fair and correct. Charles Hartley, N. Walling, D. C. Howard. Union District. June 14th, 1861. Attest: L. B. Monson, Recorder."

Eighteen sixty-one was a long time ago—68 years. The Civil War was on. The name Union District indicates that the majority of the prospectors were northerners.

Made Their Own Laws.—The method and procedure of locating and recording mining claims as told in the above record is interesting. The prospectors made their own laws, rules, regulations, and customs in each district at this date. From a composite of the laws, rules, regulations, and customs of the many districts was evolved the first general statute by which title could be acquired: "Law of July 26, 1866." "An Act to promote the development of the mining resources of the United States" was passed May 10, 1872, which with a few additions and amendments is the law under which mining rights are acquired today.

Plummer, The Road Agent.—In the early history of the territory before government was organized to protect life and punish criminals, the miners organized courts of their own to try those who committed crimes within the camp, but there were no courts to try the criminals whose work was outside of the miner's camp. As a result, crime flourished in the towns that supplied the camps and on the roads between the towns and the camps.

There were organized bands of criminals who plundered the merchant in the town, the packer and the stage on the road, and the miners on their way to and from the different camps. The members of these organizations had pass words by which they could make themselves known to each other; routes along which they operated, and stations where members of the gang were located. They also had members in every camp and town engaged in various occupations, trades, and callings. Stage stand tenders and sometimes the drivers themselves were members of the gang. When organized government was established they succeeded in getting themselves elected to the office of sheriff, marshal, etc. These men knew when every pack train started, what it had, where it went, and how much gold dust it brought back on its return; they watched every stranger and learned his business; took notice of every good horse; knew of the departure of every stage, the number of passengers and the probable treasure carried. The lone traveler was robbed of his horse by a false bill of sale. The returning packers and miners were held up, robbed, and sometimes murdered. The stage was stopped, the passengers ordered out and relieved of all their money and other valuables. Frequently the Wells Fargo box containing thousands of dollars would be among the prizes taken from the stage.

One of the most noted of these road agents was Henry Plummer. He came of good family, was gentlemanly in bearing, dignified in deportment, of strong executive ability and a fine judge of human nature. While a young man he drifted west, became a successful gambler, and acquainted himself with various phases of criminal life. In the spring of 1861 he came to Lewiston, Idaho. This town was then the head of navigation on the Snake River, and had a population of several hundred, among whom were thieves, gamblers, escaped convicts, and criminals of all kinds. These he organized into a band of highwaymen, to operate on the road between Walla Walla, Washington and Orofino, Idaho, himself directing the operations from Lewiston which was midway ground. Two sub-stations were located, one at the foot of Craig Mountain, east of Lewiston, and the other west of Lewiston at the junction of Alpowai and Pataha creeks. These were called "shebangs" and were the rendezvous of a band of robbers. Soon robberies and murders on this road were common, but the respectable, law abiding citizens were in the majority and they soon organized themselves into a law and order body, which made the operations of the robber gang dangerous and unprofitable.

The mines at Orofino were soon worked out. This, together with the citizens' organizations and the fear on the part of Plummer of being exposed for crimes committed by him while in Califorina, caused him to flee from Idaho and go to Montana. Upon his arrival there he apparently desired to reform and live the life of a law-abiding citizen. He married a nice young woman and decided upon an honorable means of earning a living. But he was a criminal by nature, environment, and practice and was not strong enough, had he desired it, to break with his old associates and habits, and, like all criminals, he was haunted by fear of detection.

When he left Idaho, a companion by the name of Cleveland went with him. They were together when Plummer was married near Fort Benton and both a little later went to Bannack. He and Cleveland had a bitter quarrel over the young lady who married Plummer. This, together with his fear of his associates in crime, made Plummer suspicious and, in a saloon brawl a short time later, he shot Cleveland. This started him again on a career of crime that has no parellel in the history of the Northwest, and, just as he had organized the criminals in Idaho, so he did in Montana on a much larger scale. These men were bound by an oath to be true to each other and were required to perform such service as came within the defined meaning of their separate positions in the band. The penalty of disobedience was death. If any one of them, under any circumstances, divulged any of the secrets or guilty purposes of the band, he was to be followed and shot down at sight. The same doom was prescribed for any outsider who attempted an exposure of their criminal designs or attempted to arrest any of them. Their chief object was declared to be plunder in all cases, without taking life if possible, but if murder was necessary, it was to be committed. Their password was "innocent." Their neckties were fastened with a sailor's knot, and they wore moustaches and chin whiskers. Plummer himself was a member of the band.

An idea of the duties of these men may be gained from the work assigned them as revealed by one of their number: Henry Plummer was chief of the band; Bill Burton, stool pigeon and second in command; George Brown, secretary; Sam Burton, roadster; Cyrus Skinner, fence, spy and roadster; George Shears, horse-thief and roadster; Frank Parish, horse-thief and roadster; Hayes Lyons, telegraph man and roadster; Bill Hunter, telegraph man and roadster; Ned Ray, council-room keeper at Bannack City; George Ives, Stephen Marshland, Dutch John (Wagner), Alex Carter, Whisky Bill (Graves), Johnny Cooper, Buck Stinson, Mexican Frank, Bob Zachary, Boone Helm, Clubfoot George (Lane), Billy Terwiliger, Gad Moore, roadsters.

But Plummer soon ran his course. He was captured and had to pay the penalty for his crimes. "Red" Yager, a member of Plummer's gang, was hanged by a vigilante committee. Before his execution he made a confession, giving the names of all the members of the band and stating that Plummer was the leader. Plummer, with two others of the organization, was at Bannack. No trouble was experienced in arresting the other two, one being captured in a cabin, the other stretched out on a gambling table in a saloon. But great care had to be exercised in the arrest of the leader of the band, who was cool-headed and a quick shot. Those detailed to capture him went to his cabin and found him in the act of washing his face. When informed that he was wanted he manifested no concern but quietly wiped his face and hands. He announced that he would be ready to go within a short time, threw down the towel and smoothed out his shirt sleeves, then advanced toward a chair to get his coat, but one of the party, by great good fortune, saw a pistol in the pocket of the coat and said, "I will hand you your coat," at the same time taking possession of the pistol. Otherwise Plummer would likely have killed one or all of those attempting to capture him. Together with the other two criminals, he was escorted in the bright moonlight night to the gallows which he himself, being sheriff at the time, had erected the year before and used in the hanging of a man. As they came in sight of the gallows the other criminals cursed and swore, but Plummer was begging for his life. "It is useless," said one of the vigilantes, "for you to request us to spare your life, for it has already been settled that you are to be hanged." Plummer then replied, "Cut off my ears, cut out my tongue, strip me naked, let me go. I beg you to spare my life. I want to live for my wife, my poor absent wife. I want to settle my business affairs. Oh, God!" Then falling upon his knees, the tears streaming from his eyes, and with his voice choked with sobs, he continued: "I am too wicked to die. I cannot go bloodstained and unforgiven into the presence of the Eternal. Only spare me and I will leave the country." But all this was to no purpose. His time had come and the leader's stern order, "Bring him up," was obeyed. Plummer, standing under the gallows, took off his necktie, and threw it to a young man who boarded with him, saying, "Keep that to remember me by," and then turning to the vigilantes, he said, "Now, men, as a last favor, let me beg that you will give me a good drop." The favor was granted and Plummer, one of the most noted outlaws ever known to the Northwest, was no more.*

The Hurdy-Gurdy Girls.

The Hurdy-Gurdy Girls.—A form of entertainment common in the mining towns was that afforded by what were known as Hurdy-Gurdy girls.

*See Langford's *Vigilante Days and Ways* for a fuller account.

The Hurdy-Gurdy Girls.

The pictures were copied from the originals now owned by a lady who was in the mining camps of Idaho in early days and knew well many of the "Hurdy-Gurdy Girls." She, as well as an old fiddler who played for them for two years and who is well known to the author, assured him that these girls were all highly respectable, and followed a calling considered as honorable then as that of the theater now.

Attention is called to two peculiarities of dress: The ladies standing each have on "hoops." These consisted of from twelve to twenty-four steel bands varying in diameter from eight inches to three or four feet. The number varied according to the height of the woman and the size varied from the foot to the waist line. Each of these hoops was made from steel strips about one-fourth of an inch wide and one-sixteenth of an inch thick and covered with cloth. They were bound together with strips of cloth running from top to bottom, the hoops being from four to eight inches apart.

Only the skirt of the dress was worn over the hoops and when she had them on, the lady looked like a boy's inverted top.

The object of these hoops, like many other fashions found in the history of woman's dress, is inexplainable from a man's standpoint.

The ladies in the other picture have their hair arranged in "nets" which were woven from large threads, the meshes varying in size. The net looked much like the "boudoir" caps worn by the ladies today around the house. The net had an elastic in the front and held all the woman's hair securely, no matter in what form she wore it.

"The hurdy-gurdy or dance houses were features of every center. One of them is described as follows: 'At one end of a long hall a well stocked bar and a monte bank in full blast; at the other a platform on which were three musicians. After each dance there was a drink at the bar. The house was open from nine o'clock until daylight. Every dance was $1.00—half to the woman and half to the proprietor. Publicly, decorum was preserved; and to many miners who had not seen a feminine face for six months, these poor women represented vaguely something of the tenderness and sacredness of their sex. Most of the hurdies were German women, who followed the business for gain—the majority homely enough, but some good dancers.' "—*Trimble,* Page 150.

"As I went by a hurdy-gurdy house on my way to address the Sunday School of the Methodist Church, South, which meets in the schoolhouse where we held services today, through its doors and windows flung widely open I saw scores and hundreds of men, and ten or a dozen women, dancing to the accompaniment of fiddles, and drinking and cursing 'between the acts.' "—*Bishop Tuttle,* Page 141.

"Saloons were more numerous in all mining towns than any other class of business, and as gambling was usually an adjunct, every effort possible was exerted to make them attractive. Talented musicians were employed at high salaries, and not infrequently girls, called 'hurdy-gurdies,' were engaged to dance with all comers who desired that kind of amusement, at the nominal price of fifty cents per dance, and the drinks for self and partner, which cost fifty cents more, or one dollar net per dance.

"The girls were engaged by the proprietors of the 'social resorts,' in sets of four, with a chaperon, who accompanied them at all times.

"They were almost invariably German girls, and although they were brought into contact with rough people and sometimes witnessed even the shedding of human blood, the rude, generous chivalry of the mountain men, some of whom were always found in these resorts, was a guarantee of protection from violence, and, strange as it may sound to those of modern times, these girls were pure women, who simply did the work they had bargained to do, and when their contracts expired, most of them married men whose acquaintance they had made while pursuing their vocation, the men who knew them best, and with the money they had earned by dancing with 'Wild Bill,' 'Texas Pete,' and others, helped to buy a home for themselves and husbands. The poor girls—and they danced only because they were poor—had kind hearts and wonderful patience and forbearance."—*McConnell*, Page 138.

The Early Theater.—The Inland Empire, in its broadest sense, is all of that territory embraced in "Old Oregon," between the Cascade Mountains on the west and the Rockies on the east.

Aside from the fur-traders and missionaries, this section was first settled by the miners and those who supplied them with provisions. The growth was rapid, and the population, chiefly male, was constantly shifting from one camp to another. Permanent settlements between the years 1860 and 1870 were few. Home life amounted to little and social amusement had to be adjusted to existing conditions. Several different forms of entertainment were enjoyed.

"An innocent form of diversion was the theaters, one or more of which were to be found in every town of any importance. Troupes of players, male and female, were often encountered by travelers, making the long journeys from town to town. A glimpse of a theater at Walla Walla is given by a newspaper correspondent. The room was a dismantled barroom, and the platform was flanked by blankets. Mrs. Leighton and a troupe presented the play 'Naval Engagements' to the 'highly marine population of Walla Walla. Thirty-five ladies graced the dress circle and 162 gentlemen laughed with delight on board benches at the expense of one dollar each.' "—*Trimble*, Page 150.

Gold Scales.

The Miner's Scales.—Every miner, or at least group of miners, carried a pair of scales which with the weights were put into a case and could be easily kept in his pocket. By this means he could always tell the worth of gold to the pan or to the yard of gravel for the day.

Placer gold is found in particles varying in size from that of a pin head to as large or larger than a bean. This is called "gold dust" and is collected in various ways, explained in the story on mining. When the miner collects his "dust" he puts it in a leather purse or other such receptacle.

Gold is the standard of value in all mining camps and towns doing business with the miner, as there is little coin. Gold dust is measured by the ounce and varies in value from $10 to $20. The miner's scales are much like those used by the ordinary druggist, except that they are not held up by a post. Instead, the miner can hold them with his hand. They are very delicately balanced and will weigh to the grain or fraction of a grain. The Troy standard of weight (twenty-four grains make one pennyweight, twenty pennyweights one ounce, etc.), is used in weighing gold.

The merchant had scales that were larger than those of the miner and were used in weighing all gold given to him in the purchase of merchandise. They, however, were on the same principle as those used by the miner, except that they weighed larger quantities.

Every person who dealt in gold dust had what is termed a "dust pan." This is a small triangular box whose sides are from four to six inches in length and from one to two inches deep. The pan is open at one corner. The gold is put into the pan and all dirt and dust blown out; then it is poured through the opening into the pans of the scales, where it is weighed.

The banker or broker who deals in large quantities of gold has a still larger pair of scales of the same kind. They ship the gold out to the mint in the form of bars, called "bricks." These bricks vary in size from a few dollars to a thousand dollars. Gold is not so very difficult to melt and when melted can be separated from impurities of any kind and run into a mould of the shape and size desired. These in turn are sent by express to the mint where they are coined into money.

The picture of the scales here represented is taken from an old pair that were used in the early days of mining in northern Idaho. They are now in the Lewiston National Bank, Lewiston, Idaho.

The Miner and His Trouble With the Indians.—" 'In the spring of 1851, after returning from the California gold fields,' said Cy Mulkey of Roseburg, 'I went to work on William Martin's farm. After digging gold and fighting Indians, plowing seemed pretty prosaic so, at the end of the month I said to Mr. Martin that he need not pay me anything if he would give me his white pony with blue eyes. He agreed to this and I rode to my home in Yamhill County.

"'A few days after I had gone home General Lane passed our place. He was following some soldiers who had deserted at Oregon City and he wanted a posse of citizens to go with him. He promised to give a reward of $30 for each deserter captured and returned. These soldiers were mounted dragoons who had come across the plains the year before. A good many of them were soldiers who had served under General Lane during the Mexican War.

"'Stories of the fortunes being made in the California gold fields were too much for them. A large number of them had deserted and had started for California. General Lane knew that the men were not prepared to make the 800-mile trip. They had left without supplies except what they could carry on their backs. We overtook 83 of them at Grave Creek in the Rogue River Valley. Their clothes were worn out; they were out of food and were not at all unwilling to be captured. We took them back to Oregon City and General Lane paid the reward to those of us who had gone with him.

"'On this trip General Lane told me that he, himself, was going to California on the first of June and on his way he was going to stop, hold a peace council with the Rogue River Indians and try to get them to cease their attacks on the miners traveling through their country. As I had lost two good horses and a silver mounted saddle, bridle, and spurs, besides $3600 in gold dust, the fall before, I was anxious to go along in the hope that I might recover some of my property.

" 'General Lane offered me a position as interpreter. I gladly accepted his offer. At this time there were a great many Klickitat Indians in the Willamette Valley. Their chief was very anxious to make a raid on the Rogue River Indians to get the horses, which they had stolen from miners and packers. They had several hundred stolen horses.

" ' "Quarterly," the head of the Klickitat Indians asked General Lane if he would let 40 of his warriors go with him so that if General Lane failed to make the treaty, the Klickitat Indians could make a raid on the Rogue River Indians and secure the horses. General Lane agreed to this and took the Indians along.

" 'We had with us, about 500 head of beef cattle which belonged to General Lane, Phil Thompson, Mr. Martin, and Mr. Angel.

" 'We reached the South Umpqua River, near what is now the town of Canyonville, without special incident. We camped there several days while the Klickitat Indians were out scouting to find the Rogue River Indians. They located a small band near the head of the South Umpqua. They brought these into camp. With them there was a boy about 15 years old whom the Rogue River Indians had captured from the Calapooia Indians. This boy could talk good Chinook, so could I. General Lane would give me his message which I would translate into Chinook to the boy and he would translate it into the tongue of the Rogue River Indians. The Rogue River Indians agreed to send runners out and get all of the tribe together at a council on the Big Bar on the south side of Rogue River, just above where the town of Gold Hill is now located. They kept their promise and met General Lane as agreed.

" 'After a two-day council they signed a treaty. We named the chief who signed the treaty for his people, Chief Joseph, naming him after General Joseph Lane. General Lane killed two beeves and gave the Indians a big barbecue. In return, the chief of the Rogue River Indians made General Lane a present of an Indian boy whom they had captured from the Calapooia Indians. During the council I saw an Indian on one of my horses which had been stolen from me the year before. General Lane had my horse returned to me and one of the Indians gave me $100 of the gold dust that had been taken from me. The rest of it, about $3500, they had thrown into the river. They had taken from our party the year before, over $20,000 in gold dust and of this entire amount they had saved only $100 in nuggets, throwing all of the rest away.

" 'General Lane was afraid that as soon as he left, the Klickitat Indians would make a raid on the Rogue River Indians, steal the horses and break the treaty he had just signed. He called the chief of the Klickitats and told him that I was his personal representative and would go back with them to the Willamette Valley and that he would hold him responsible for any harm his Indians did on the way back.

" 'The Indians made no trouble whatever on the way back. General Lane went on to California while I returned to Oregon City where I spent that winter.' "—*Fred Lockley.*

The Story of a Little Burro and a Great Mine.—Gold was discovered near Orofino in 1860. This was

"Jack," Discoverer of the Bunker Hill Mine.

followed by other discoveries on the Salmon River, in the Boise Basin, on the Owyhee River, and in various parts of central and southern Idaho. But no discoveries of any consequence were made in the Coeur d'Alene section until about 1883, when a miner by the name of Pritchard, a strolling prospector, while wandering around the sources of the Coeur d'Alene River, came upon a little stream which now bears his name. There he found a small amount of placer gold.

The discovery of gold on the Pacific Coast from Alaska to southern California, has always, or at any rate since 1849, attracted thousands of miners. Among those who were drawn to the new mines in Coeur-d'Alene, was a man by the name of N. S. Kellogg. He was a quiet, intelligent fellow, a good prospector, and one of the few men "who stood you off from the intimacy of a nickname," and was probably the only man in Idaho who was honored by the prefix of "Mr." Even his most intimate acquaintances always addressed him as "Mr. Kellogg." He had been on the Pacific Coast for a long time, and was now nearing three score years of age. His life had been a checkered one; he had made and lost several fortunes in mining and lumbering camps, and now he had arrived at an age when it was difficult for him to get work for any length of time. In the recent years, he had attempted working on a railroad, but because of physical infirmities and approaching old age he was soon dismissed, being unable to perform the required labor. On top of all this, he had an invalid wife. After having spent every penny and going deeply into debt, he left his wife in the care of his daughter and struck out into the world again to see if he might make a new stake.

He had mined in the Boise Basin in Idaho twenty-five years before, and had gone thence to the fresher fields in northern Montana, then farther north to the Kootenai district of British Columbia. The remembrance of what had been found in the country adjacent in the early days stimulated in him a belief that at last in this Coeur d'Alene country he would find the mine of his dreams, and that the hopes which had led him on for a lifetime would at last be realized. So he decided to return to the north and seek his fortune in the region he had abandoned a year or two before.

As has been said, the report of the discovery of new mines in any country brings thousands of men thither, and the Coeur d'Alene discovery was no exception. These men must be fed, supplies must be brought in for this purpose, and since there were no roads, the usual method was by pack train. Such a train had been brought into the Coeur d'Alenes from Colorado the winter before Mr. Kellogg arrived.

Mules and burros are most often used in the packing business, and in this Colorado pack train was a little Spanish burro which had strayed away from its owner, and being considered of little value was left near the mines. "He is described as a diminutive but thoroughbred specimen of the Spanish jackass. He was mouse colored. His ears were nearly as large as his head and when he laid them back in obstinacy they reached almost to his withers. He was noted all through the Coeur d'Alenes as one of the best pack animals ever cinched, although he was a most cunning and tricky little brute."

Mr. Kellogg arrived at the camp without funds, and was given the little burro by his friends, Cooper and Peck, who "grub-staked" him, that is, furnished him with provisions, tools, blankets, etc., that he might prospect throughout the surrounding country. He was known as a good prospector and a man of wide experience. During July and August of 1885 Mr. Kellogg explored the hills bordering on the south fork of the Coeur d'Alene River, and while on this trip he located what afterwards became the famous Bunker Hill Mines.

There are various accounts, fanciful and otherwise, of the discovery of this mine. One is to the effect that Mr. Kellogg, in a dream while in southern California, had a vision of what afterwards became the famous mine. Another was that while he was leading the burro up the mountainside, it suddenly stopped and when he tried to lead it on, it refused to come. He then got behind it and with a stick tried to push it on. But still the little burro held his ground and finally turned and faced the opposite hill, braying loud and long; when Mr. Kellogg looked across, he saw the glittering galena, which he recognized as that of his dream. Neither story has much foundation. The story as told by Mr. Kellogg is as follows:

One night he camped close to the site of the present town of Kellogg, and turned his burro loose. It wandered up Milo Gulch in search of grass. Next day in looking for the burro, Mr. Kellogg found the outcroppings of the Bunker Hill Mine. These outcroppings showed the bright galena, and he picked up a number of specimens and returned to Murray, taking his samples of ore, which he showed to Cooper and Peck, who had grub-staked him. But they were interested only in Placer Mines.

Mr. Kellogg was much discouraged and did not know what to do. He had no funds of his own and Cooper and Peck did not seem disposed to finance him further. As an example of how poor his credit was, the local merchant refused to trust him for the price of a pair of shoes. But he had other good friends, Phil O'Rourke and Con Sullivan. The former had been in the silver-lead district of Leadville, Colorado, and at once recognized the value of the specimens. They immediately made preparations and returned to the location made by Mr. Kellogg, re-locating the Bunker Hill Mine; Sullivan located another adjoining it, the two together afterward constituting the Bunker Hill-Sullivan Mines.

The news of Kellogg's discovery had leaked out at Murray, and although Kellogg, O'Rourke and Sullivan took great precaution to conceal their movements, on their return to the mine they were followed. Among those who followed them was Jim Wardner, and while the former were staking out their claims, Wardner went above and appropriated practically all the water necessary to work the mines, and a mine without water is of little value. When the three men approached Wardner, he showed them where he had peeled the bark from a big fir tree and written upon it a full and complete location of all the water in the stream. To make this location perfect, witnesses were needed, and, although the three miners saw that Wardner had them at a disadvantage, they signed as witnesses to his water right, and made him a partner.

The nearest road to the mine was at Cataldo Mission 17 miles distant, the nearest railroad was over 100 miles and it was over 1000 miles to the nearest smelter, San Francisco, California.

The outlook did not seem very promising. An attempt was made to mine and ship the ore, but it failed. The final result was a law suit which, according to one of the parties concerned, Jacob Goetz, "Dutch Jake," terminated as follows:

"When Cooper and Peck's suit for grubstake was brought in the district court at Murray the jury gave a verdict against them. However, Judge Norman Buck, who presided, reversed the jury's verdict and held that the real discoverers of the Bunker Hill were Phil O'Rourke, Kellogg, and the jackass, which was the property of Cooper and Peck. He gave Cooper and Peck a quarter interest in the Sullivan and a half interest in the Bunker Hill. It was shown in the trial that Messrs. Cooper and Peck grubstaked Kellogg only to the amount of $22.85. He had paid $2.40 of it and the balance is unpaid to this day. The late W. B. Heyburn, senator from Idaho, and Major Woods of Wallace, Idaho, were counsel for Cooper and Peck. Our attorneys were Albert Allen, Judge Clagett and Frank Ganahl. The lawyers all got interests in the mine for their fees. We appealed the case to the supreme court of the state, but while it was pending a deal was made to sell the mine to Sim Reed of Portland, Oregon, for $1,500,000. It was necessary to give him a clear title, so we compromised by paying Cooper and Peck $76,000.

"The sale was made in May, of 1887, and it was put through by Colonel 'Jim' Wardner. Harry Baer and I, who were partners in all our mining operations, got $200,000 cash in one lump for our interests. Phil O'Rourke got over $200,000, Kellogg got $300,000, Con Sullivan got $75,000, and Alex Monk, a sort of side partner of O'Rourke's, got $75,000. He is a lucky fellow."

Since the sale of the mine $42,772,510.00 in dividends has been declared, and the mine is still one of the richest in the world. It comprises about three thousand acres and has one tunnel over two miles long. It has many thousand feet in drifts, raises, and short tunnels, and has placed Idaho first among the lead producing states in the Union, as well as giving it the distinction of having one of the greatest mines in the world located within its borders.

INDEX

www.ingramcontent.com/pod-product-compliance
Lightning Source LLC
LaVergne TN
LVHW020529100826
845148LV00010B/1402

* 9 7 8 0 7 8 8 4 4 3 8 8 6 *